The Other Side of Salvation

The Other Side of Salvation

Spiritualism and the Nineteenth-Century Religious Experience

John B. Buescher

Skinner House Books
Boston

Cover design by Jill Feron.
Text design by Communicáto, Ltd.

Printed in Canada

ISBN 1-55896-448-7

07 06 05 04 03
10 9 8 7 6 5 4 3 2 1

Library of Congress Cataloging-in-Publication Data

Buescher, John B. (John Benedict)
    The other side of salvation : spiritualism and the nineteenth-century religious experience / John B. Buescher.
        p. cm.
    Includes bibliographical references and index.
    ISBN 1-55896-448-7 (alk. paper)
    1. Spiritualism—United States—History—19th century. 2. United States—Religion—19th century. I. Title.

    BF1241 .B84 2003
    133.9'0973'09034—dc21

                                                    2002030868

Contents

Introduction

IN THE SPRING OF 1848, Americans heard reports that the glorious spirits of the dead had started person-to-person correspondence with the living inhabitants of Earth. Americans also heard that these heavenly communicants had confounded the proud by selecting three young sisters named Fox from rural New York to receive their first messages.

Many found these reports easy to dismiss, but many were not sure. Their religious beliefs were already being challenged by the new revelations of science and by humbling discoveries about foreign cultures and the historical and scriptural record. What they held as firm truths seemed to be dissolving. Who could be certain of what might be possible? Perhaps humankind was about to enter a new era of history. If spirits really had been contacted—and had answered in the form of telegraphic taps, as supporters of the Fox sisters alleged—the consequences were unimaginable.

Spiritualism, at its simplest, was the belief in this simultaneously wondrous and quotidian conversation with the dead. It seemed to require walking a course between blind faith and blind skepticism about matters of spirit.

Religious liberals were recasting their relationship to the Christian tradition at this time. Among the denominations, Universalism and Unitarianism were small in number but large in influence. Both had been born in New England during the last decades of the eighteenth century and the first decades of the nineteenth. And while both were strongest in the North, their ideas were felt throughout the United States. Universalism and Unitarianism provided fertile ground for the development of a variety of liberal religious beliefs in the modern world.

Universalism spread the joyful idea that God would not condemn anyone to endless misery but would ultimately bring everyone to salvation. Its optimistic judgment that difficulty and punishment were temporary and adventitious appealed enormously to people in the struggling lower and middle classes. They envisioned the progressive development of both the individual and society, believing that human nature was not fixed and predetermined but free and changeable and that God's will could be effected by human action in the world to bring each and all to ultimate salvation.

People from every denomination and from no denomination (and even those who were explicitly antireligious) became spiritualists. Universalists, however, were quite disproportionately drawn to this belief, and no denomination lost more of its leaders to it. Universalists and non-Universalists alike noticed this at the time, as have a few modern historians of spiritualism. But historians of Universalism have generally ignored it.

For example, nineteenth-century Universalist minister and historian Richard Eddy never mentioned it in his book *Universalism in America*. This seems odd, considering that while he was a young minister in Canton, New York, Eddy served on the Fellowship Committee of the St. Lawrence Universalist Association as it dropped from fellowship Universalist ministers who had turned to spiritualism. When he wrote his denominational history, Eddy presumably believed these ex-Universalist ministers had forfeited any place in it because they were no longer Universalists, whether by choice or not. One exception among Universalist histories is Russell Miller's two-volume work *The Larger Hope*. In the few pages he allots to spiritualism, he treats it as if it were an exotic virus that briefly gave a mild rash to the body of Universalism.

The silence on this subject has only recently been broken, most notably by Ann Bressler in *The Universalist Movement in America*. Nevertheless, her brief treatment of spiritualism simply places it alongside other pseudo-sciences of the time, such as phrenology and mesmerism, about which some Universalists became enthusiastic. On the whole, however, spiritualism was more than an enthusiasm. It presented a serious and sustained challenge to the denomination, capturing the interest of many of its clergy and members. And this interest was often not a mere hobby but a profound reordering of individuals' understanding of God's providence, of human destiny after death, and of the relationship between Heaven and Earth.

Today, nineteenth-century spiritualism may seem like a revival of an antique necromancy, an atavistic reversion to primitive irrationality. But it did not necessarily seem so at the time. Rather, many saw spiritualism as a rejection of superstition and supernaturalism and an endorsement of the universal application of natural law and evolution—even to the afterlife. Moreover, it provided a new area in which to conduct empirical experimentation. These scientific elements were often submerged under sensational images of trance possessions, weird excitements, and mentalist jugglery. Even so, as a philosophy, spiritualism was generally undogmatic, attentive to new revelations, and respectful of the individual imagination and judgment. As such, it found many sympathizers not only in Universalism but also in Unitarianism, which was similarly noncreedal. Indeed, the two denominations consolidated much later, in 1961.

Unitarianism had grown up within the Puritan-descended Congregationalist churches but turned away from the Calvinist doctrines of original sin, the total depravity of human nature, and predestination and toward views that were amenable to science and democracy. Unitarianism held to no privileged religious elect or arbitrary authority (even though Unitarian blood was famously "blue"), no sacrosanct point of view (even though Unitarian theology was famously intellectual), no miracles that were impossible to investigate and understand in natural terms (including the divinity of Jesus), and no setting aside of part of creation (either on Earth or in Heaven) as ungoverned by natural law. In fact, these views—seeking to reconcile religion with science, democracy, and the modern world—spread far wider than denominational boundaries. They came to permeate the common beliefs of the members, if not the official doctrines, of many of the orthodox churches. Although Unitarianism was not affected by spiritualism in quite the same way that Universalism was, many of its members were similarly drawn to the belief and practice of contacting the spirits.

The pivotal experience of the spiritualist was personal and individual. It was a communication from one person, living as a spirit in the afterlife, to another, still "clothed in the flesh." The community the spiritualists built, at heart, extended upward to Heaven; it did not extend outward over Earth. Thus, spiritualists made effective prophets and visionaries but not particularly good group members. Their formal organizations and associations were fragile, as were their doctrinal formulations. By and large, spiritualists believed they had gone beyond sectarianism. They were wary of binding themselves into an organization, and their efforts to do so were often confounded by internal dissension. Many people did not declare themselves spiritualists publicly but participated in informal spirit circles or happily accepted in silence the reports of spiritual contact, despite what condemnations of spiritualism they may have heard from the church pulpit.

Nevertheless, in 1854, the New England Spiritualists Association estimated the number of spiritualists in the United States as 2 million, and *The North American Review* gave its opinion that that figure was reasonable. *The Spiritual Register,* a popular annual serial compiled by spiritualists, estimated the number of spiritualists in 1860 as 1,600,000 but suggested that the number of nominal believers was 5 million. In 1861, in "The History of Modern Spiritualism," spiritualist editor Samuel Byron Brittan put the number of spiritualists in the United States at 3 million but admitted, "No one has so much as attempted to ascertain the number . . . and hence no authentic information can be given. Those who profess to prepare such statistics, either depend on the conjectures of persons who know as little as themselves, or they draw entirely on their own imaginations for what they are pleased to publish as the facts." A few modern scholars, working with no new evidence, have suggested that 1.5 million Americans practiced spiritualism during the period of its greatest influence, the decade before the Civil War, when the U.S. population was just 30 million.

These numbers require some qualification, however. Both spiritualists and their opponents sometimes stretched the meaning of the word *spiritualist* to include, for instance, anyone who had once assembled an ad hoc séance as an amusing party game or who had developed into a medium and made a living by giving public trance lectures. Spiritualism was therefore not so much a belief system to which one declared his or her faithfulness as a loose set of experiences and practices. One became a spiritualist simply by trying the spirits and being encouraged by the results. In this respect, spiritualism was a volatile, charismatic movement that spread across denominational lines. But individuals' interest in spiritualism often waxed and waned. Many who devoted their attention to spiritualism when it emerged in the late 1840s and early 1850s had cooled in their enthusiasm by the mid 1870s. And by the 1880s, many followers had drifted into other newer movements that had historical ties to spiritualism, especially those known as *Mind Cure, Christian science, New Thought,* and *Theosophy.* Some followed still different paths toward *Free Thought* or socialism and even psychoanalytic theory.

Others moderated their original enthusiastic investigation of spirits through séances into a vague interest in creative inspiration and the hidden powers of the mind, an interest that was felt in the culture at large. In that respect, spiritualism and Universalism shared a similar fate during the second half of the nineteenth century. The belief in universal salvation began to permeate nearly all the Protestant churches, even while the number of people affiliated with the Universalist denomination leveled off and then declined. Universalists could claim victory for their core belief, even while complaining that their membership would be five times greater if all those who believed in universal salvation would declare themselves Universalists.

Universalists assumed positions of leadership in the early days of spiritualism, and their collective contribution was decisive to its development. In particular, their influence drew other Universalists to spiritualism, and these new devotees found the movement both fascinating and familiar. Some felt they had returned to the original "fountain," or the source of true religion, while others believed they were continuing the journey begun by the founders of Universalism.

The importance of spiritualism perhaps can be best understood by looking at the lives of those who played a part in it. *The Other Side of Salvation* tells the stories of many of the Universalist clergy and laypeople who labored for spiritualism. For the purposes of this book, these individuals have been organized into three groups. In reality, they all knew and influenced one another, but considering them in turn will help clarify important aspects of spiritualism. In presenting these accounts of contacts with spirits and other extraordinary events, this book makes no claims about their truth, but to avoid tedium, it refrains from qualifying these accounts by using phrases such as *he claimed* and *as it appeared to her.*

The first group, considered in "The Reconciliation of Religion and Science," consisted of the Universalist clergy who investigated mesmerism and associated themselves with clairvoyant seer Andrew Jackson Davis. These followers migrated to New York City and organized themselves there. They developed spiritualism as a rationalist challenge to traditional beliefs in the plenary truth of the biblical revelation and in miracles as incomprehensible suspensions of natural law. From the beginning, spiritualists were standard-bearers for pre-Darwinian evolutionary theory and for a comparative approach to religion. They believed that spiritualism, at its core, tried to reconcile religion with science.

The second group, considered in "The Conversation with Spirits of the Dead," invested itself more in another aspect of spiritualism—a wilder one. Far from being merely a rationalist philosophy, spiritualism was also bound up with individuals' intimate experiences of the uncanny, the entertaining, the weird, the gothic, the romantic, and the bizarre. It was attentive to *phenomena:* materializations, disembodied voices, psychic displacements, physical levitations, and sensory contact with individual spirits of the dead in the séance circles that began with the spirit rappings in rural New York. The members of this group all had ties to the Fox sisters.

The third group, which clustered around Boston, is considered in "The Annunciation of the New Age." These followers saw spiritualism as a powerful tool, integrated with and inspiring other radical and reform movements of the day. Spiritualism spread with fiery enthusiasm, not as a science but as a millennial movement. Spiritualists believed that the kingdom of Heaven had begun to pour itself out upon Earth and that the spirits had just begun an intimate intercourse with humankind that would bring about the communion of saints. Spiritualists were confident that because a turning point in history had arrived, a revolution in human affairs was more than possible. One might become an angel—or sleep with one, give birth to one, place one at the head of an army, or send one to the White House.

Spiritualism coursed through the heavens of the nineteenth century like a comet, burning brightly, reaching its zenith, and then falling back into the dark below the horizon. Five decades after it began, almost no chronicler regarded spiritualism as a movement of any real significance in the course of human progress. But in its heyday, many people believed that it illuminated the warring claims of religion and science or spirit and matter, solving one of the great questions of the age.

The stories of the extraordinary characters that inhabit these pages detail how a liberal tradition confronted spiritualism. Similar though less spectacular stories were enacted throughout organized religion in the United States, as it struggled with the force of modernity and the questions it raised: What impact should worldly evidence have on faith? What place should individual experience and judgment assume against tradition and external authority? What place should women have as religious prophets, priests, ministers, preachers, and spiritual advisors? What relation does one religion have with another? What are the sources of revelation and scripture? Are they closed or fixed, or are they still open and continuing? Is the exploration of the psyche a path into religious truth? What does the body have to do with the spirit? What does heaven have to do with Earth? What is the meaning of a single life and of a single death?

These questions are at the heart of the stories that unfold in these pages—particular stories not only of Universalists but of the universal.

John B. Buescher
September 2003

The Reconciliation
of Religion and Science

IN THE EARLY NINETEENTH CENTURY, many of the people who had embraced the Enlightenment ideal of reason and accepted the power of science to explain the natural world also recognized that science had left religion and spirit behind as either false or irrelevant. The material realm of science and the immaterial realm of spirituality seemed far apart and mutually hostile. But the investigation of electricity and magnetism made the immaterial visible in the material world, and a mysterious connection between the spirit and the human body became apparent with the investigation of *psychology*. This was the time that spirits began returning to the human world. Trance, dreams, visions, and kindred phenomena—a mysterious opening for the immaterial—flashed into the material world of the nineteenth century.

Doctor of Electropsychology

ONE SUNDAY IN 1809, thirteen-year-old Johannes Bonfils walked through the forest near Amsterdam, New York. He lived with his uncle and had just finished visiting his impoverished, widowed mother. On his walk back to his uncle's house, Johannes encountered his father, who had died two years before but now appeared and spoke. He told Johannes, "The spirit-world was not what people supposed—that great darkness and error hung over the religious world—that the sects differed as widely from the truth as they did from each other—but that a new era of light was soon to dawn on earth."

The frightened boy ran on and told his family about the vision, but they thought it was "a mere hallucination and a subject for mirth." Nevertheless, the following Sunday, in the same place, the boy again encountered the spirit of his father. He told Johannes not to tell anyone any more about the things he revealed, "as the world was not yet prepared to receive them," and then "proceeded to explain to him the spirit-life." After that, the boy kept the visitations secret.

Johannes Bonfils was born in 1795 in the town of Florida, New York. He was the son of Jane Dods and Jacob Mathias Bovee Bonfils, a Swiss Huguenot who had immigrated to the United States. When Johannes's father died in 1807, the boy was adopted by and went to live with his maternal uncle, who lived nearby.

Johannes's uncle raised him in the Congregational Church, and his religious disposition drew him to prepare for the ministry, which he did under the name John Bovee Dods, in honor of his uncle. Dods became a clergyman in 1823 and first settled in the town of Levant, in Penobscot County, Maine. Not long after he began, however, his father's spiritual admonitions about the afterlife intruded into his mind in a dramatic way, for he was visited

3

several times by the spirit of another relative, who had committed suicide by drowning.

During one of these visits, the relative appeared to Dods and his wife, Mercy Ann. After retiring for the night, they heard "a distant rumbling sound, as if a wagon on the frozen ground" was rolling up to their house. The door burst open, and in a "peculiar light" that filled the room, the spirit appeared, "clad in shining robes, with a most angelic countenance and eyes of great brilliancy." She told Dods that "she had been appointed to come to him to prepare his mind for an important work to which he was to be called in enlightening mankind" and "some of the doctrines he was preaching were erroneous." She said she would give him lessons that would "satisfy himself to proclaim" the spirit life to others.

For the next three months, beginning in January 1824, Dods's house was the scene of extraordinary phenomena: "sounds like the striking of heavy stones forcibly thrown against the building, rumbling sounds, explosions as of a cannon near the house, violent shakings of the whole building, the movement of various articles of furniture, even to that of a bed with a heavy man upon it, across the room, with great force." Dods's in-laws, staying at his house, found their bedspreads pulled out of their hands and off their beds. One group of curious gentlemen visitors encountered something like an invisible cannon ball, which fell from the ceiling; rolled, hopped, and bounded about the room, up and over the furniture and careening off the walls; and then hopped up on a bed, where the apparent depression of its weight on the bedclothes moved from the head to the foot of the bed. "A gentleman in the room walked towards the bed, with the seeming intention to take hold of, or arrest its progress," wrote one narrator of events, "but one of the company caught hold of his arm, and said, 'Do not touch it *for your life.*' It then dropped on the floor, and rolled out of the side of the house."

The house was visited by hundreds of curious visitors, and Dods and his family finally had to move. But before they left, the spirit of his relative bade him farewell for a time with a proof that "the exalted spirits had power over material substances." She said to him, "See, I can yet handle dead matter, for the immortal form I wear is made out of original eternal matter, which is the body of God!" With that, "she reached forth her hand, *took his hat from his head, or rather it seemed to be attracted by the hand, and floated off, carrying the hat with her, over the top of his house, also over a neighboring house, described a circuit of about a mile in diameter, or three miles in circumference, and then returned the hat to him!*" And then she disappeared.

Dods kept many of these experiences to himself, but they led him to renounce his previous religious beliefs, especially about eternal damnation. (After all, the spirit of one who had committed suicide had been made glorious.) Dods also shifted his allegiance to Universalism, "although he considered that sect a long way from the truth"—or, at least, he did years later in retrospect. A skeptical Unitarian minister, Bernard Whitman from Waltham, Massachusetts, wrote that a neighbor of Dods's had told him that the phenomena in the house were caused by "the spirit of God, haunting [Dods] to forsake Calvinism and declare universal salvation." The spirit moving Dods's hat through the air demonstrated a divine energy that *could* act in the world, in ways neither imperceptible nor impersonal, and a divine energy that *would* act in the world, revealing the truth and bringing individual souls to sanctity. It was evidence of a providence whose saving grace extended to all. Contrary to Whitman, who characterized the event as a "haunting," Dods believed this spirit's purpose was to comfort, teach, bless, delight, and guide, not to terrify or punish.

In 1826, Dods, who was now a Universalist minister, preached at the Eastern Association Universalist Union. The Reverend Sylvanus Cobb wrote in his journal that the sermon affected the other ministers deeply. Dods moved to Union, Maine, and Cobb, who was settled nearby, transferred to him some of his preaching duties. Dods carried out these duties over the next six years, preaching in Levant and farther afield in other Universalist pulpits.

Dods resolved his theological difficulties in private consultations with the spirits of his father and the Apostles Paul and John, who explained such doctrines "as the resurrection, the person and mission of Christ, atonement, second death, etc. . . . in a manner which seemed to him rational and philosophical." He used these explanations in his own preaching and, as he said later, sometimes found them spread through books and newspapers, without the borrowers knowing their ultimate source, and even generally adopted within Universalism.

Dods's in-laws lived in Virginia, and during a visit to see them in 1830, he spent ten weeks in Richmond, helping the scattered Universalists and Unitarians there organize a Unitarian-Universalist Society (the so-called Uni-Uni Society) before returning to Maine. He soon moved again, however, and in June 1832, Dods was installed as pastor of the First Universalist Church of Taunton, Massachusetts. He remained there until 1835, when he went to Provincetown, Massachusetts, as pastor of the Christian Union Society, the Universalist church. While there, he opened an academy for young students and was helped with the teaching duties by Universalist minister Nathaniel Gunnison. Dods also became known as a powerful preacher, often traveling to preach in nearby Wellfleet at the Universalist Society there, and as a progressive rationalist, who taught his audiences about a God who made his universal love available to all. From time to time, he also returned to Maine to preach.

In 1836, Dods had the opportunity to view the New England exhibition tour of French mesmeric experimenter Charles Poyen St. Sauveur. As a result, he became interested in mesmerism and in electricity, which he believed was the cause of mesmerism. He was surprised that mesmerists could induce in their subjects experiences similar to his own—namely, "visions of angels, the spirit-world, their departed friends, &c."—and could "cause them to think they saw what did not exist, and to believe that movements of physical articles took place when they did not, etc." He began to wonder whether the phenomena of what he called *psychological states* could sufficiently explain his own visions or whether he also needed to believe in the reality of disembodied spirits.

Dods was transformed into a dedicated amateur of science: a "doctor," an intense and energetic experimenter. He used his wife, his four daughters, his son, his friends, and members of his congregation as subjects for trance induction and treatment with insulated wands and rods that conducted static electricity into various parts of their bodies. In some of these subjects, he induced experiences that amused him—for example, having them taste water as lemonade—but in others, he induced religious experiences. A clerical colleague, William Fishbough, described his inductive powers as follows:

> Any vision of which the imagination can conceive, however absurd or impossible, may thus be made to pass before the mind of those most susceptible, with all the appearance of absolute reality, causing them now to weep with sorrow, now to shriek with terror, and now to exclaim with ecstasies of delight, according to the nature of the picture that is made to appear.

Dods concluded that his subjects' experiences were not real and that his, too, must not have been. This did not make him happy. Recounting Dods's narration of his earlier life, a reporter later wrote,

> Anxious to teach nothing beyond the truth, he felt compelled to give up his long cherished faith in communion with departed spirits, the belief in his own inspiration and appointment to a great work, and all the expectations of distinction which had floated before him. He wept like a child over these supposed delusions, and thereafter became doubtful and materialistic, though he at times had misgivings on the subject.

Interestingly, the combination of mesmeric, electrical, chemical, and massage treatments that Dods provided for his subjects helped to ease their physical and mental problems. Realizing this, Dods incorporated electrical and mesmeric experimentation and treatment into the curriculum at his academy. Some of his students, including those he was guiding into the ministry, took up his interest in combining mesmeric healing and religion as a way to reconcile science and religion, matter and spirit. In explaining mesmeric trance, Dods also offered as a synonym for *animal magnetism* a word he liked better, *spiritualism.*

Dods's naturalistic explanations had theological implications and vice versa: God was the ultimate energy source, emanating into the universe in various forms. Substances were the expressions and thoughts of God. Trance induction was a sacrament that allowed one to see God's spirit taking shape and to align oneself more fully with God's energy. The process of salvation was progressive, evolutionary, and cumulative. It was also a growth into ecstasy, however, and could be induced through *natural means,* which turned out to be identical with God's means and God's grace, expressed through the medium of electromagnetic energy. Dods believed that "all motion and power originate in mind, and as the human spirit, through an electromagnetic medium, comes in contact with matter, so the infinite Spirit does the same, and through this medium he governs the universe."

Dods crafted an explanation for spiritualistic phenomena that treated them as the products of *two brains:* A lower mind, hidden from the ordinary mind, was capable of imagining and making manifest to the higher mind phenomena such as levitation, the appearance of spirits, and the production of mysterious sounds. These phenomena would occur *psychologically,* through the automatic emission of electromagnetic charges that entered the brain from the atmospheric ether through the organ of the lower brain, the cerebellum. The charges collected there until the higher brain, the normal inhibitor, was suppressed. At that point, the collected charges were released in the form of visions and what would today be called *telepathic* and other *paranormal perceptions.*

Some of Dods's contemporaries found this explanation incredible because while it dispensed with the notion that external, intelligent, disembodied spirits caused the phenomena, it attributed them to a cause that they saw as far less believable: two minds in a single person, with the electrical discharges of one mind becoming conscious to the other. One individual summed up Dods's views in exasperation, writing,

In other words, every man is engaged in thinking thoughts of which he is profoundly unconscious! He carries in his own brain a separate world of mind, endowed with the power of sustaining masterly arguments, imparting various and astounding information before wholly unknown, and answering with readiness many difficult questions—*without his own knowledge of the fact!*

The notion that there existed a second mind, whose operations were hidden from the higher part of the mind, was just "too fanatically foolish to require any comment," although comment was certainly offered. Dods's critic continued,

To say that every body who testifies to the plain facts of table-moving, bell-ringing, guitar-playing, etc. [by spirits], is *deceived* or "psychologized" is as silly a defense as can be set up. I might, with equal propriety, coolly inform Dr. Dods that although he firmly believed his wig to be properly adjusted on the top of his head, yet he was only laboring under a delusion in that respect; that the aforesaid useful appendage was, in point of fact, plainly attached to the end of his nose; although he couldn't *see* it in that light, being under the all-pervading "psychological influence."

Landscape and portrait painter and spiritualist Josiah Wolcott wrote to *The Spiritual Telegraph* to report messages he received from the spirits of deceased physicians who were critical of Dods's theory. Another spiritualist, Wilshire S. Courtney, disputed Dods's ideas in a lawyerly fashion in his *Review of Dr. Dods' Involuntary Theory.* Sylvanus Cobb described the same discovery of crossed purposes within the same mind but used another metaphor: "It is quite evident that in the organization of the human mind, there is, as it were, a wheel within a wheel—a class of powers which are capable of acting independently of our volition, will, or even knowledge."

Dods applied his theory of dual minds to the macrocosmic scale as well. It provided an explanation for the existence of suffering and evil in a universe governed by an all-loving providence. In the person, one mind was voluntary and one mind was involuntary. In the same way, the entire material universe was the manifestation of God's mind, and it, too, was dual, having both voluntary and involuntary parts. Suffering and difficulty were the result of God's involuntary mind acting (or at least seeming to act) at odds with his voluntary mind, in which there was only love for humankind.

Dods stayed in Provincetown until 1842, when he resigned his ministry and went to Fall River, Massachusetts, to the First Universalist Society, just when the mechanics in the area were organizing for labor reform in the mills and agitating for a ten-hour workday. Dods became a speaker and organizer on the workers' behalf.

While in Fall River, Dods also enhanced his reputation as a scientific theorist by lecturing throughout New England on the relationship among mesmerism, psychology, and electricity. Other Universalist ministers also explored mesmerism and joined the lecture and demonstration circuit. Among them were one of Dods's students, Theophilus Fisk, whose demonstrations were about what he termed *electrobiology*, and Sylvanus Cobb, who preferred to use the term *living magnetism* to describe his technique. During one lecture series that Dods gave in Boston on "the science of the wonderful power of the human imagination to charm all pain," some two thousand people attended each lecture over the course of six nights.

Dods also began teaching courses on mesmerism, which by now he called *electrical psychology*, charging ten dollars for a man and five dollars for a woman. By 1850, he had trained over one thousand people, some of whom had formed a Psychological Society. He also constructed his own equipment for electrical experimentation and treatment. (Decades later, his widowed last wife, Phoebe, supported herself as an "electrician," selling a line of his equipment.) Dods found himself in competition with other exhibitors of mesmerism and jockeyed with them about who had first discovered the various techniques now in common use.

By this time, Dods had also developed a less than cordial relationship with the Universalist establishment. The Reverend Thomas Whittemore kept on hand (and later passed down to the Universalist Historical Society) a letter of testimony from a young woman named Olive Fairbanks, who had sometimes taken care of the Dods children when the family lived in Maine. She accused him of attempting, in her words, "to take a greater freedom with me than I thought proper to allow." Whittemore also had a letter from a group of Dods's neighbors, however, who declared the whole thing a misunderstanding that had been blown up into a deliberate slander. The incident had occurred, Dods said, when the children's regular nanny was away. He had slipped into bed one night with the children and discovered another person there in the dark under the bedclothes, whom he had not recognized at first. It turned out to be Miss Fairbanks, whom Dods's wife had brought in to take care of the children.

The controversy might explain the story told about Dods's gift for publicity by Universalist minister Cyrus Augustus Bradley. Bradley wrote that Dods

> had difficulty with the Maine Fellowship Committee. They advertised that the Rev. J. Bovee Dods was not in fellowship with the Maine Universalist Convention, and that it was in no way responsible for him. He retorted with an advertisement that the Maine Universalist Convention was not in fellowship with J. Bovee Dods, and that he would be responsible for none of its acts.

Dods became a freelance preacher for a while, lecturing on both Universalism and mesmerism. Whittemore criticized him for holding a public discussion with an orthodox clergyman "on the merits of Universalism." Writing in May 1848 in his newspaper, *The Trumpet and Universalist Magazine*, Whittemore remarked, "Mr.

Dods is in no way connected with the Universalist denomination. He does not preach under the approbation of Universalists." In fact, the Massachusetts General Convention of Universalists had just dropped Dods from fellowship.

By 1850, Dods had moved to Brooklyn, New York, and was spending all of his time lecturing, experimenting, and treating patients. He was still devoted to religion, although he was inclined to take the spiritual doctrines and beliefs of Christian experience and derive a materialist or naturalist meaning from them. He denied the possibility of true immateriality and held that one's spirit was an electrical emanation of God, sometimes assuming a ponderous existence as a substance. Electricity was "the body of God," and so all other bodies were his body's "emanations, and all other spirits are emanations from his spirit. Hence all things are of God. He has poured himself throughout all his works."

In his own way, then, Dods was able to be consistent in his writings. In 1850, he published *The Philosophy of Electrical Psychology*, which was met with great success. His theories created so much notoriety throughout the East that in 1851, a group of senators— including Daniel Webster, Sam Houston, and Henry Clay—invited him to Washington, D.C., to give a series of lectures on his ideas. Then, in 1852, Dods published *Immortality Triumphant; The Existence of a God and Human Immortality Philosophically Considered, and the Truth of Divine Revelation Substained.*

When spiritualism first blossomed during the early 1850s, Dods assumed that spiritualists, who attributed their experiences to real spirits, were mistaken. In order to explain the manifestations in a materialistic way, he took issue with one of spiritualism's most prominent proponents, John Worth Edmonds, by publishing *Spirit Manifestations Examined and Explained; Judge Edmonds Refuted; or, An Exposition of the Involuntary Powers and Instincts of the Human Mind.* In doing so, Dods provided one of the main arguments of the time against spiritualism. He did not attribute the manifestations to demonic or devilish spirits, as others had done, but to the natural and mechanical operations of the brain. And while the book made him no friends among the spiritualists, the scientific community hailed it as a major contribution.

Not long after the book's publication, however, things changed for John Dods. In August 1855, four spirits appeared to him— among them, his father and other relatives "whom he supposed were living in the body" in Norfolk, Virginia. These spirits told him "they had just passed to the spirit-world, having died suddenly of yellow fever, and that his daughter and another relative, residing there, had been attacked by the same disease, but would recover." When he subsequently confirmed this surprising information, "his unbelief in spirits was somewhat staggered, but he tried to persuade himself that this was a psychological impression."

Dods was shaken further by the reappearance of the female spirit whom he had encountered earlier in his life, that of his dead relative. She was now more gloriously robed in light. She criticized him "for his want of faith, and his over-reliance on human philosophy, by which he had been led into error, and assured him that he should have further demonstrative evidence, which would settle the question of spirit-agency beyond doubt in his mind." She commanded him to be faithful to the mission she had given him years before and then disappeared again. Soon after, a "series of astonishing physical phenomena" erupted in Dods's room, including rappings and flights of heavy furniture from one corner to another, even when he was sitting on it, "until he had all the evidence that the senses were capable of receiving, that these things were real, and that he was in his normal state."

At the beginning of 1856, Dods publicly revealed himself as a spiritualist. It was now "his duty to proclaim the glad tidings of *immortality demonstrated* to his brethren of the human race." His transformation from a public explainer of spiritualism to a public expounder occurred in his lectures, in which he began to incorporate some of his own spiritualistic experiences as illustrations. These narrated experiences were so many, so varied, and so rich that audiences became suspicious and questioned him. For example, one audience member questioned Dods about his report that the spirit of Universalist minister Hosea Ballou, who had recently passed away, had visited him:

> A Voice [from the audience]—At a certain place the other night you saw Father Ballou; he told you the [spirits'] rappings were true. What do you make of that?
>
> Dr. D.—No telling tales out of school.

Over the course of a few lectures, Dods admitted with quickening conviction, urgency, and even relief that he had now become a believer in the objective reality of the spirits.

Newly declared a full believer in the truth of the spirits, Dods took to the public pulpit in New York City and elsewhere, speaking constantly in the name of spiritualism. (Until his death in March 1872, he was a leader of the spiritualist movement in New York City.)

By 1855, Dods's daughter, Jennie, had become a powerful spirit medium, and he worked with her in his experiments. He had a new set of expectations, however, as he had come to believe in spirits as personal entities who served as the intelligent intermediaries between an impersonal God, who was a universal energy or life force, and living beings. The spirits were first-line mediums who manipulated, directed, and transmitted that energy to humans in the form of a magnetic fluid.

Dods's turn to spiritualism also had another effect: In the eyes of the scientific community, it tainted the credibility of his previous theories. Materialists now thought they had to look elsewhere for a theory of spiritualism. "Mr. Dods, the well-known expert in animal magnetism," wrote a reviewer in the *New Englander and Yale Review,* "develops a theory of involuntary mental and muscular action, setting spirits wholly aside. But unfortunately for his logic, since his book was published, he has burst the shell of his own theory, and come out a full-fledged spiritualist."

After his reconversion to spiritualism, Dods also continued to administer medical treatments. He had previously attributed their effectiveness to the mental force of the individual being treated and to the electromagnetic power of the healer. He believed he had a natural gift for diagnosing disease, even if the patient was far away, because of his unusual magnetic power. As he explained in a letter to a spiritualist newspaper, "I am, sir, in the *electro-psychological state*. I am *naturally* in it—I was born into existence in it. I require no extraneous aid from other persons to put me in it."

Now Dods's healing sessions took an overtly spiritualistic turn. In the summer of 1857, for example, in a public session back in Provincetown, Mrs. Betsey Cook was brought before him, unable to walk. She had been diagnosed with neuralgia, nervous spasms (or hysteria), and diabetes. Dods caused a sensation with a spirit-controlled faith healing. "Betsey," he intoned, "in the name of the great Master Medium of our race, *be whole in your infirmities. Arise and walk.*" And so she did. "But how was it done?" Dods asked rhetorically in his description of the episode. "Answer—From beginning to end, the *whole* was done under *spirit-direction* and by *spirit-skill.*"

Dods experimented with ether and other drugs to induce an exalted mental state, entry into which constituted the death of the old self and the birth into sanctity that revivalists sought with different means. In this exalted state, one was in rapport with the mesmeric operator but also with the larger forces of the universe. One could align himself with God in this way and, by so doing, increase his well-being and even conquer disease. Disease, pain, and disability were believed to be caused by being out of touch with the forces flowing from God through the universe into his creatures. Like pain and sin, sickness was the result of a mental reaction to the world, not a part of the world itself. It followed that the mind could do away with sickness, as it could do away with pain.

Dods and his contemporaries, especially physician Phineas Parkhurst Quimby, laid the groundwork for the *mind cure* and *new thought* movements that blossomed in later years, especially in the teachings of Mary Baker Eddy. Quimby lived and practiced in

Belfast, Maine. In 1836, he, too, had attended mesmerist Charles Poyen St. Sauveur's lectures in the area. Dods, who was preaching in Levant at the time, had also influenced Quimby. Quimby describes in his notebooks at least one meeting with Dods and a discussion with him about his *Six Lectures on the Philosophy of Mesmerism*. Lucius Burkmar, Quimby's protégé and mesmeric subject, with whom he traveled on an exhibition tour from 1843 to 1844, recorded similar observations. A few years later, Burkmar traveled with Dods on an exhibition tour, and some years after that, Quimby treated Mrs. Patterson (that is, Mary Baker Eddy) to free her from her invalidism, inspiring in her the idea of mental cures.

Quimby, Dods, and a few other itinerant mesmerists in the region, including James Stanley Grimes, all interacted with one another. Dods's and Quimby's method for trance induction, for example, did not put their subjects into a state of unconsciousness but allowed them to remain awake and alert, although still under control. Grimes always gave a nonreligious or nonspiritual explanation for mesmeric and spiritualistic phenomena, and he debated against spiritualists on the subject.

Dods also experimented with alchemy. When he was lecturing to the senators in Washington, D.C., in 1851, he told them that he believed that there was nothing in the world (at least, nothing solid and visible) that was not a composite. Henry Clay suggested to Dods that if his theories were true, then he should be able to manufacture gold. Dods began experimenting, and almost two years later, "he succeeded in producing gold in all its qualities save one." He believed, at that point, that he would be able to "produce gold equal in quality to any found in California," even though the process was slow. Nevertheless, the newspapers reported, "He thinks that in less than a year he will be able, by the assistance of ten men's labor, to manufacture *one* if not *two tons* of gold per day!"— a prediction that clearly never panned out.

Calvinist orthodoxy held that humans could in no way compel God's grace through their actions. But the logic of revivalism brought this into question, for humans could at least *act* to make themselves fit vessels for the grace that God had promised to those who repented and turned to him. In practice, this amounted to specifying a natural means of inducing God's grace in an experience of personal salvation.

Charles Grandison Finney explained his techniques for bringing people into a state receptive to grace in his *Lectures on Revivals*. Finney made spiritualism equivalent to Universalism on the basis that neither ever "saved a man from sin" but made people happy despite their not being "fit for heaven." Each was, therefore, "a refuge of lies." But Dods's methods of inducing the experience of grace, which he explained in *Six Lectures on the Philosophy of Mesmerism* and in more detail in *The Philosophy of Electrical Psychology*, also assumed that humans could use natural methods to achieve salvation. For Dods, nature was the means through which God worked in the world and the means by which it could be regenerated.

With this formulation, Dods was able to reconcile science and religion, for it made the study and use of the natural world a religious and moral activity. It treated even the spirit as a natural phenomenon, susceptible to scientific explanation and manipulation. For Dods, entering a trance or ecstatic state provided the bridge between Heaven and Earth. Doing so effected an inner alchemy that transmuted spirit into matter and joined the soul and body. In this, Dods was following in the path trod by George de Benneville, America's first preacher of universal salvation.

De Benneville was an eighteenth-century French Pietist who had joined hundreds of other religious enthusiasts at gatherings in the French mountains, where spontaneous visions and trances spread through the crowds. After an experience of receiving God's grace, he became a preacher of universal salvation and later fled to America to escape persecution. On one occasion around 1750, he fell into a fever and then into a coma, in which he seemed to have died. Three days later, during his wake, he revived, emerged from his coffin, and described having been transported into a realm of angels, saints, and universal love. In his vision, Heaven was brought into the world over a bridge of visionary enlightenment. As the spirit of Adam told him during his heavenly sojourn,

> My dear brother, rejoice with universal and eternal joy, as you are favored with the heavenly visions. It is in this manner that our adorable Royal High Priest, mediator, and intercessor, shall restore all my descendents to the glory of our God. And their eternal and universal salvation for the kingdom of eternal love hath power sufficient to draw all mankind out of their bondage, and to exclaim and say, "O death, where is thy sting, etc."

The experience was spiritualistic but also had a more overtly occult meaning. De Benneville was a Universalist preacher and a physician but also a Rosicrucian and alchemist. He had settled among a community of German Pietists in the Wissahickon Valley in Pennsylvania and become close friends with the most mystical wing of another group of Pietists within the Ephrata cloister, further west. This radical wing engaged in practices based on the Hermetic notions of religious *regeneration and generation,* to which they gave an alchemical (and physical) meaning. The practices were meant to effect the internal transmutation of mind and matter through the *leading of the spirit,* a notion that was reinforced by German Pietist medical ideas, according to which elementary, lifeless matter transmuted itself into living matter.

The mystical wing within the Ephrata cloister formed a Brotherhood of Zion, which conducted ceremonies based on those of the irregular orders of Freemasonry. De Benneville supplied the alchemical laboratory at Ephrata with a gold tincture for transmuting base elements into gold. Ephrata member Ezechiel Sangmeister was de Benneville's good friend, and either he or his alchemist friend Jacob Martin was the intermediary who supplied de Benneville's universal tincture to the community.

De Benneville's own experience of death and rebirth lasted *forty hours.* The Brotherhood of Zion's most important ceremony of death and rebirth lasted *forty days*. Perhaps they never actually performed the rite but always held it out as a goal—the ultimate stage of initiation for members of the Brotherhood. In theory, anyway, the rite regenerated the mind and body through the administration of alchemical preparations, some of which induced loss of consciousness, perhaps even death and revivification. This resulted in regaining the *state of primitive innocence.*

A disposition to credit the mind's or spirit's magical manipulation and shaping of matter would be necessary in order to accept spiritual contact as true. The mixing of the realms of spirit and matter, which is at the heart of alchemy, provided the philosophical bridge that reconciled de Benneville's identities as physician and mystic. It would also connect spiritualism's simultaneous fascination with experimental science and with religion, for like alchemy, spiritualism was a technology of the spirit.

Many Universalist clergy would also cross this bridge as they became spiritualist mediums and healers, activists both in the radical politics of liberation and in experimental utopian communalism. At the point at which spirit and matter intersected, women and men were to be reborn in spirit and society as a whole would be transmuted by an egalitarian providence whose material creation was a vast systematic catalog of signs expressing the mind of God. Spiritualism's goal was to revive the corpse of religion, killed by materialism. As Ralph Waldo Emerson said of Swedish seer Emanuel Swedenborg's spiritual visions of angels in the niches and cracks of the material world,

> To the withered traditional church yielding dry catechisms, he let in nature again, and the worshipper, escaping from the vestry of verbs and texts, is surprised to find himself a party to the whole of his religion. His religion thinks for him, and is of universal application. He turns it on every side; it fits every part of life, interprets and dignifies every circumstance.

The Seer of Poughkeepsie

Gibson Smith, one of John Bovee Dods's students, believed his teacher to be the era's most able theologian and followed him in mixing religious Universalism with experiments in mesmerism and so-called electrical psychology. He also followed Dods into the Universalist ministry, into mesmeric experimentation, and then later into spiritualism and alternative medicine. In addition, Smith joined one of Dods's projects, explaining away miraculous aspects of the Christian tradition.

Smith edited and published an apocryphal gospel of Matthew and some supposed letters of the Apostle Peter, represented as having been found in the catacombs in Rome. The letters revealed that the Apostle Paul had converted to Christianity as a trick in order to lead the faith astray and therefore destroy it. Dods wrote a letter as an introduction to Smith's work, in which he said that while he did not question Smith's honesty regarding the letters, he could not believe that Paul was such a villain. This interest in alternative narratives of the Christian story would blossom in a few years in spiritualism at large. That is, new narratives of the life of Jesus and his disciples would be delivered through mediums from the spirits of Jesus and the Apostles, in which they revealed secrets about their real teachings.

The Maine Convention of Universalists had ordained Smith in 1835, when he was living and preaching in Dexter, Maine. From 1844 to 1845, he was the pastor of the Universalist church in Poughkeepsie, New York. He also experimented with mesmerism and discovered and cultivated a seventeen-year-old youth in town who was a sensitive clairvoyant subject. That youth, Andrew Jackson Davis, had become interested in mesmerism during an 1843 public exhibition in Poughkeepsie of mesmerist lecturer James Stanley Grimes, who had mesmerized members of his audience.

Davis was born in 1826. He had been close to his mother, but she died when he was still a boy and he had little contact with his alcoholic father. After the youth gained practice at being mesmerized, he became a ready clairvoyant, traveling through the cosmic ether, as far as his mesmeric operator commanded. He traveled to distant places but also into bodies of people who were sick, where the sources of their diseases would become transparent to his vision. While still under trance, he prescribed herbal remedies or physical exercises for these individuals.

When Davis first manifested his clairvoyant abilities, Abner Rogers Bartlett was pastor of the Universalist society in Poughkeepsie. Born and raised in New Hartford, New York, Bartlett had become a Universalist minister in 1839 and had served as pastor at Bath, Maine, before coming to Poughkeepsie. Bartlett had given Davis the youth's only clerical example of love and sympathy and had become his spiritual teacher, although Davis wrote later that he did not relish studying biblical criticism and other such bookish pursuits, as Bartlett's denomination practiced. Rather, "owing solely to the attractive influence of pure friendship," he wrote, "I allowed myself one day to be openly recognized as a brother in the Faith!"

Bartlett eventually left the ministry, however, and Gibson Smith took his place as pastor in Poughkeepsie. With these two Universalist mentors, it is not surprising that Davis's clairvoyant visions took on a Universalist tone. He saw the sanctified glory in which all beings already partake through an indwelling of the spirit and by which they will, in the future, be brought into salvation. His was an ecstatic vision of universal love and luminous energy, one that was filled with colors and flames, "like the breath of diamonds," and in which the spiritual beings wore "crowns of spiritual brightness decorated with shining crescents and flaming jewels." What he saw was the natural correspondence between this world and the glory of the next. "What is thus natural to the human brain in this, its first stage of existence," he wrote, "is preserved and indescribably improved in the Spirit-Land to which we are all surely tending. . . . Thus I saw not only the real physical structures themselves, but also their indwelling essences and vitalic elements." Disclosed to his vision was "that festive illumination which the ten thousand flames of the golden candles of life imparted to every avenue, pillar, chamber, window, and door, of the human temple!"

Under Bartlett's tutelage, Davis's trance experiences grew beyond mesmeric clairvoyance and glittering mystic visions of cosmic interconnection. Disembodied intelligences of deceased humans began to contact and guide him. For the spiritualist movement that was to come, this was an important development. Dods had prepared the way, but out of the many mesmeric experimenters, only he and a few others had also used theological language to frame the phenomenon of mesmerism and to explain clairvoyance as a religious experience.

When Smith took over as pastor from Bartlett, he acted as Davis's impresario for a while, initially sending him on astral tours via his spirit in order to envision people and places as far back as Maine, from where Smith had come. Smith's Universalist minister friends also came to Poughkeepsie to visit and test the youth. One of them, Luke Prescott Rand, from Orono, Maine, wrote a glowing tribute to Davis's diagnostic abilities. Smith included this testimonial in a pamphlet he published in 1845, *Lectures on Clairmativeness; or Human Magnetism,* in which he described teachings that Davis had given in trance.

The trance lectures that young Davis gave Smith are reminiscent of Dods's amalgam of mesmerism, electrical psychology, theology, and medicine. Davis mirrored back to Smith the theories that the minister brought to the subject to try to understand what was happening. Davis was reluctant to declare himself a Universalist, and the Universalist ministers and laypeople who clustered around him also tended to discount his ties to the denomination.

Minimizing his education, his level of literacy, and the influence they had over him maximized the general impression that Davis's discourses came from the beyond, because on his own and

others' testimony, he had been incapable of producing them out of
his own intellectual resources. Even so, while writing later that
Davis had had very little education, Bartlett did say that he "possessed an inquiring mind—loved books, especially controversial
religious works, which he always preferred, whenever he could bor-
row them and obtain leisure for their perusal." And Davis's later
associate, William Fishbough, wrote,

> I know, however, as others know, that Mr. Davis has a remarkable
> aptness in catching, appropriating, and expanding such matters
> as his eye may casually rest upon as floating through the channels
> of newspaper literature, and especially such as may be thrown out
> by his intelligent friends (of whom he has many) during his con-
> versational intercourse with them.

In trance, Davis expounded on the nature of the brain, the
"structure of the muscular and sympathetic nerves," the "production of Mind," and "the Duality of Mind." He explained that magnetic and electric fluids in the atmosphere affected the brain and
served as the intermediary between mind and matter. On Smith's
suggestion, Davis traveled far into space, out among the planets,
and reported back in trance the nature of comets, for instance.
Davis also reported on a visit to the planet Saturn, which he revealed was inhabited. Moreover, the people on Saturn were more
beautiful and intelligent than the people on Earth. They had very
high foreheads, translucent skin, and perfectly symmetrical bodies.
They lived to one thousand years of age without sickness, strife, or
sin and "worship God with willing hearts, all as one."

Having the subject travel outside the body was a typical part of
a mesmeric exhibition. On tour with Phineas Quimby, Lucius
Burkmar described an exhibition (or "experiment," as he called it)
they gave one night in which Burkmar left the hall, while his body
remained on stage, and went to the house of someone from the audience, whom he had brought up on the stage. "Our experiments
last night proved very satisfactory to the audience," Burkmar
wrote. With the first person brought up on stage that night, Burk-

mar had traveled psychically to the gentleman's house and then returned to describe its rooms, including the study where Burkmar saw in his vision a map lying on the floor. As the gentleman left the stage, he told the audience "that before he left his house he put a map upon the floor."

Smith went on tour to Albany, New York, and elsewhere with Davis and the youth's mesmerist, a tailor from Poughkeepsie. At demonstrations, Smith gave lectures or sermons, after which Davis, mesmerized, exhibited his clairvoyant powers, including his ability to diagnose and prescribe for the illnesses of the audience members. By the end of the tour, it was clear to Smith that the audiences had not come to hear his sermons but to gaze on the clairvoyant boy wonder and be healed.

As a consequence, Smith returned to Poughkeepsie to occupy his pulpit at the Universalist Society. He found, however, that traveling about with Davis had not increased his congregation's affection for him. Davis later wrote that they, "being in quest of respectability and popularity, refused to extend as cordially as before the right hand of fellowship" to Smith, which gave him an opportunity to revise the lectures he had transcribed from the entranced Davis and publish them.

Later, Smith moved to South Shaftsbury, Vermont. In the fall of 1851, he began seeing angels and was himself "endowed with the faculty of seeing the internal organs of the body"—of seeing disease, and, simultaneously, its remedy. Like Davis, he also claimed that he traveled psychically to other planets. By the early 1860s, he moved back to Camden, Maine, from where he toured, giving lectures in spiritualism and giving demonstrations of clairvoyant medical diagnoses. Like Dods, Smith, too, left the Universalist ministry. And years later, his physiological views still echoed Dods's notion that the living world was an emanation of God. "Universal life is the inner *Temple* in which the infinite *spirit* is enshrined," he wrote, "and physical organization is the outer *Court* of that temple, and is a faithful record of the doings of the august divine *worker* within."

Smith's friend, Universalist minister Luke Prescott Rand, who had written a testimonial for Davis, was born in 1816 in Canaan, Maine. He served Universalist Societies in Cumberland and Kennebunk and then became the pastor of the Universalist church in Orono. He developed an interest in mesmerism and participated in demonstrations when they were first conducted in Portland. In 1845, Rand moved to Poughkeepsie to take over the pastorate of the Universalist Society in place of his friend Smith, while Smith "suspended his clerical labors . . . in order to devote himself more effectively to the theory and practice of Mesmerism." The Poughkeepsie Universalist Society did little better at keeping Rand's attention away from mesmerism than they had done with Smith, and so the society dissolved and sold their church to the Baptists.

Rand moved back to Bangor, Maine, and participated in the spirit circles that formed there in the early and mid 1850s. He was converted to spiritualism by the messages given during these séances. "These communications, thus received," he wrote later, "were fraught with suggestions of inestimable significance and power in relation to momentous considerations, touching the elevation, purity and improvement of our race."

The spread of the gospel of spiritualism resembled that of Universalism in its earlier years. Universalism had grown through itinerant preaching and the gathering of small groups into a community of the spirit. In small, Pietistic study circles, the early Universalists found a way to the heart. In the backwoods gatherings of the evangelists of universal salvation, small communities felt the living present. It was the meeting point of the past—the experience of the first, primitive Christians—with the future—a foretaste of the ultimate salvation of humankind in God's love. In spirit circles, too, those gathered in the present felt themselves intermingling with the lives of those in the past and entering into their own future blessed immortality. Spiritualism opened wide the gates of Heaven.

In the charmed circle of the séance, a group would share an experience in which the dark obstructions and pains and limitations of this life became transparent and even dissolved. The boundaries between the realms encompassed by memory would dissipate, and those living in the present would commune with their friends and loved ones from the past, clothed in angelic robes of glory in a reconciliation of ecstasy, joy, and peace. Heaven and Earth would again become one, under blessed providence, in a union so intimate that when leaves skittered across the ground, they seemed to trace the intentions and actions of angels.

Even those Universalists who did not defect to spiritualism could appreciate, given the Pietistic past of their denomination, that spiritualism renewed the sense of the spirit that had begun to disappear from the faith. Heaven was not far away from Earth; the spirit (and the spirits) was close by. Angels were busy in this world, for God wasted nothing. As described by James Martin Peebles in *Seers of the Ages; Embracing Spiritualism, Past and Present,* "God has a use or employment for all the creatures he has made, for every saint on earth, for every angel in heaven. He would that none be idle. He has a mission for every one."

The atmosphere in Maine during the 1850s, when Rand began attending séances, seems to have been electrified by spiritualism. Consider the experience of Elihu Baxter Averill. He entered the ministry and served a Universalist Society in Hampden, Maine, before settling in Dover, Maine, as pastor. He was converted to the gospel of angelic visitation, however, and through his preaching, had a strong influence on the Universalists in Maine, drawing many of them to spiritualism. A Congregationalist minister wrote a history of the region, in which he described the times:

> At length, "spiritism" arose. Many, before indifferent to all shades of belief, and other neglecters of the Bible, were fascinated by its [spirit] rappings, and eagerly swallowed its pretended communications. The great majority of Universalists adopted it, and some of other sects. A part of the ministers went with the majority, a part kept silent, and a part openly opposed it. Their meetings dwindled, some were suspended, their churches also expired.

Although Averill remained beloved by many in his congregation, the Universalist authorities dropped him from fellowship. A genealogical history, avoiding any mention of the controversy, says that when he left the ministry, he took a position in Dover as registrar of deeds, "an affection [sic] of the throat having made it advisable for him to cease preaching."

In 1857, two boys from Buffalo, New York, Ira and William Davenport, who were building reputations as mediums and escape artists, traveled with their father on a tour to Maine and stayed there for almost a year. Luke Rand was extraordinarily moved by the phenomena that manifested at their spirit circles, such as phosphorescent spirit hands that appeared in the darkness of the séance room and floated about in the air, writing out communications from the dead. As proof of their innocence, the boys invited participants to tie their hands to their chairs. As their performances evolved, the boys incorporated the untying of the ropes' knots in the dark as proof of the power of the spirits.

Rand became devoted to the boys, and with a missionary's conviction about the new religious dispensation that he believed the spirits were initiating, he accompanied them on a performance, lecture, and séance tour through New England and then across New York State. The three were arrested in Oswego, New York, however, and prosecuted under a local ordinance prohibiting jugglery, a charge at which Rand was indignant. They were jailed for almost a month, Rand said, "on account of propagating our religious principles."

A couple of days before their jail sentence ended, he later wrote, angelic spirits granted him a sign to demonstrate to others the spirits' power. Late one night, the spirits unlocked his cell door and a voice addressed him. "Rand, you are to go out of this place this night. Put on your coat and hat—be ready," it said. The cell door was "immediately thrown open," and he heard the voice speak to him again. "Now walk quickly out and on to the attic window yonder, and let thyself down by a rope and flee from this place. We will take care of the boys—There are many angels present, though but one speaks."

Convinced that his jailbreak was accomplished to let others come to understand the power of the spirits, Rand did not flee town. He waited outside on the street until morning, when he presented himself to the alarmed constabulary, who in the end did not press any further charges against him. Perhaps Rand had convinced others that the episode bore a striking resemblance to the angels' freeing of the Apostle Peter from King Herod's prison. Years later, Rand's self-published pamphlet describing his jail escape and his adventures with the Davenports made its way into the hands of Harry Houdini, who knew the Davenports' performances well, for they continued to tour for another two decades in the United States and Europe. Some of Houdini's most famous escapes were from locked jail cells, a stage act that was perhaps bequeathed to him by Rand's angels.

A Voice to Humankind

AFTER PARTING WAYS WITH GIBSON SMITH, Andrew Jackson Davis surprised an enthusiastic Universalist clergy, William Fishbough, with a commission in a letter in November 1845 to act as his amanuensis or phonographer, writing down what came out of his mouth while in the superior state. Fishbough, born in 1814, was trained for the ministry in Philadelphia by Abel Charles Thomas. Although he was living in New Haven, Connecticut, and without a congregation at the moment he received Davis's letter, Fishbough had been a pastor in Massachusetts at the Taunton Universalist Society and before that at the First Universalist Society of Southold, on Long Island, New York. He met Davis early in 1844, when he stopped in Poughkeepsie to preach to the Universalist Society there. Fishbough was no doubt impressed because he eagerly accepted Davis's offer.

Fishbough's first public description to his Universalist colleagues of Davis's powers came in November 1846. He wrote to *The Universalist Union* that Davis, in the clairvoyant state, had discovered an eighth planet of the solar system, something that scientists had later inferred from perturbations they observed in the orbit of Uranus. (Actually, Davis had described an eighth and a ninth planet.) In that article, Fishbough asked,

> Who will shrink from any light on such a subject, or having such objects and tendencies, in a blind and bigoted affection for some paltry, despicable, sectarian *tweedledum* or *tweedledee*? And what folly so foolish as to close the mental eye to the almost *demonstrative* evidence which this very *phenomenon* presents, of future and immortal existence, the goal of the highest and holiest hopes of man? Reader, let *truth* prevail, though all hereditary and conventional forms of belief be sacrificed!

The editor of *The Universalist Union,* Philo Price, introduced this claim of astronomical discovery with a caveat. He wrote that he knew Davis and Fishbough well and did not doubt their honest convictions. Also, he had seen Davis at work and found "something perfectly inexplicable" in his clairvoyance, but he could not give credence to everything claimed about him:

> We are not ashamed to confess our inability to answer it satisfactorily, even to our ourselves. We know not what to say of it. We are neither prepared to admit his claims, or reject them, in toto; but may be said to be in a glorious state of *between-a-tive-ness,* if we may be allowed to coin an expression.

Samuel Byron Brittan was another Universalist clergy who joined the circle around Davis at this time. Brittan was born around 1815 in Massachusetts "of Puritan ancestry." He was educated in the Baptist church but became "a believer in Universalism from an instinctive opposition of reason" to the idea of eternal damnation and from an "innate sense of justice." He decided to become a minister, and his first settlement after ordination was as pastor of the First Universalist Church of Albany, New York, from 1842 to 1843.

Brittan then moved to Connecticut with his wife, Elizabeth, where he became pastor of the First Universalist Society of Bridgeport. Brittan was also active in radical reform movements, writing and lecturing on temperance and abolition of the death penalty. He remained in Bridgeport until he was convinced by his previous congregation in Albany to return and lead an expansion of their society from 1846 to 1847.

At that time, Brittan was studying the new phenomena of mesmerism, clairvoyant healing, and psychology, and he had begun to lecture about them. One of his protégés during this time, Semantha Beers Mettler, achieved great success in her spiritualist career. Through Brittan's liberal preaching in Bridgeport, Mettler had converted to Universalism and soon also developed into a clairvoyant healer and spirit medium. She made journeys throughout the region, sometimes following Brittan's own peripatetic lecturing and healing tours and sometimes under the guidance of her own spiritual influences, who led her where her powers were needed.

Mettler also formulated and sold nostrums from recipes dictated to her by the spirits. Decades before Lydia Estes Pinkham (another Universalist turned spiritualist) began selling her tonics and elixirs, Mettler became famous throughout New England for advertising her mail-order products: Mrs. Mettler's Celebrated Dysentery Cordial, Mrs. Mettler's Restorative Syrup, and Mrs. Mettler's Cholera Elixir. She was a healing clairvoyant, "instrumental for the working of 'miraculous cures,'" according to spiritualist historian Emma Hardinge. "The suffering and afflicted crowded her rooms from morning till night, whilst the records of the cures she performed under the avowed influence of spirits would fill a volume."

Brittan estimated that over the first ten years of Mettler's mediumship, three years were completely lost to her because she was in trance most of the time. Moreover, he estimated that she had treated with her clairvoyant healing power thirty thousand patients, of whom only a handful had not been fully satisfied. "Owing to her extraordinary success, her name has found its way into almost every city and hamlet in the United States," Brittan enthused, "and scattered abroad all over the continent are the people who rise up and call her blessed."

Mettler also provided an open channel to the spirits for some of her friends and clients. Alvin Adams, for example, the entrepreneur who founded the successful delivery service Adam's Express, was a devoted believer in spirit contact, a vice-president of the New England Spiritualists Association, and one of Mettler's most frequent clients. She acted as a medium for him to receive business advice from the spirit of Daniel Webster. After Mettler's husband, Johnson, ran into financial difficulties in his own business, he became her assistant and partner in her healing work.

Under the control of spirits at circles, Mettler would sometimes be guided to dance, do pantomime, or play out impromptu and improvised dramatic scenes that carried some "great moral or spiritual truth" and often described the transition of the soul at death into the wonders of the next life. Others present at the circles also participated, all in trance and thus transfigured into representations of spirits and angels. Mettler's biographer explained,

> As there is no programme of the performances, and therefore the spectators do not know what is coming till it is nearly or quite past, and at the same time the actors, themselves, do not remember any thing of what has happened, when they return to the normal state, these representations seem to go by with a kind of meteoric splendor, which arrests the attention, and thrills the heart for a little while; and then it is extremely difficult to give any thing of a definite idea of what has passed.

In 1846, while attending to his pastoral duties in Albany, Brittan became ill and had a near-death experience during a twelve-day fever. As a result, he believed that he had achieved the power of clairvoyance. He had also made contact with spirits of the departed and gained an exalted spirit guide, a "*strange spiritual visitor*," who "engraved on his mind a set of impressions wholly distinct and at variance from those which his former life's images had left." Brittan testified,

> I was attended, almost constantly, by a glorious and majestic being, an angel in superhuman loveliness, benevolence and wisdom—in a word, this blessed companion was all that we have ever dreamed of archangelic perfection, save the fabled wings and the no less fabled distance between poor humanity and celestial love.

This was the pivotal experience that turned Brittan to spiritualism. He wrote,

> New avenues were opened between the soul and the world, and life presented novel and beautiful aspects. The currents of thought and feeling were mysteriously changed, or directed into channels before unknown. Darkness fled from every subject that occupied the mind, and all things appeared to be transparent.

Nevertheless, what Brittan saw in his heavenly travels was in accord with his Universalism because the afterlife appeared to be an opportunity for the rehabilitation of all souls and their evolution into salvation:

> I saw many whom I had known on earth in different stages of progression, and with some of these I conversed, and learned that all were on their upward way according to the strength of individual purpose by which they endeavoured to tread the path of good and reform. Let me add, as the last and most solemn revelation that I brought with me from this land of the hereafter, that though I saw thousands of Christ-like spirits teaching, comforting, and aiding the souls of the guilty to reform and come up higher, I never discovered throughout that universe of sphere life any *Saviour* in the Christian sense of redemption, or any vicarious means of atoning for sin; I saw none, in short, but angels of love and mercy, teaching and inspiring guilty-stained souls to forsake the criminal tendencies they had acquired on earth, and save themselves by penitence and a purer and better life.

Brittan began preaching on the subject of intercourse with the spirit world. Although his society was surprised at this turn of events, the size of the congregation soon doubled. Even so, it is clear that not everyone in the society was pleased with Brittan's new teachings, for he wrote, "I was earnestly solicited to continue the existing relation with the Society, but four months after resigned the pastoral responsibility for the sake of unlimited freedom of thought and expression."

Brittan met Davis when the youth passed through Bridgeport on a public tour. Davis had engaged Brittan's brother-in-law, physician and Universalist Silas Smith Lyon, to act as his mesmeric operator during his stay in Bridgeport. Brittan's meeting with Davis allowed the minister to give a shape to his new religious experiences. It was "the rock that ground the dry bones of his old theology to powder."

Davis had become convinced that tremendous revelations were about to be delivered to the world through him, and he strongly believed that they should enter the world in New York City. He and his amanuensis, Fishbough, moved to New York with Lyon, who abandoned his thriving Bridgeport medical practice. According to Fishbough, they opened up a healing clinic to support themselves while awaiting the revelations.

Not all Universalist clergy were well disposed to Davis and his clairvoyant powers. William Allen Drew, for example, previously editor of *The Christian Intelligencer,* reported in George Quinby's *The Gospel Banner* (and reprinted in *The Universalist Watchman*) that he had "successfully floored the pretensions of Mr. Davis" through a scheme of his own.

Part of Davis's clinical work was to diagnose and prescribe for patients through the mail. To do so, he required only a description of the individual's symptoms and a lock of his or her hair; the latter provided the physical connection that Davis would use to psychically read the patient. To test this, Drew sent Davis locks of hair from the same person but in separate envelopes under the signatures of different people and with descriptions of varying symptoms. He received back from Davis varying diagnoses, which convinced Drew that "his whole art is shown to be the art of humbuggery, and *nothing else!*" Fishbough replied to Drew, however, defending Davis, and received a letter from John Dods's previous Provincetown associate, Universalist clergy Nathaniel Gunnison in Maine. Fishbough wrote Davis that Gunnison "says my reply has been extensively read and much talked about, and that it is the general opinion that it is not all a humbug after all."

Davis began delivering a series of trance lectures—perhaps not from his own exalted spirit exploring the universe but from other spirits he believed were those of the ancient Greek physician Galen and the Swedish seer Emanuel Swedenborg. Davis said that the state from which he uttered these revelations corresponded "almost precisely to that of *physical death.*" Interested observers attended the lectures and watched the slow process: Davis would utter a few words, Lyon would repeat them, and Fishbough would write them down. More than 150 sessions were required to complete Davis's revelations, which were collected in a single volume.

As a whole, the work presented itself as an extended "scientific" lecture on the origin and evolution of the cosmos that was delivered, in effect, through the peculiar mechanics of trance as a self-authenticating religious revelation. It described the development of life on Earth, human evolution from animal life and from primitive to advanced states, and the future of society, which would be organized on the socialist principles of associations and affinities.

The writings of French social philosopher Charles Fourier and other radical socialists had taken the form of utopian prophecies about the revolution of society (and of nature itself) that could occur through social engineering, allowing natural affinities to associate together without hindrance. The notion owed much to the eighteenth-century electromagnetic theories of Anton Mesmer.

Spiritualist mediums believed they dealt in human *magnetisms* and were sensitive to individuals' particular and subtle affinities. If the health of the individual (and indeed, of the entire society) depended on the communion of true affinities of the spirit or the soul, then health and truth depended on separating those who were not affinities with one another (even if artificially bound by an institution or convention) before joining those who were affinities. In many cases, one could do this by provoking a *crisis*, to use Mesmer's word, either within the body (when applied as a medical technique) or within the body politic (when used as a justification for revolution).

This "social science" provided the basis for the spiritualists' critique of the adventitious and therefore unnatural institutions of society—the church and the state—in favor of individual freedom. That freedom could be exercised in a healthy way, however, only when all individuals were brought into communion with higher powers or principles. It is not surprising that one of the few regular visitors to Davis's series of trance revelations was Albert Brisbane, a disciple and populizer of social theorist Charles Fourier.

Despite the length of Davis's collection of revelations, the seer refused to be questioned on matters of detail. At one point, he said,

> I am not impressed to descend into the *particulars* of any subject, inasmuch as "particulars are the unreal ramifications of *general principles*, unfolded to the external observation of mankind." *Minutiae*, therefore, are, according to my impressions, *unreal* and *excrescent*, though these are often collected as evidences to establish metaphysical hypotheses.

This describes Davis's method fairly well: expostulating worlds of detail while preempting discussion of them as unimportant.

The teachings that emerged from Davis on the origin of mythological theology took aim at traditional Christian doctrine. They construed Christianity as a primitive religion with a symbolic history, which, in its literal reading, had "no foundation in Nature." Rather, it existed as shorthand "in the language of correspondence." Cain and Abel, for instance, were not actual people but symbols of two groups of primitive, warring tribes—say, one from Asia and one from Africa—embodying different "incipient stages of civilization."

Fishbough, who had been convinced that he was receiving the truth from Davis, suffered a crisis of faith when he heard this critique of Christianity. "He labored with a heart full of disappointment," Davis later wrote. "The divine origin of the Bible, its superterrestrial derivation and value, was an idea which involved his sentiments and religious experience." After a days' long struggle, however, Fishbough was somehow able to reconcile what he had heard from Davis with his own religious beliefs—at least for a while.

Fishbough would later say that he regarded Davis's utterances in trance as those of "a spirit freed, by a process of nature from the obstructing influence of the physical organization, and exalted to a position which gave access to a knowledge of the structure and laws of the whole material and spiritual Universe." Moreover, Fishbough said that he regarded "*Truth* with infinitely more reverence" than he regarded "a certain *book*," meaning the Bible. The one was a stable principle, he said, while the other was "mere paper and ink, composed of certain well known chemical elements." In fact, like Dods, Davis had made God and nature coextensive. There was no special dispensation except from natural causes and conditions. The works of nature were identified as the means through which God's providence was effected.

Although Fishbough's biblical faith was challenged, others found the lectures that Davis delivered in trance to be in harmony with Universalist doctrine. The revelation, for example, attributed the origin of evil not to innate depravity but to circumstances that could be remedied through education, "the various conditions that were *incidentally* established among mankind in consequence of the uncultivated state of their mental and moral faculties, and of these being improperly directed." The devil was a personification of primitive people's socially misdirected feelings of vengeance and retaliation. Human nature was "divine, perfect, and harmonious" and "represents the divineness of its great Origin and Cause." In addition, "retrogression is a word, like death, having no meaning. Everything is unfolding life and beauty, according to the law of progressive and eternal development." Jesus was not God or even a miracle worker but a prophet, a reformer, and an "exemplifier of the true moral and spiritual qualities of man."

One skeptical observer told Fishbough, "The theology of the work is inclined toward Universalism, of which you are an intelligent preacher. . . . Now don't he get *that* from association with *you* and others of like faith?" One Methodist critic later wrote of Davis's book that it "abounds with unmistakable internal evidence that it was written by one familiar with Universalism and its methods of interpreting scripture." By this, he meant Davis's readiness to explain away as allegorical or mythological or parabolic the aspects of the scriptures that suggested anything less than universal law and love.

Brittan stopped by one night at the small apartment that Davis and Fishbough shared with Lyon in New York City, where he found "a tall and slender youth, ungainly in appearance, awkward in gesture" and "with a pale, thin visage, and long unkempt black hair," who, he was told, had never been to school. When the lights were turned down, the youth, Davis, went into a trance and began to speak. As described by Brittan, "In a voice deep, firm but exquisitely modulated, and in accents as pure, noble, and high toned as those of the most accomplished orator, the now transfigured rustic" began a lecture that described "the creation, the origin of all things, the nature of matter, force, and spirit; the order of the heavens; the stellar firmaments, known and unknown."

Brittan moved to New York City to join Davis and his associates and attended the young man's trance lectures. He helped find funding for the publication of Davis's lectures in book form, for which Fishbough was the editor (despite Fishbough's avowed disdain for mere paper and ink). The publication of that book, *The Principles of Nature, Her Divine Revelations, and a Voice to Mankind,* in the late summer of 1847 was one of two events that precipitated spiritualism out of the swirling religious atmosphere of the time. Davis's work—despite its mysticism, its recourse to fantasy, and its attribution to disembodied spirits of the dead—was widely received as a radical but progressive, rationalist critique of revealed religion.

The Spirit of Inquiry Run Riot

BECAUSE IT WAS ACCOMPLISHED by a group of Universalist clergy and because it touched so many theological nerves in Universalism, the publication of Andrew Jackson Davis's *The Principles of Nature, Her Divine Revelations, and a Voice to Mankind* caused a sensation in the Universalist press. Some of that sensation was positive. Universalist minister John Murray Spear, for example, in the briefest of notices in *The Prisoner's Friend*, the newspaper he worked on with his brother, Charles, wrote, "I have not yet thoroughly read this work, though I intend to do so; therefore I am incompetent to express an opinion of it, farther than to say that it now appears to me, as far as I have examined it, to be the most wonderful work ever made by mortal man." But some of the sensation was negative. The Reverend Thomas Whittemore later wrote in *The Trumpet and Universalist Magazine*, "We were exceedingly sorry to see Br. J. M. Spear showing an inclination to foster the infidelity of A. J. Davis' revelations."

Univeralist minister William Stevens Balch had known Davis for a few years, since he had gone to New York and seen several exhibitions of Davis's clairvoyant powers. At first, Balch was cautiously but somewhat favorably disposed to Davis, whom he found "a sincere and pure-hearted young man." Balch allowed that he had known Davis to make mistakes but believed that they were unintended. He had also heard Davis enunciate "some of the sublimest truths and sentiments" he had ever heard.

Balch had read portions of the transcription of *The Principles of Nature* in manuscript as the work went on. He later reviewed the book in *The Universalist Union* based only on those early selections, not on a reading of the final book, which would not be published until a month after his review. And so while he did not then express a final opinion on the book, he did describe it as claiming "to consist of the consecutive reasonings and revelations of a spirit freed by a process analogous to physical death, from all the darkening and obstructing influences of the flesh, and elevated to a higher sphere of knowledge and observation, even to the spiritual world." He also judged its aim to be "the establishment of a lofty spiritualism" and "the destruction of all sectarism, and other social antagonisms, and a uniting of the race in the bonds of one vast Brotherhood."

The first impression of the Reverend Sylvanus Cobb, whose judgment was sought because of his experience with mesmerism, was not favorable, although it was not extremely negative either. He explained how Davis could have achieved his results by combining Swedenborgian and transcendentalist ideas. "He had no doubt obtained, from some source, a smattering of these sentiments," wrote Cobb. "And then, with all his mental powers quickened and expanded in the clairvoyant state, and the faculty of sympathetic correspondence in vivid action, he traced out and delineated in full the sentiments and writings, forms of expression even, of those minds for which he had an affection."

More typical of the Universalist press, however, were sustained attacks, not only on the work but also on the Universalist clergy who had presumably nurtured it. Especially harsh was a series of denunciations by Whittemore in *The Trumpet and Universalist Magazine* from Boston. Balch published another attack in *The Christian Ambassador* after he completed a full, considered reading of the published book. In *The Christian Messenger* of New York, Thomas Jefferson Sawyer wrote of Davis, Brittan, and Fishbough, "From the first to the last they have exhibited a quibbling, shuffling, trickish course" in propagating "a second Book of Mormon." Sawyer then, in what Whittemore called "a manly and pithy manner," accused the three of duplicity and deceit. He wrote,

> Is this honest? Can it be honest? Are these men *mad-men* or *idiots,* that they do not know that the Bible and Davis' Revelations cannot stand together; that Christianity and Davis' pretended philosophy have no harmony? There is but one alternative, sir,

and that, harsh as it may seem, is that they are *dishonest*. . . . It is *not* ignorance, sir. They know themselves to be rank infidels, and yet persist in claiming to be Christians, because they are aware of the advantages which even the profession of this religion affords.

Sawyer declared that *The Principles of Nature* was "directly and utterly opposed to the Bible and the religion of Jesus Christ. The two works cannot stand together; one or the other must fall." He cautioned, "Let Universalists be on their guard" against this "duplicity" and "knavery." And he called on the Universalist associations to officially and publicly withdraw fellowship from those ministers who associated with Davis.

Fishbough responded by reporting a dream, in which he and his colleagues were sparrows being menaced by an eagle tracing out the letters "T J S" in the sky. Feeling secure, however, the sparrows remained perched where they were, while the eagle rushed down onto them. Fishbough wrote,

> He thrust forward his beak, clenched his huge talons, and grasped—*the air*. It appeared that from long visual effort in gazing at those objects which no eagle's eyes are made to gaze at, his eyes had become affected with a species of *amaurosis*, which caused things to appear *where they were not*, and *what they were not*; and hence the aberration of his flight. The fall stunned and wounded him, and caused a vast derangement of his plumage.

Sawyer explained his main objection to spiritualism at a public discussion in New York City that had been addressed earlier by Charles Partridge, of *The Spiritual Telegraph*, and others. Sawyer said,

> I am not satisfied with the view these gentlemen express of the Bible and of Christ because it does not seem to me to come up to the view which the Bible itself expresses, and which Christ took. If I understand him, he was not merely a Christ—a medium of communication between God and men—but *the* Christ. He stood forth pre-eminent. "I am the vine," said he; "ye are the branches"; and God was the great Husbandman over all. If they

abided in him they would share his love. And he spoke of himself as "the light of the world"; and the great good that God was pleased to confer upon the world. If I caught the full meaning of these gentlemen's remarks this evening, they do not believe that Christianity is complete, or that Christ is the Author and Finisher of our faith, but that we are to have it modified by revelations, made to us from day to day.

A few years later, still unreconciled to spiritualism and to Davis's writings, Sawyer gave this advice to Universalists:

Stand back a little from this rampant, mis-named Spiritualism. You can see quite as well and may save yourselves future neglect and trouble. It is by no means proved that Spirits have any thing to do in these exhibitions, and it is quite certain that they are too frivolous and too false to deserve any human attention, even if they were the sole cause of all that was done.

And twenty years later, he was still fighting against Universalist ministers who had turned into spiritualists. At that time, ex-Universalist minister Joseph Osgood Barrett, one of the editors of the Chicago-based spiritualist newspaper *The Spiritual Republic,* noted sarcastically that Sawyer, "the 'iron-clad,' is firing bombshells at certain 'inconsiderate gentlemen,' who have lately been struck by spiritual lightning, and consequently have got their denominational polarity almost reversed."

After Sawyer first published an attack calling for Davis's clerical associates to be disfellowshipped, Brittan, in mock earnestness, wrote,

A solemn *protest* has gone forth to the whole Christian world, Catholic and Protestant, denying our claims to the Christian name and character. Up to this time, there has been no general response from the people, and we believe it is not yet determined whether it be lawful to regard us as "Christians in any sense whatever." We hope this question will be settled soon; this suspense is terrible!

In another note, Brittan explained that Sawyer "believes in plenary inspiration: that the grand old prophets, Jesus and his apostles, absorbed and monopolized all the revelations of God; and hence, that [all] we poor followers of the 19th century get is second-handed, stereotyped forever!"

Spiritualism jettisoned tradition and authority in its search for novel sources of inspired truth. A spiritualist could expect to change his or her beliefs over time through the influence of the spirits. Universalists had a history of coming out of the traditional authority of the old religious dogma, so coming out of Universalism was more of the same. Henry Knapp, a Universalist convert to spiritualism, felt he had left his former denomination behind. He wrote proudly about those

> who refuse to go to mill with the grist in one end of the bag and
> a *stone* in the other, *merely* because their *"fathers* did." [Others]
> seem to think that their theological food has all been mumbled
> for them by their *fathers*; and that all they have now to do is to
> recline on sofas of ease and, young-robins-like, swallow whatever
> happens to have been cherished by their predecessors, though
> the offspring of superstition cradled in credulity. Hence the
> preaching and publications of the denominations are little
> else than a stereotyped edition of the *fathers*.

For Knapp, spiritualism had progressed even beyond the progressions of Universalism.

In returning his letter of fellowship to the St. Lawrence Universalist Association, Edwin Augustus Holbrook, a new spiritualist from Watertown, New York, wrote to his former clerical associates that a true religious sensibility should always be open to new revelation. He wrote, "Pardon me for saying that I believe the Universalist denomination has accomplished, as a sect, a greater work than it can ever do in the future; while the true principles imbodied in it, and which can not be sectarized or made the exclusive property of any, will eternally continue their conquests."

Another Universalist turned spiritualist, Harvey Jones, re-sponded to criticism of spiritualism from George Washington Quinby of Augusta, Maine, editor of *The Gospel Banner and Family Visitant,* a Universalist newspaper. Jones compared "the inspira-tions of a *living faith,*" which he found in spiritualism, to Universal-ism, which, as he wrote to Quinby, "you crystallize into a stationary creed, containing, of course, all there is to be learned from God, the angels, or from man!" Jones believed that spiritualism was the replacement for a moribund Universalism:

> Universalism once had it in its power to have controlled the liberal element of this country; the sun of that day is setting, and the era of its crystallization seems to have begun; while many of the noble and fearless men it called into being are being driven to the wall. The "mother has turned upon her children," and that Church that once so fearlessly courted theological investigation, now shuns it. There is a mighty strife going on in the Universalist ranks, the one side contending for a larger liberty, the other for a narrower creed.

Quinby had written in order to criticize the Reverend Hiram P. Osgood's declaration that he was leaving the Universalist ministry because of his new conversion to spiritualism, his "accession of light." Quinby wrote,

> The Athenian tendency to "new things" has ever been the curse of our ministry. Every nine days' wonder winnows us, and sweeps away a portion of us. Biology, Thusology, Magnetism, Mesmerism, or by whatever name it should be called, has already slain its thousands, and we know not but under its new develop-ment it will carry off its tens of thousands. We need their labors.

Brittan suggested the idea for and then edited and published the first spiritualist newspaper, *The Univercoelum and Spiritual Philosopher.* The word *univercoelum* (pronounced "univer-*see*-lum,*" according to Brittan) was one of many invented by Davis in the trance state. He said that it meant "the united revolving heavens," but in *The Principles of Nature*, he used it to mean something like "the universe of universes" or "the universe, in all its vast interconnectedness."

The newspaper began publication in 1847, soon after *The Principles of Nature* was published. It focused on the so-called harmonial philosophy of young Davis, to whom Brittan had rented a room in his house. Others in the emerging group of Universalist clergy who were turning to spiritualism also worked on the paper. Fishbough was a major contributor of articles to *The Univercoelum and Spiritual Philosopher*, but he had also begun work on *The Macrocosm and the Microcosm*, which would be published in 1852. In it, he developed a theory that combined science and prophecy in suggesting that all natural phenomena existed in cycles and that understanding their periods could allow prediction of the future.

So many Universalists associated themselves with *The Univercoelum and Spiritual Philosopher* that letters to the editor speculated about whether spiritualism was simply a sect of Universalism. One reader, for example, suggested that if Brittan and his colleagues wished to make sure that they were not confused with Universalists, they should cease giving lectures in Universalist churches and find a secular venue and they should refocus their lectures on science, rather than theology.

Some of the Universalist clergy who opposed this interest in spiritualism accused their colleagues of repudiating the Bible and the Gospel message. Some even accused them of a deliberate deception, in which they fed Davis information that he then repeated under trance. Especially galling to the mainstream Universalist commentators (as they reckoned it) was that their former colleagues were "using the credit of the Universalist denomination for the furtherance of views and principles which that denomination does not recognize."

In an unsigned article, one of the clerical editors of *The Universalist Quarterly and General Review* wrote of "certain weaknesses in our own denomination, which have been somewhat aggravated by it [spiritualism]. There are evils among us, which if suffered to grow, would be fatal to our permanence. . . . Now, we have got, somehow, to put a stop to this teeming fecundity among us, or it will put a stop to us." He gave two reasons for why so many Universalists, including clergy, were flocking to Davis's revelations. One was "the great want of systematic mental discipline among us," requiring more rigorous clerical training and examination. The second was that

> our organization is so very loose, that many find a way into our ministry apparently from other than religious motives, especially from ambition to "make a noise in the world" and whose principal qualifications (we mean for making a noise, not for preaching,) are an unfurnished head, a voluble tongue, and a cockerel smartness. They preach a little while, full of zeal; but anon, some novelty agitates the public mind, and, as they have neither stability, nor any settled or well digested faith in religious principles, they are soon off in full chase of the new topic.

He argued that for many people, Universalism was just a transient point on a religious trajectory that led from the strictures of Calvinist orthodoxy into unchartable regions of chaos.

One short career that would illustrate this trajectory was that of Jeremiah Goldsmith Anderson, born in Indiana in 1833. His parents sent him to a Presbyterian academy to prepare him for the ministry, but he resigned, writing an essay declaring his belief in universal salvation. This new, young Universalist soon passed into spiritualism, however, and then perhaps into apocalyptic visions. He moved to Kansas and enlisted in the service of John Brown. He died in October 1859 from bayonet wounds in the stomach after Robert E. Lee's command charged the armory engine house at Harper's Ferry.

Cobb wrote in *The Christian Freeman* that while it may have been necessary for Universalism to be militant and revolutionary

during the previous generation, as it opposed the "illiberality, bigotry and superstition, which were then supposed to enter largely
into all the religious creeds of the times," the situation had
changed. He now proposed that Universalism take a conservative
stance and oppose innovations, which had, in fact, resulted from
the liberal notions that Universalism helped usher in. Cobb wrote,

> It may become necessary to contend for the very *existence* of
> Christianity itself, instead of employing ourselves in freeing it
> from the incongruous materials which human hands have sought
> to incorporate into it. If such a necessity shall be found to exist,
> I trust we shall not be found wanting in our duty. Having given
> the first impulse to the spirit of inquiry, it becomes us to see
> well to it, that it does not run riot with all that is most dear and
> interesting to us.

Brittan and his associates were content to quote Cobb—in effect, to use his own words to convict him of impeding the progress
of truth. Cobb objected to the movement, born within Universalism, that was now leading some, as he saw it, not to a purified and
primitive Christianity, shorn of its priestly baggage, but rather to a
view that was shorn of the Bible and other "primitive myths." As
Davis had put it, while in trance, "Thought, in its proper nature, is
uncontrolled. It is free to investigate, and rise into lofty aspirations.
The only hope for the amelioration of the world is free thought and
unrestricted inquiry." The ideal of untrammeled thought was, in
some sense, the glory of Universalism. Its latitudinarian position
on doctrine, apart from that of universal salvation, was its strength.
However, its mainstream commentators now wondered if its loose-
ness was to be the cause of its undoing.

Cobb, despite his conservative caution, was a moderate within
Universalism in the controversy. His practice as a mesmerist had
convinced him that "mind can silently commune with mind, and
act upon other minds" and "minds of those in the spiritual body,
which are more elevated and powerful, may act upon our minds."

He was also prepared to believe that much of the information that spirits were supposed to give a séance's eager participants through inexplicable means actually came from the clairvoyant medium, who had left the body for a while and traveled to some other place or time. Nevertheless, he was a spiritualist, for he believed that some cases of spirit contact were real.

Cobb objected, however, to whatever in the new revelations of Davis and others was at odds with traditional Christian doctrine. His spiritualism affirmed the truths of religion, as they were already believed. He advised those spiritualists who held to Christian doctrine that

> even if your minister does not happen as yet to have gone fully with you in the actual greeting of the immortalized departed, if he is a Christian, you will find no occasion to abandon him, for he will faithfully and feelingly preach unto you the same spiritual truths in which your communings have enlivened and confirmed you, and the same spiritual life.

For Cobb, true spiritualism led nowhere else than to Christianity: "I find in it some beautiful confirmations of the hopes of Christianity; and nothing more. There is no *substitute* for Christianity here, and there never can be. It is perfect. It is the ultimate religion." He published letters from Universalist spiritualists, such as the Reverend Moses Ballou, who saw spiritualism as a vivification of their Christian lives. One correspondent wrote,

> Now the question comes up, what shall I do? Shall I tear myself away from my former religious associates, simply because I have been blessed with more light? I believe none the less in the ultimate salvation of the human race; I have none the less reverence for God and his government. I read the Bible with increased interest, and pray with greater fervor than ever before.

Cobb's son James had died as a child from a wasting disease, but the boy had felt in his final days that he had been visited by heavenly beings. Cobb believed this proved that "to some of the dying, the door of the Spirit world is kindly opened even before they are quite departed from the earthly." His wife, Eunice, became a partial medium and received messages of comfort from their son. In 1852, she wrote *Memoir of James Arthur Cobb*, detailing the boy's final passing and his subsequent contact with his loved ones.

When Cobb criticized some spiritualists for their versions of spiritualism, they raised the issue of his family's postmortem communications from the boy. Cobb replied in anger that his little James had "urged a devoted love of the Scriptures, and a profound reverence of the Sabbath, and a religious punctuality in attendance upon public worship and secret prayer, and a vigorous support of the Universalist Christian ministry." In addition, he wrote, "Since his resurrection to the high spirit sphere, he maintains the same sentiments" and urges "an entire separation from the whole anti-Bible, anti-minister, anti-Sabbath, anti-Universalist, and anti-Christian school" of spiritualism.

Cobb's other son, adventure novelist Sylvanus Cobb, Jr., wrote a biography of his father, in which he reproduced a loving letter that his father had written to his mother. It stated that if one of them died before the other, they would still have constant, real communication with each other. In fact, Cobb had explicitly and repeatedly declared his belief in contact with spirits. In a letter he sent to *The New-England Spiritualist* as a rebuttal to the Reverend Asa Mahan's criticism of spiritualism as "demonic," Cobb wrote, "I believe and rejoice in spirit manifestations, not as a substitute for Christian revelation, but as a happy confirmation."

Luther Colby, editor of the Boston-based spiritualist newspaper *The Banner of Light*, remembered after Eunice Cobb's death that she had encouraged him to begin this publication. He said that she had told him, "You will be opposed by the clergy; but fear not. In our Heavenly Father's own good time you will reap the reward of well-doing." As for Eunice's having become an inspirational medium, Colby wrote, "She did not wish us at the time to make the fact known, for the reason that her husband was a Universalist minister and editor of a Universalist paper." Sylvanus Cobb, however, did write a series of articles in *The Christian Freeman* during the spring and summer of 1858, in which he tried to separate the true spiritualism that sustained his Christian faith from what he regarded as delusory, false spiritualism.

Spiritualist and ex-Universalist minister James Martin Peebles, ever ready to detect and encourage Universalists' moving into spiritualism, wrote an obituary for Cobb in *The Banner of Light*. He wrote that Cobb "was a Spiritualist at heart, although he did not publicly endorse our grand philosophy, from fear of injuring his popularity among his immediate associates, probably." Spiritualist and ex-Universalist minister Joseph Barrett also named Cobb as a "Christian Spiritualist," the label designating that subgroup of spiritualists who were unwilling to part with Christianity.

The problem with the label "Christian Spiritualist," however, was that applying it was a matter of emphasis and interpretation. One person's reasonable interpretation of the essence of Christianity was another's infidelity. If one set out to separate the excrescences that had grown upon Christianity over the centuries in order to find its true core, he or she was treading a common dissenting Protestant path. Despite or perhaps because of that, the Universalists who turned to spiritualism found it ironic that the "little sect" of Universalism, so often branded as infidel by the mainstream churches, should in turn seem ready to establish a Christian orthodoxy, crystallize it in a creed, and disenfranchise those who did not accept it.

While some spiritualists saw themselves as having shed Christianity for something better, others saw themselves as having progressed into the fulfillment of its highest and original purpose. They were not seeking the enthusiasm of the revival meeting but something just as immediate and personal. They wanted a living, essential religion. Spiritualist Uriah Clark described a Universalist congregation in search of a pastor that could lead them to it:

> All they want is right representations of the gospel, and manifestations of a corresponding nature. Ranting, canting, hobby-riding, destructive, denunciatory, Bible-hating and church-demolishing ranters are not wanted. The people are hungering for the apostolic gospel, which not only preaches but practices, reaching forth the hands of healing to the afflicted, and manifesting spiritual gifts in demonstration of the celestial powers.

Many Universalist clergy who did not declare themselves spiritualists were skeptical of particular instances of purported spirit contact but still accepted the basic fact that spirits could and did inspire the living. As the Reverend Eli Ballou put it, "We believe it as probable that all angels in the spirit world, or in the spheres above us, were once men in the flesh; and that when necessary, and under favorable circumstances, angels from the world of spirits *have* and *do* communicate with spirits in the flesh."

Why Seek Ye the Living
Among the Dead?

ANOTHER UNIVERSALIST MINISTER IN THE GROUP that formed around Andrew Jackson Davis was Joshua King Ingalls. Born in 1816 in Swansea, Massachusetts, Ingalls was trained for the ministry by William Balch. After preaching on Cape Cod and then gaining fellowship with the Universalists as a minister in 1840, Ingalls settled in Southold, on Long Island, where he remained for three years, following Fishbough's tenure there. Then he went to Danbury, Connecticut, and back again to Southold, wrote Samuel Brittan, "until the New York Association of Universalists, alarmed at the growing liberalism of the younger ministers—reduced the theological platform to such narrow dimensions that our friend [Ingalls] fell off, with several of his brethren." Brittan also wrote, "There was no one hurt, and the principal loss sustained was on the part of the denomination." And he commented, "Ecclesiastical councils have very little to do in making and unmaking such men as Ingalls, who found outside the church standing ground so broad and firm that he never troubled himself to so much as attempt the recovery of his old footing in the sectarian institution."

In November 1846, influenced by the heady liberalism of the group around Davis, Ingalls published a long article in *The Universalist Union*. In it, he questioned miracles, and adopting a stance similar to that of controversial Unitarian minister Theodore Parker, he suggested that such questioning was born from a Christian imperative. "It appears to me a mark of skepticism," he wrote, "for us to *doubt* that the miracles, so called, wrought by our Saviour, were the results of fixed laws, and that it is but little, if any thing, short of superstition, to believe that they were effected only by a suspension of laws, or contrary thereto."

The following October, Ingalls continued with this line of thought in another article, writing that Jesus, in order to accomplish what were called miracles, used natural means—perhaps, one might wonder, his magnetic powers. Ingalls doubted that miracles ever consisted in the suspension of the natural law of causation and declared that the evidence for God's existence was to be found in the "wonderful order and harmony of nature" and "in the progressive tendency of all things, material and spiritual."

Using highly charged images drawn from the biblical account of the resurrection, Ingalls asked why anyone would look to the old ways of thinking or the stories passed down from the ancients, all of which relied on human tales. He looked to a new dispensation, in which outmoded and lifeless forms and conventions were set aside in favor of living revelations that would look directly at the natural world and find God there. "And the enquiry propounded to [the women at Jesus' tomb] may not be inapplicable now," he wrote, "'Why seek ye the *living among the dead?*'"

The evidence suggests that spiritualism's appeal in the culture at large was strongest among the middle class, which was also true of Universalism. The concerns of that class centered on the home and the family, and spiritualism was believed to domesticate Heaven (or so its opponents said). The middle class was even turning the pursuit of spiritualism into a parlor game. Over that domesticated religious landscape, women, particularly mothers, came to hold sway. Spiritualism centered religious experience in the home, not in the church.

In domesticating Heaven, however, spiritualists also tamed or rationalized the afterlife in a way that was familiar to Universalists, many of whom would agree with the claim that natural causation and conditions extended beyond death into the afterlife. When Laverna Matthews, from New York State, first read in her newspaper about communications with spirits of the deceased, she had a natural Universalist reaction: "Mrs. Matthews had been reared a

Universalist, so when reading of those wonderful manifestations, she exclaimed: 'How pleasing! How reasonable, that the same law that permits the spirit to depart from the body, will permit it to return, and with its magnetic power control other bodies susceptible to its influence.'" Matthews moved to San Francisco after the Civil War and was installed as the pastor not of a Universalist church but of a large spiritualist congregation.

To those Christians who criticized spiritualism as superstitious, spiritualists could point out that the sensory evidence for the phenomena of spirit contact was plentiful and available everywhere and to everyone. The same was not true of the evidence for Christianity's central event—the resurrection of Jesus—which even his own disciple Thomas had doubted until he had received the evidence in a form (according to spiritualists) not unlike that reported by latter-day spiritualists in their contact with the departed. Moreover, the Christian evidence had become more and more indirect and remote as the centuries had passed. To spiritualists, attending a Universalist service and sitting in a pew listening to a sermon was like hearing about the glorious land that borders this life; attending a spiritualist séance, on the other hand, was like embarking on an exploratory expedition into that far country.

Spiritualism felt *scientific* in that it was open to practical testing. Realms that had always before been susceptible only to religious explanations—the etheric atmosphere and lightning, for example—were now open to rational investigation. What had been invisible and untouchable to a previous generation had been materialized and brought to serve a later generation. Even the spirits seemed susceptible. A large part of a séance's preliminaries was spent *trying the spirits*, or conducting practical proof tests to ensure that the spirits were genuine and were intent on and capable of helping the humans who were participating.

Spiritualism's scientific air appealed to Universalists, given their respect for Enlightenment rationalism, as did its democratic, populist dimension. Everyone could conduct this experimentation themselves, with no complicated instruments. This understanding of science, however, was a particular one. To increase the likelihood of a favorable outcome, the spiritualist experimenter was advised to be uncritical and well disposed. The spirits were known to refuse to cooperate with harsh experimenters. This revealed an essential aspect of spiritualist belief: If expectations and attitudes influenced the outcome, it was evident that spirit or mind affected matter. Matter was not dead but could be enlivened. It was a form of spirit, a thought that had materialized.

For progressive spiritualists, uncanny experiences that an earlier generation would have regarded as miraculous suspensions of the natural order were not considered miraculous at all. Rather, they were thought of as manifestations to a mind made sensitive to subtle electricity—of phenomena that could enlighten one about the nature of matter and spirit. Unitarian minister Giles Stebbins, for example, related the experiences of his friend, Universalist minister Sims Paine, of Friendship, New York. On two occasions while riding through the woods, Paine saw the spirits of relatives who told him that acquaintances of his—Universalists Elijah Baker and Joseph Phelps—had just passed away. Paine told Stebbins,

> I was in a very happy and tranquil state, so that the sunlight seemed to shed new glory on the landscape, and my thoughts were rich and spiritual; but the persons whom I saw were not at all in my mind, yet their coming seemed natural and pleasant, and did not disturb me at all, while the impression made was vivid and indelible, just as clear now as on the days when these things occurred.

On both occasions, Paine was afterward able to verify what his spiritual visitors had told him. Stebbins commented on those experiences that "these are not miracles, but natural results of the opening of the inner vision, and of the power of spiritual beings to become visible under fit conditions, and to rouse our torpid faculties to a sense of their nearness and intelligence that we may come to know ourselves better."

In November 1847, just a few months after publication of Davis's *The Principles of Nature,* the New York Association of Universalists authored a creed that ministers would be required to sign each year in order to remain in fellowship. The association, which pointedly held its meeting in Southold, where Ingalls was pastor, defined its creedal pledge as "I sincerely declare that I receive the Bible as containing a special and sufficient revelation from God." It was designed as a response to the seemingly anti-Christian teachings of Davis, although Davis's spirits seemed to have been mainly following Theodore Parker's sermons and lectures. The Reverend Abel Thomas wrote that the creed was created because several ministers "had given heed to seducing spirits and doctrines of demons which turn from the truth, and others had taken ground in denial of miracles and the authority of the Christian revelation." Five ministers refused to sign it, all of them associates of Davis: Joshua Ingalls, William Fishbough, Samuel Brittan, Zephaniah Baker, and Thomas Lake Harris.

The New York association's creed was like many others adopted by the similar regional associations, the first of which had been the Boston association. That creed resolved, "In order for one to be regarded as a Christian minister with respect to faith, he must believe in the Bible account of the life, teachings, miracles, death and resurrection of the Lord Jesus Christ."

After this resolution was passed, George Severance left the Boston association and retired to a farm in Vermont, and Joseph Baker resigned from his pastorate at Glens Falls, New York, even though his congregation asked him to remain. Similarly, David J. Mandell resigned from his society in Winchester, New Hampshire, and became a successful spiritualist lecturer. He wrote, "As to Spiritual Manifestations, I dislike many things connected with them as much as do many who bitterly oppose them. But I know, from actual experience, that a decent respect for the true principles on which the thing is predicated, will do away entirely with those features which form the basis of the complaints alluded to."

The proponents of the Boston association's creed had pointed an accusing finger at *German rationalism,* meaning the influence of Theodore Parker. His most notorious philosophy was his rejection of Christianity's supernaturalism, including miracles, which he explained in an 1841 sermon, "A Discourse on the Transient and Permanent in Christianity." Among the eight Universalists ministers and laypersons who voted against the resolution establishing the creed were two ministers—Charles and John Murray Spear—who had been raised in Universalist luminary John Murray's (and then Hosea Ballou's) Boston church. When the Spears moved back to Boston in their adulthood to begin work among prisoners and to abolish capital punishment, both attended Parker's services, rather than Ballou's.

Thomas Whittemore, one of the leaders of the movement to establish creedal tests, saw the issues as adherence to the Bible and devotion to Jesus. These two issues appeared in every regional creed. The creed of the Michigan State Convention of Universalists read "that in order to be a Universalist, it is necessary to believe in the Old and New Testaments, as containing a sufficient revelation; and that the life, teachings, miracles, death, and resurrection of Jesus Christ, as given in the Gospels, are divine truth."

The Chautauque Universalist Association in New York State adopted a creed that read:

> We believe in the divine authenticity and genuineness of the scriptures of the Old and New Testaments that they contain a special revelation from God to the world, and are a sufficient and a perfect rule for Christian faith and practice; and we hereby express our firm belief in the life, miracles, death and resurrection of our Lord Jesus Christ, as set forth in the Sacred Scriptures; and we pledge ourselves as far as we have the ability to preach the doctrine of Christ, and render practical obedience to its divine requirement.

Then it voted "that all ministers in order to retain the fellowship of this Association, be required to subscribe to this declaration of faith and pledge" and "that all preachers, who shall hereafter receive the fellowship of this body, be required to assent to the above declaration and pledge."

The Reverend Philip P. Fowler returned his letter of fellowship to the association, accompanying it with this charitable comment: "I am unchanged in faith and feeling, except in their growing brightness and intensity and desire for you all that *spiritual prosperity* which the faith you cherish can alone pre-eminently bestow and which you are so well prepared to *appreciate*." Fowler became involved in reform politics, immigrated to Kansas in 1854, and was elected to the first territorial legislature as a Free-State candidate but refused his seat by the proslavery faction. He became "an intimate associate of old John Brown, and concealed and defended that notorious champion of freedom, on several occasions."

The Vermont Convention of Universalists lost one of its most esteemed clergy, Henry Partridge Cutting, when it adopted a creedal test. In response, the convention noted that Cutting "still sympathizes with our views, and desires our welfare and prosperity, and that he will continue to preach to our people." But in fact, he made a name for himself on the spiritualist lecture circuit over the next few years. He told a large spiritualist convention in Vermont that "he was a Universalist in the large sense of the word—it includes all truth, and, therefore, in this large sense, it takes in all the good there is in any ism in the universe."

Cutting's fellow minister, Harvey Elkins, told the same convention, "He [Elkins] was a Universalist, insofar as he was in search of universal truth. . . . Universalism looked upon Spiritualism as a *sort of wing* to the Great Edifice, and he was anxious that there should be a union between the two, in order to make more strong the hosts against paganism or popular theology." Elkins may have counted himself primarily a Universalist, but he believed whole-heartedly in spirit contact as a reasonable extension of biblical and Christian beliefs. "If spirits ever could appear unto men, they can to-day," he said. "If man ever had intercourse with spirits he may to-day; but

no doubt certain physiological and psychical conditions are necessary, else all men could hold intercourse."

Not every dissenter in the Vermont Convention of Universalists handled the pledge in the same way. Opposition arose, as it had
elsewhere, not primarily because people disagreed with the creed's
articles but because they disliked the very notion of an organization imposing a creedal test on its members. Russell Streeter wrote
years later from Woodstock, Vermont,

> The Universalist Convention of this State decided that all our
> ministers must sign a Resolve that the Scriptures of the Old and
> New Testaments are a *sufficient* Rule of Faith and Practice, &c., or
> forfeit their right of fellowship. And, to please, "the boys in *black*,"
> I signed it, when sent to me. Those suspected of *heresy* might
> have done the same, by giving their own definition of the word
> "sufficient."

The controversy lingered in the Vermont convention. In 1871, it
considered but failed to pass a resolution that would have barred
the use of Universalist churches to anyone, including spiritualists,
who did not accede to the unique truth of the Christian scriptures.

Well-known minister Linus Smith Everett withdrew from the
Buffalo Association of Universalists in the early 1850s after it
adopted a creed similar to the others, and he went on to find his future in spiritualist lecturing, writing, and editing. Born in 1795 in
Worthington, Massachusetts, Everett received fellowship as a Universalist minister in 1822 and then ministered in Buffalo, New
York, where he also co-edited *The Gospel Advocate and Impartial
Investigator.* He established a pastorate at the First Universalist Society of Auburn, New York, and ministered to Universalist churches
in Charlestown and Salem, Massachusetts; in Baltimore, Maryland; and in Hartford and Middletown, Connecticut. With fellow
Universalist minister Theophilus Fisk, Everett managed a political
paper, *The Boston Daily and Weekly Reformer.* At different times, he
also edited *The Universalist* and *The Western Evangelist* and helped
Whittemore edit *The Life of John Murray.* Upon resigning from the

association, Everett declared himself a spiritualist, and his wife announced that she had become a medium. At the beginning of 1857, he began publishing a short-lived newspaper in Cleveland, Ohio, *The Spiritual Universe*, which was followed by an even shorter-lived effort, *The Spiritualist*.

Controversy surrounded the idea that Universalists should have to sign any creed or hold to any particular doctrine (that is, apart from a belief in the ultimate salvation of all). The promulgation of creeds was a "theological contraction" within Universalism, in Brittan's words. It was meant to oppose the findings and methods of the philosophical and historical "Higher Criticism" of the Bible, which was an attempt "of German Rationalism to rear its head among us," according to Whittemore.

That rationalism invited questioning of the divine origin of the Bible and placed it not only alongside other holy books of all kinds but alongside other so-called myths, as well. Insofar as this leveled all religious beliefs—old and new, orthodox and heterodox—it indirectly supported the new revelations of Davis. But by a further turn of logic, Davis's supporters regarded his revelations as not just level with the Bible but as superceding it, because his revelations described the historical context out of which they had evolved. Because the Bible did not do the same, Davis's followers claimed it was the product of a more primitive stage of religious sensibility.

Universalist clergy who were interested in the new religious universe being opened by clairvoyance and trance vision felt caught by what they saw as the denomination's retrenchment into dogmatism. But they were not the only ones who objected to the new creeds. For many, the idea of stripping away the authority of a society or congregation to determine its own minister, and placing it instead under the jurisdiction of a local or regional ecclesiastical body, challenged freedom of thought. The New York Convention of Universalists resolved, "In no case, shall Fellowship be granted" when a clergy moved from the boundaries of one association to another "until the applicant subscribe" to its creed. Not only that, but the clergy had to "bring satisfactory testimonials of good standing in the Association from which he removes," in order to ensure that he had not crossed borders in order to escape doctrinal scrutiny.

In the midst of this general effort to enforce and standardize doctrine, Whittemore professed to have "been taken somewhat by surprise" by the action of the Susquehanna Association of Universalists. That association's members unanimously resolved, "Several of our ecclesiastical bodies have established tests of fellowship hitherto unknown in our denomination, and in our opinion inconsistent with the freedom of the human mind and the liberty of thought, speech and opinion." The members of the association also voted that they "disclaim all right to dictate to those who profess to believe in the Christian religion, the grounds on which they shall base their faith." They therefore resolved "that we disapprove of the establishment of any other test of fellowship than the following: to wit, a professed belief in the theoretical and practical doctrines taught by Jesus Christ and a life consistent with such profession."

The association's secretary, Aaron Burt Grosh, of Reading, Pennsylvania, proudly reported the resolutions to Whittemore, and Henry Bacon, one of the association's most distinguished members, defended the action in the columns of *The Trumpet and Universalist Magazine*. Brittan republished Grosh's letter in *The Univercoelum and Spiritual Philosopher*, commenting that Grosh had spoken the truth in repudiating the idea of creeds for Universalism. Thomas Sawyer wrote a reply to Grosh, in which he asserted, "As a denomination we never favored the stupidities of Davis, or the more learned fooleries of Parker. We never denied the truth of the Bible, or its inspiration; we never questioned the miracles, or their proof of Christ's mission."

This controversy led to discussions about the denomination-wide Winchester Profession of Faith, first formulated in 1803. That creed, as amended from 1870 through 1896, assumed one's assent to certain ideas, not to a particular and precise set of words. Nor was that creed envisioned as a litmus test for maintaining people in fellowship. The proponents of creeds believed the Winchester Profession needed amendments, extra requirements and strictures, and an enforcement clause. Local authorities within the denomination added these elements under new "articles of religion," as were specified, for example, by a Boston-area meeting criticized even by William Balch, who was no disciple of Davis. Balch wrote about the so-called article of religion,

> A modest name for a narrow, stringent, dogmatic creed. It also proposes a "government" and "rules" after the high church ritualistic precedent. It ignores, does not so much as mention or allude to the "Winchester Profession," the "Baltimore Interpretation," the "evident intention of our denominational fathers," or the fathers themselves. Perhaps they wanted themselves to be fathers—they doubtless will be to the poor, pinched bantling they have brought forth.

To the objectors, Universalism seemed to have lost its flexibility and openness in the effort to standardize its doctrine and give weight to its institution. The Reverend Elijah Case, from Osseo, Michigan, for example, wrote to the spiritualist newspaper *The Banner of Light* that Universalism had degenerated into a "Mutual Admiration Society." He wrote of Universalism,

> The very errors and follies that, with stentorian lungs, it has for years past cried out against in others, it is now adapting as fast as it can. Look at its costly churches, its high salaried ministers, its organs, and choirs, and bells, and stained windows, and frescoed walls where thousands of dollars are more than wasted away, while poverty and misery, squalid want and sin, lie starving and dying around the doors of its churches.

Case had been criticized by members of his congregation and other Universalist clergy for his lectures to groups of spiritualists, and he eventually left the denomination. "For many years," he wrote, "I have felt the untold curse of denominational thraldom and ecclesiastical tyranny resting like an incubus on my soul, and have felt more and more determined to throw it off."

As institutional Universalism tried to confront the burgeoning interest in spiritualism within its ranks, it became quite important in determining whether an individual clergyman was still to be granted fellowship whether he clung to the word *Christian* in the phrase *Christian spiritualist.* Many of those individuals who had dissolved the bonds of fellowship looked back at the unease of their colleagues within the denomination who kept the word *Christian* hypocritically to preserve comfortable ties to convention. One noted that "hundreds" of Universalists were "*Spiritualists*—not fanatical Spiritualists, but earnest, candid, *Christian Spiritualists.*" However, the same individual also responded sarcastically to the writing of another, who was "very prudent in his language, careful to preserve the precious adjective that renders all things respectable—Christian—a '*Christian* Spiritualist.'"

One's commitment to the core of Christianity or its tradition could change back and forth over the years. Among those who called a convention in 1876 to establish a national organization of Christian spiritualists were many Universalist clergy and laypeople who had years previously severed their connection to the Universalist denomination (or had it severed for them) when they became spiritualists.

One such person was John Henry Watson Toohey. Although he had refused to sign the New York Universalist Association's creed and was therefore unable to obtain fellowship papers, he published *The Christian Spiritualist* in New York City in the mid 1850s. Toohey was born in Ireland in 1802 but immigrated to New England. There, he left Roman Catholicism to become a Baptist and then a Universalist. Uriah Clark later wrote, "Mr. Toohey was one of the *heretical* ministers who was never able to get his *credentials;* and in this particular, perhaps, was much more fortunate than those of us who, having once got into the ministry, were not able to get out without leaving our heads or reputations behind as an offering on the altar of ecclesiastical inquisitions." After Toohey left *The Christian Spiritualist,* he moved to Boston, where he practiced an eclectic version of medicine and served as an officer and lecturer for the Massachusetts Spiritualists Association.

Davis's revelations questioned the biblical account of creation, opting instead for a version of evolution espoused by French naturalist Jean-Baptiste Lamarck, according to which characteristics developed in an individual's lifetime can be passed on to later generations. Davis's spirits had also perhaps read *The Vestiges of the Natural History of Creation,* published in Britain by Robert Chambers in 1844 and in New York in 1845 and available, therefore, while Davis was in the city, dictating *The Principles of Nature.* Davis's circle of Universalist ministers were familiar with Chambers's book and even used an argument justifying the need for a new revelation of the truth based on the notion that evolution in religious thought was just as natural as it was in geology and biology.

Davis's description of evolution elicited amused barbs from conservative quarters, such as from the Reverend George Quinby of Augusta, Maine. Quinby wrote of Davis, "He says men were first *tad poles,* then they came to be *monkeys,* but it required much time; then after a long lapse, they *progressed* to be *human,* with intellects and all that sort of thing." For Universalists, the issue of evolution raised a concern with which they had already been struggling: the continuity of the individual soul in the afterlife. The idea of evolution seemed to threaten the persistence of the personality, or at least it confused the issue.

In an 1853 article entitled "The Condition of Men after Death," published in *The Universalist Quarterly and General Review,* renowned Universalist minister Hosea Ballou II denied that any spirits in the afterlife still needed perfecting, for the spirit's life, after having cast off the body, was fixed and unchanging. He contrasted this with the idea of evolution, in which, according to him, the identities of individual creatures changed:

> According to the late hypothesis, called the Development Theory, we, the men and women who now live, were once clams and oysters, tadpoles and bats, or something of the kind. But we have never seen it argued, even on this hypothesis, that it is a matter of felicitation, to oysters and tadpoles that their being is to be developed, at length, into the glorious rank of human creatures, of whom they know nothing, and who in turn will have no self-consciousness reaching back to them.

Spiritualist lecturers became strong advocates of evolution (at least as Lamarck had conceived it), sometimes combining in the same lecture a discussion of the new discoveries in the realms of the spirits with those in the areas of geological history, paleontology, and archaeology. This became another part of their rationalist critique of biblical revelation, and for the Universalist clergy who were tending toward spiritualism, it became another source of difficulty with the denominational authorities.

At the time when Davis's teachings first appeared, Joshua Ingalls declared himself a spiritualist and made the rounds as a lecturer and propagandist, offering articles to *The Univercoelum and Spiritual Philosopher*. After the New York Universalist Association passed its creed, he stayed on as pastor at Southold for a few months but then left to become minister of a Unitarian congregation in Southington, Connecticut, where he stayed for almost two years. Then he set off into secular life as a social theorist and reformer. He became interested in labor reform and in the abolition of the private ownership of land. His central idea was "an effective limitation of the right of private property in the soil, and in the crude material gratuitously supplied by Nature—out of which all wealth is developed—must constitute the initial step in any rational solution of the social problem." He also "distinguished himself by his uncompromising . . . warmth, earnestness, and intelligence with which he ... defended the just claims of Labor against the unrighteous exactions of Capital." The subjects of the articles he contributed to *The Univercoelum and Spiritual Philosopher* and then to Brittan's later newspapers, *The Spiritual Telegraph* and *The Spiritual Age,* changed to reflect his new interests.

The Universalist Society in Southold was drawn into spiritualism. Many of its members became enthusiasts and mediums, and traveling spiritualist trance lecturers found they were welcome there. Charlotte Tuttle visited Southold in the summer of 1854, for example, and gave three trance lectures to crowds in the Universalist church. When she traveled to nearby Greenport, however, she found a cooler reception. One correspondent to *The Spiritual Telegraph* wrote, "I am told she occupies a hall there, the church edifices being of *too sacred* a character for her admission." The church in Southold was closed for a dozen years beginning in 1864, likely due to a rift within the society over spiritualism.

One of the ministers who voted against the Boston Universalist Association's creed, David Henry Plumb, pastor of the Universalist Society in Chardon Street, spent a year tending toward the new dispensation, standing before his society "as a disbeliever in the supernatural character of Christianity." In the spring and summer of 1848, he sent several articles to *The Univercoelum and Spiritual Philosopher,* chafing at the conservatives in the denomination. In one of them, he wrote, "The old notion of a miraculous and special revelation, for a (comparatively) little handful of women and men, for the long period of 4,000 years, has made more bigots and exclusives, than all other causes combined."

In August of that year, Plumb announced to his congregation that he would resign, admitting that he was in the midst of a religious crisis. A small portion of his congregation followed him to the chapel in Philip's Place, where he "assumed an independent Christian position." He almost immediately reversed himself, however, and was enfolded back into the care of the denomination, having decided that Christianity had to maintain miracles and the inexplicability of the supernatural. He declared in the columns of Whittemore's *The Trumpet and Universalist Magazine* that "the tendency of the Rationalistic or natural theory is manifestly downward, tending to a denial of all religion. Those who have commenced with a denial of miracles have not stopped there, but have found themselves doubting the truth of all religion, and neglecting the worship of Almighty God."

The Pebble and the Angel

WOODBURY MELCHER FERNALD was another former Universalist minister active in publication of *The Univercoelum and Spiritual Philosopher*. Born in New Hampshire in 1813, he eventually served as pastor of the First Universalist Church in Cabotville, Massachusetts, and became the first settled pastor of the First Universalist Church in Newburyport in 1840. By 1847, when he began associating with the group in New York City who were attending Andrew Jackson Davis's trance lectures, he "had abandoned the Universalist denomination because it no longer represented the true spirit of religious progress."

Of Davis's book *The Principles of Nature*, Fernald wrote, "The work is honest and it is the most stupendous psychological phenomenon the world ever saw. The only effect the work has had on my own mind is an increased and calm faith in God, a vivid realization of immortality, and a profound conviction of its truth and usefulness to mankind." Fernald was no longer in fellowship with the Universalists; however, he made himself part of the group of ex-Universalist ministers whose religious progress was catalyzed by Davis's revelations and so received his share of criticism from the Universalist press.

When Fernald and others associated with Davis were accused of having departed from the Christian faith into pantheism, he denied it, arguing that *pantheism* meant the belief that God and nature are one. But God and the world were not one, and neither was God exterior to the world. Rather, God was interior to it. His philosophy was "that God is united to Nature, as the soul of man is to the body—that God, in fact, is the Great Interior, Actuating Soul of the Universe."

For a while, Fernald published his own paper, *The Christian Rationalist and Theological Reformer,* in order to propagate "the principles advocated by that class of men who call themselves 'Rationalists,'" as Whittemore put it. In judgment, Whittemore said of Fernald, "He is wandering in the darkness of unbelief; and it is not possible for Universalists to hold fellowship with him as a Christian preacher."

Fernald always saw himself as a *rationalist.* By this, he meant he was convinced that Heaven, the afterlife, and all the region of the spirit—that is, the supernatural—were as much under the providence of God as was everything on Earth, in this life, in this universe. In sum, all were subsumed under natural law. In this sense, God's providence was not *partialist,* which was the term that Universalists used for the orthodox belief that God would save only a portion of the human race.

In another sense, Fernald's rejection of partialism meant that he rejected the idea that portions of God's creation, such as Heaven and the afterlife, were not governed by the same providence that extended everywhere else. Natural law therefore operated both on Earth and in Heaven, on matter and on spirit, in all times and places, among the first Christians and those of modern times. As Fernald put it,

> We look out upon Nature, and we see the order and regularity
> of things. No jarring miracles—nothing, at least, contrary to law,
> or independent of law, and yet we pick up a pebble, and we say
> God made it. If God made the pebble, then the pebble is a pro-
> duction of personal agency. But does it look so, thus simple in
> its structure, when it rolls upon the shore, driven and polished
> by the winds and waves? Now I say, God made the angel no more
> than the pebble.

Coming from a Universalist background, in which God's providence was held to be impartial and constant, like natural law,

Joshua Ingalls wrote, "Idolatry, we are taught, arose from neglecting to discern God in his works, and to acknowledge him as the source of all blessings." As he explained,

> The impartiality and unchangeableness of the divine gifts must be assumed as the very foundation of all faith in the Divine Goodness. If God is partial in his gifts, if *he is a respecter of persons*, and acts *specially* in the operations of his spirit of grace and truth, then some partial system must be true, and the hopes of man are made dependent upon innumerable contingencies and the caprices of a changeful Deity.

This interpenetration of spirit and matter, Heaven and Earth, high and low, eternal and contingent was akin to Ralph Waldo Emerson's musings on the ultimate as the hidden inwardness of nature.

Fernald continued his esoteric studies with George Bush of New York City, a professor of Near Eastern languages and a minister in the Swedenborgian church. He also had attended Davis's trance lectures, as had several other well-known figures, including Universalist and *The New York Tribune* editor Horace Greeley and author Edgar Allan Poe. In private letters, Poe made fun of the pretensions of Davis's revelations. Even so, Poe had published his short story "Mesmeric Revelation" the previous summer, and as Davis's lectures began and gossip spread about the Universalist clergy who were participating, Reverend Eli Ballou reprinted Poe's story in *The Universalist Watchman*. The following year, while disdaining Davis's *The Principles of Nature,* Poe wrote "Eureka," a work that, at once visionary and theoretical, was briefer but similar in scope to Davis's. Poe appeared to be in a trance when he read "Eureka" in front of an audience.

Influenced by Bush, Fernald eventually turned to the Swedenborgian New Jerusalem Church. He moved to Boston and began writing on Swedenborg's philosophy. He even engaged in a series of debates with Universalists such as Adin Ballou and tried to prove the existence of an eternal Hell, as Swedenborg had described.

The dissemination of Swedenborg's philosophy during the 1840s had helped prepare the way for spiritualism. Swedenborg had emphasized that all humans were free to shape their destiny and salvation. He had also spent many of his later years in conversation with angels and spirits, leading by example, as it were (although institutionalized Swedenborgianism did not encourage its followers to do as the master had done). His reports on his experiences with the spirit world provided a survey of the universe that spiritualists explored. Perhaps most important, Swedenborg provided many people with the conviction that the afterlife corresponded to this life, that spirits were like living people, and that Heaven and Hell were the spiritual counterparts of Earth.

Swedenborg's ideas merged in spiritualism with other components of the intellectual climate. One of these was the *Romantic sensibility* that gave value to intuition, feeling, and nonintellectual experience—to being driven by impression and impulse. Another of these was *idealism*, which suggested that the material world was an expression of mind, or that mind had primacy or dominion over matter. To some, this made plausible the seemingly magical phenomena that manifested at séances.

Over the years of spiritualism's expansion, Samuel Brittan remained in the top ranks of its leadership and inspiration. In August 1851, he was a founding member of the New York Circle, a weekly séance group that grew into a large public organization that sponsored lectures by such advocates as John Bovee Dods (who had by then moved to Brooklyn) and William Fishbough as well as lyceum discussions and trance exhibitions. Beginning in 1852, Brittan guided the members of the New York Circle in their effort to spread their views through a series of public addresses. He also joined with wealthy New York match manufacturer Charles Partridge, another ex-Universalist, to publish a series of spiritualist books. These included new titles as well as such older works as the English translations of Louis Cahagnet's account of French clairvoyants' psychic journeys (under the title *The Celestial Telegraph*) and of Justinus Kerner's German account of a clairvoyant, *The Seeress of Prevorst.*

In 1854, Brittan also helped found the Society for the Diffusion of Spiritual Knowledge, an association of respectable businessmen, public officials, and clergy who meant to lend their collective weight to propagating spiritualism. In April of that year, in a similarly high-minded effort, he presented to the U.S. House of Representatives a petition that he had drawn up and for which he and his colleagues had collected thirteen thousand names, asking Congress to appoint a scientific committee to investigate spirit communication. The petition was never acted on, however, apart from being met with facetious suggestions to refer it to the committee that handled postal matters or the committee on foreign affairs. *The New York Times* commented on the failure of Brittan's petition to Congress:

> It was probably the reputed fondness of gentlemen residing in Washington for spirits, that induced the presentation of the petition and perhaps led its author to hope for an investigation; but the subject is too ethereal, and if the believers desire the individual attention of the powers, they must present spirits with more body in them. The Misses Fox may be able to "call spirits from the vasty deep" by some mysterious agency, but that is of no particular interest to Congressmen, for a majority of them see tumbler after tumbler come forth every night of their session by a simple up-and-down motion of the handle of a beer-pump.

Brittan's most enduring contribution to the spiritualist movement was as an editor. In New York City, in addition to publishing *The Univercoelum and Spiritual Philosopher,* he published a series of newspapers and periodicals, including *The Shekinah, The Spiritual Telegraph, The Spiritual Age,* and *Brittan's Journal of Spiritual Science, Literature, Art, and Inspiration* (the motto of which was "The Trumpets of the Angels Are the Voices of the Reformers"). Of these, *The Spiritual Telegraph* was most widely disseminated during its six years of existence, from 1852 to 1857, and was the most popular spiritualist newspaper during the first decade of the movement, when spiritualism was at its height. When the other main spiritualist newspaper of the era, *The Banner of Light,* began in Boston in 1860, Brittan was its regional New York editor.

Many other Universalist clergy who turned to spiritualism also edited and published spiritualist newspapers, perhaps because as Universalists, they were used to conducting theological debate through newspapers. As an editor, Brittan was a genial but unflinching controversialist. Although he was a firm defender of spiritualism, he was an acute observer of its often oversized and eccentric manifestations.

In his later years, like some other old-line spiritualists, Brittan became disenchanted with the spiritualist movement, as it devolved into an amalgam of magicians' stage tricks and proof tests. While never losing his belief in spiritual contact, he refocused his interest on alternative healing. He graduated from the New York Eclectic Medical College and successfully practiced medicine for many years in New York City and in Newark, New Jersey. He died in July 1883. The memorial service was held at New York's American Spiritualist Alliance in New York City, which he had helped found. At the service, trance medium Cora Richmond placed herself under the control of his spirit, which allowed him the opportunity, as it were, to address the crowd that had gathered to honor him.

Fishbough also distanced himself from the mainstream spiritualist movement. His devotion to the Bible reasserted itself, and by 1854, he had declared himself again a Christian—although still a Christian spiritualist. He sought to distance himself from Davis and other spiritualists who held Christianity to be merely one more creed and one more hidebound institution. In 1847, when he had been editing Davis's trance lectures, Fishbough had addressed his letters to Davis with the salutation "Dearly Beloved Prophet" and had closed them playfully with "Yours affectionately, the right reverend most excellent great grand scribe, cabinet maker Esq. Bill Fishbough." In 1854, however, he wrote an icy letter to "Mr. A. J. Davis," detailing their estrangement:

> I have been constantly pained to see what I am forced to regard as the most sacred truths, and on which I believe the salvation of the world depends, ignored, misconceived, misrepresented, and virtually (though of course ignorantly, and therefore unintentionally) abused *by* and *through* yourself and a majority of the more prominent spiritual mediums and writers who adopt the essential principles of your philosophy and theology.

Even Davis eventually slipped away from the spiritualist movement he had helped to found. He had become unhappy with its pursuit of spiritualism's sensational phenomena, rather than its progressive philosophy.

Divine Respiration

Thomas Lake Harris and Zephaniah Baker were the two other Universalist clergy who associated early on with Andrew Jackson Davis and refused to sign the New York Universalist Association's creed. Harris, who was born in England in 1823, was the son of a strict Calvinist who had brought him to the United States during his youth. He rebelled at his father's theology and became a Universalist and a minister. In 1844, he was made pastor of the Fourth Universalist Church of New York City. When Davis and his Universalist entourage came to New York and began their mesmeric exhibitions and trance lectures, Harris was one of the eight or ten who attended regularly, and his life was altered by the experience. In 1847, when the New York association adopted its creed, he resigned his pastorate and his fellowship with the denomination.

Zephaniah Baker had edited *The Gospel Messenger* in Providence, Rhode Island, and then moved to New York City to minister to a congregation on Fourth Street. He also refused to sign the statement, for many of the same reasons as did Harris (and William Fishbough, Joshua Ingalls, and Samuel Brittan).

Both Baker and Harris became regular contributors to *The Univercoelum and Spiritual Philosopher*. Baker's congregation, however, voted to keep their minister, even if it put them outside the Universalist fellowship. Harris continued to occupy the pulpit in that church until he found another venue in the autumn of 1848. Then, a group of interested individuals, led by The *New York Tribune* publisher Horace Greeley, declared themselves the Free Church and asked Harris to be their pastor. They convened at the Coloseum and took the name of the Independent Christian Society.

Baker vacated his pastorate but continued to preach in Universalist societies without the approval of the regional governing associations. Thus, it is clear that despite the associations' requisite creedal pledges, individual Universalist societies still invited free-lance preachers into their pulpits. In January 1853, a member of the Universalist Society in Dudley, Massachusetts, wrote to Thomas Whittemore, complaining that a certain clergy had been preaching in the Quinebaug Universalist Association during the previous year "to the detriment of the cause" by "denouncing the Bible and its sacred institutions." That preacher was Baker; the Dudley society had previously been under his pastoral care.

The Reverend Baker's wife, Frances, had been a regular attendee at Davis's trance dictation sessions in New York City and also contributed articles to *The Univercoelum and Spiritual Philosopher* and gave enthusiastic lectures on the new dispensation. Her friend Fannie Green also attended Davis's trance revelations, and her byline often appeared in the newspaper.

Green was born Frances Harriet Whipple in Smithfield, Rhode Island, in 1805, to a Baptist family, but she had demonstrated a fierce independence of mind. While still young, she published poetry and novels with reformatory themes (such as the rights of labor and antislavery agitation) and edited two newspapers. One of them, *The Wampanoag and Operatives Journal,* gave a voice to the radical labor movement in Fall River, Massachusetts. During her time in Fall River, Green ultimately fled the confines of her orthodox Baptist religion. The Reverend Abel Thomas presided over her wedding to artist Charles Green in Thomas's Universalist church in Lowell. Her marriage to Green lasted only five years before she divorced him, but she retained and deepened her religious and social radicalism.

Green became so interested in Davis's trance lectures that she moved to New York City in 1846, boarded in Brittan's house, and included herself in the small group who were regularly present, "congregated 'in the dead of night' to receive a revelation from an other world!" as another Universalist attendee, Henry J. Horn, put it. He, too, found the occasion to be "characterized by an impressive solemnity" and the "slow, distant, and measured utterances of the seer" to cause "sensation that cannot be described."

After Brittan and Fishbough began publication of *The Univer-coelum and Spiritual Philosopher,* Green contributed articles and poetry to it and had no further obvious connection to organized Universalism. Instead, she worked closely with Brittan for a while, helping him edit *The Young People's Journal of Science, Literature and Art,* and then with ex-Universalist minister Russell Ambler and his wife, a spirit medium, in their editorial work at the head of *The Spirit Messenger and Harmonial Guide.*

Green was a dedicated worker in the field of spiritualism for the rest of her life, writing, for example, the *Biography of Semantha Mettler, the Clairvoyant* in 1853. Yet she also made a successful career as a mainstream essayist, poet, and novelist. Like many other spiritualists from New England, she eventually moved to California. There, she was often entranced by the spirit of deceased California senator Edward Baker and delivered trance lectures from him, in which his opposition to slavery, it was noted, had intensified since his death.

Fannie Green remarried, and as Frances Green McDougall, she published two so-called trance novels in California, which she supposedly received from spirits. The first, published in 1866, was *The Love-Life of Dr. Kane,* told by the spirit of the Arctic explorer Elisha Kent Kane; in it, he explained his great devotion to young spirit medium Margaret Fox, whom he had secretly married. The other novel, published in 1878, was *Beyond the Veil,* told by the spirit of deceased medium Paschal Beverly Randolph.

Just after Davis's first series of revelations in New York City in 1846, Green's fellow devotee, Thomas Lake Harris, traveled as far west as Cincinnati and as far south as New Orleans to lecture on the new dispensation. Along the way, he occasionally wrote to Davis, asking him to use his clairvoyant powers to determine where he (Harris) should go next on his lecture tour.

Universalists and Swedenborgians—more threatened than other groups, perhaps, by Davis's teaching and Harris's lecturing—organized opposition to Harris. A correspondent from Cincinnati wrote to Whittemore, proudly describing a vocal and very public protest that was mounted against Harris when he attempted to lecture. He closed his letter to Whittemore with the words "I thank you for the stand you have taken in this matter. *Defend the Gospel—Defend the Bible till death.* You can not do a better work."

The Universalist papers reported with distaste that before Harris returned to New York City, he "became acquainted with a new sect in Cincinnati, called, we believe, the 'Spiritual Brotherhood,' a kind of Swedenborgians, who believe by complying with certain disciplinary rules they can hold intercourse with departed spirits in another world." This mesmeric brotherhood was organized by radical abolitionist and Quaker John Otis Wattles and had settled south of the city in a commune called Excelsior.

By the time Harris and Davis's other clerical associates had made themselves anathema to institutional Universalism, they had begun to fragment in their mutual allegiances. While boarding with the Brittan family, for example, Davis had enticed (or at least gladly accepted) the attentions of a wealthy married woman, Catherine DeWolfe Dodge, who was twenty years older than the twenty-one-year-old Davis. After Dodge divorced her husband, Davis married her. Brittan was not happy with the resulting scandal.

Financial disagreements arose concerning the newspaper. In addition, the members of the group, all stubbornly independent thinkers, began to find themselves, each in a different way, unreconciled with Davis's trance utterances on the nature of reality and religion. Although a regular contributor to the early issues of *The Univercoelum and Spiritual Philosopher* (with articles with names such as "Asthma—Its Cause and Cure"), Davis even disappeared from its pages in its second year because of these disagreements. After a few issues, his articles reappeared, but his relation to the rest of the group had changed. In September 1848, Harris pointed out in an article in *The Univercoelum and Spiritual Philosopher,* "It ought to be borne in mind that Mr. Davis' book contains errors and contradictions, in the midst of much that is truthful. It ought to be remembered that he has made grave mistakes and at any time is liable to repeat them."

By December 1848, Brittan had resigned the editorship of the paper. It passed to Fishbough and then, in a somewhat different form, as *The Spirit of the Age,* to William Henry Channing. But Harris now also became a kind of law unto himself in his independent church in New York City. He had become a medium who was connected with "great, ennobling spirits," and he began receiving poetry from them. Some reviewers were impressed, but many were not. One wrote of his massive *The Epic of the Starry Heavens,*

> Mr. Harris dictated this poem in a state of entire unconsciousness as to surrounding objects, and it is well adapted to induce such a state in the reader. . . . It is the work of certain spiritual beings, who made Mr. Harris their medium; and . . . might authorize the belief that the spiritual life is a retrograde career as to all the elements of intellectual culture and wisdom.

Harris's spirit experienced an undeniable afflatus, as writers of the time phrased it. In 1850, he joined with another spiritualist minister, a Seventh Day Baptist itinerating missionary named James Leander Scott, to take over the spiritual guidance of a large group of believers from Auburn and New York City. This Apostolic Circle used their séances as occasions for revival-like visitations of the gifts of the Holy Spirit. These included mediums personating the spirits of the Apostles of Jesus.

Harris was excited at the idea that "St. Paul would and could condescend to speak through a mortal." He arranged for medium Eliza Benedict and others from Auburn to come to Brooklyn and, at Harris's boarding rooms, "deliver the oracles of St. Paul to twelve chosen persons, and if possible develop or remodel Mr. Harris, so that henceforth he should be Paul's oracle to the world." Harris and Scott co-edited a newspaper during this time, *Disclosures from the Interior and Superior Care of Mortals.*

Scott set off into the wilderness with one hundred followers and wandered until spirits bade them to halt. At that place, in the mountains of Fayette County, Virginia, from 1851 to 1853, they established a community at a place called Mountain Cove and published *The Mountain Cove Journal.* They renamed the town the

Gate of Heaven, and there, they awaited the second coming of Christ. By the fall of 1852, Harris had joined Scott there and they had proclaimed to their followers that they were the two witnesses from Revelation 11:3–8.

The community fell apart in recriminations, however, as the two leaders assumed not just earthly authority but something approaching that of the Godhead, whose wishes, they told the community, were equivalent to the utterances and wishes of his instruments: Harris and Scott. Harris/Jehovah enunciated these words, for example: "I am that I am now inquireth of thee; and prepare to answer thou me. . . . None other than God, thy Redeemer, calleth for thee. None other than He who hath the keys of death and hell addresseth you through one of your members."

Matters came to a head when some of the "Mountain Covies," as *The New York Times* called them, refused to sign over all their earthly goods to their leaders. But also contributing to the rapid dissolution of the community was Harris's idea that he had found a spirit bride for himself, with whom he could unite in spirit when his body was united with a counterpart female. All people, he believed, could also find their spiritual consorts in this way. But he had the privilege of initiating the women of the community into this mystery himself, as the physical instrument through which they might come into contact with their spiritual counterparts.

Although the utopian colonists would balk at this notion, this form of "spiritual intercourse" would underlie the ideas that carried Harris onward in his career, becoming the person that William James referred to in his *Varieties of Religious Experience* as "our best known American mystic." James referred to Harris's idea that God emanates the universe through a process of divine respiration, which Harris connected to a practice of breath control accompanying the sexual intercourse meant to unite the practitioners to their higher spirits (although James may not have known this).

After the Mountain Cove community dissolved, Harris made his way back to New York City, where he associated himself with the Swedenborgian Church of the New Jerusalem. In 1860, he went to England on a long lecture tour to gather devotees. By now, he was insisting that he was no spiritualist, and by this, one can only assume that he meant, more or less, no *ordinary* spiritualist (which is to say that he believed himself to be *sui generis*). He said that spiritualists had diverged from Christianity and that he was a devoted Christian. The British press often reported his lectures as antispiritualist, but having found no place of honor among other spiritualists in the United States, he decided that all spirits, except those who communicated with him, were demonic and evil.

Harris returned to the United States, where he founded the Brotherhood of the New Life. He became what would now be called its *guru*. In 1861, he funded its settlement, which he called *The Use,* with huge donations from a couple of wealthy disciples. It was first located at Wassaic, in Dutchess County, New York, and then in 1863, it was moved across the county to another small town, Amenia. In 1867, wealthy from the donated funds of his followers, Harris bought two thousand acres in Brocton, New York, in Chautauqua County, on the shore of Lake Erie.

There, Harris exercised his energies in the belief that he was the "'pivotal man' between the forces of heaven and hell," while his followers cultivated vineyards and constructed a winery. By all accounts, however, the practical life of Harris's followers was no Elysian Fields but rather a descent into their own frailties, as Harris forced them through spiritual cleansing. Arthur Conan Doyle, recounting their story later, called their living arrangement "virtual slavery save that it was voluntary." He added, "Whether such self-abnegation is saintly or idiotic is a question for the angels."

In 1875, Harris took a few of his disciples to California, where, in Santa Rosa, they established another settlement of the Brotherhood of the New Life. They planted another vineyard at a place they called Fountain Grove. In 1881, a minor rebellion arose among Harris's followers back in Brocton, but he weathered the resulting public revelations about the poor living conditions of his followers (compared to his own) and about their irregular sexual arrangements. He quit the community in 1892, retiring to New

York City, where he died in 1906. True believers to the end, some of Harris's disciples refused to allow his body to be moved for more than three days because they were convinced he would rise from the dead.

The practices of Thomas Lake Harris were far from the 1845 electrical experiments of John Bovee Dods or the trance lectures of Andrew Jackson Davis. Those who participated in the birth of spiritualism conceived of it at the time as a rational evolutionary philosophy, a progressive cosmology, a purified religion, and an advanced science. Whatever spiritualism became and whatever it was mixed with, the strand of it that found its expression in the mesmeric utterances of Davis that seemed so prescient, so *clairvoyant*, was at its beginning a high-minded enterprise aimed at investigating the hypothesis of spirit communication and freeing thought from narrow and outmoded conventions.

The Universalists who embraced spiritualism believed they were bringing their faith to a higher level, one in which its earlier form would be superseded. Samuel Brittan had this spiritualism in mind in 1873, when he proposed the formation of a National Association for the Advancement of the Occult Sciences. That organization, which would have been something like a precursor to the Society for Psychical Research, would have put the investigation of all the uncanny phenomena associated with spiritualism on a high, ennobling, objective, and scientific basis—he hoped.

Universalist minister Olympia Brown, who served as pastor at Bridgeport long after Brittan had left, wrote to him to endorse his project. She believed it would offer a way to separate the truth at the core of the spiritualistic phenomena from all the varieties of "humbug" and "claptrap" that accompanied it. Two years later, in 1875, she wrote to her friend Isabella Beecher Hooker that most Universalist ministers were spiritualists and made no secret of it. Brittan, however, never established his association, nor would he ever reconcile himself to the Universalist denomination.

The Conversation with
Spirits of the Dead

IF SPIRITUALISM WAS TO RECONCILE SCIENCE AND RELIGION, it would need to prove a connection between Heaven and Earth that was real in substance and detail, not just in the imagination or abstract. The connection had to make possible the exchange of messages between particular inhabitants of the spiritual and the material worlds—to allow conversations between the living and the dead and to pass intelligence and comfort from one realm to the other. Like the new technology of the era, the magnetic telegraph, the connection between Heaven and Earth had to eliminate distinctions of time and space, bringing this world and the next into communion. All evolved and progressed together: the old and the young, the male and the female, the saint and the sinner, the spirit and the body.

Spiritual Automatists

IN 1849, CHARLES HAMMOND, pastor of the First Universalist Society of Rochester, New York, visited the house of the Fox family, who had recently moved to Rochester. Hammond, who was born in 1805, had grown up in the area and had begun preaching the gospel of universal salvation in 1830. After receiving a letter of fellowship from the Western Association of Universalists, he had preached in several places in the region before settling in Rochester in 1842. He had taken over the new First Universalist Society there and begun a weekly Universalist newspaper, *The Western Luminary*, which had lasted until 1846.

The Foxes had been living nearby in the town of Hydesville. In March 1848, the two youngest sisters, Margaret and Catherine, ages twelve and fifteen, had demonstrated to their family that mysterious knocking sounds—such as rappings on wood, ranging from loud thumps to pattering cascades—could be heard in their presence. These sounds represented a haunting, a visitation, but with something new: The "haunt" would reply to questions.

Just a few years before, the electric telegraph had revealed to an amazed public that the limitations of time and space could be annihilated. The spirits that ultimately made themselves known to the Fox sisters demonstrated that they had either borrowed the technology of the telegraph or inspired its invention, as some would come to believe. The living could communicate with the dead through the rappings. The departed could be asked questions, and they could answer with raps in a simple code. A telegraphic line had opened between this life and the afterlife, between Heaven and Earth, wrote Andrew Jackson Davis after he had visited some of the rappers. He decided the rappings were in harmony with his revelations and wrote them into his so-called harmonial philosophy in a book entitled *The Philosophy of Spiritual Intercourse*, published in 1851.

This phenomenon was a scientific fulfillment of the intense millennial expectations common of the western New York frontier, which was permeated with religious revivals during this time. Communicating with the deceased could set aside doubts about the existence of an immortal soul, resolve controversies about the claims of revealed religion, and most importantly, reassure and comfort those among the living who grieved and pined for those who had passed away. Universalists took note that the spirits who contacted those they left behind were not crying from out of an eternal fiery pit but were telling about a better state in the afterlife. They were still making progress but in another form.

The rappings of the Fox sisters spread like wildfire across the country, manifested in the presence of other spirit mediums. Hundreds and then thousands of spirit circles were formed, gatherings of the idly curious, the emotionally wrought, the seriously interested, and the intensely scandalized. The gatherings crystallized in form, at first containing elements of revival meetings but then rapidly emulating mesmeric circles, in which people sat in a circle with their hands joined. Doing so was meant to increase the electrical charge of the group and the power of those who were sensitive to the subtle influences of the spirit world. As with mesmeric circles, other physical "phenomena" appeared in séances, such as the movement and levitation of furniture or even the participants themselves.

Spiritualists came to regard the Fox girls' first rappings as the nativity of what they called *modern Spiritualism*. It was Samuel Byron Brittan who gave the emotional lecture that would later be recognized as the first to bring together all the elements of this movement in a comprehensive philosophy. He spoke in response to a series of public demonstrations at Stuyvesant Hall, in New York City, given by the Fox sisters in November 1850.

The two youngest sisters had moved to Rochester, New York, with their mother in 1849, soon after newspapers began to report their rappings. Amid intense interest and skepticism, the girls conducted spirit circles for curious visitors to their home. Their Methodist pastor in Hydesville had disavowed them (despite the fact that the spirits they contacted had first taught that, in accord with orthodoxy, some souls were destined for endless misery). In Rochester, other clergy exhorted the girls to abandon their ties with the devil and even offered their services to exorcise the girls' demons.

Hammond, however, was much more sympathetic. He had come to a sitting as a somewhat skeptical but interested observer. He proposed test questions for the spirits but received only rapped assurances that his questions would be answered if he returned for another sitting. When he came back, the spirits answered some of his questions—correctly, according to Hammond. On his third visit, he was singled out to sit with the sisters and their mother in another room, which filled with sounds—not just rapping but also buzzing, scraping, and roaring. The furniture, too, came alive. Hammond's chair took leave of the floor and traveled through the air.

Hammond had no explanation for these events other than a spirit intervention. He became a regular participant in spirit circles, and over the next two years, he traveled around the region to find other circles forming and to help spread the gospel of spirit contact. He also served as a traveling correspondent for Brittan's *The Spiritual Telegraph*.

In the fall of 1850, however, the spiritualistic phenomena began manifesting in Hammond's own family. The doors and windows of his home opened and shut without any visible cause, and his six-year-old daughter "was exercised by control of her limbs" with such vigor that Charles and his wife, Sybil, took the girl to a clairvoyant. She told them that the spirits meant the girl no harm and would soon desist, which they did.

Lying in bed one night before falling asleep, Hammond felt his right hand and arm move "without any volition" of his will. As he described it, "Being satisfied that spirits were present, I said mentally, will the spirit take my hand and throw it forward over the bed clothes. Gently my hand was carried to the position I asked." The next day, the spirits drew his hand across a sheet of paper. When he placed a pen in his hand, they formed words on the paper and then wrote an entire book. He wrote the introduction while he was not under spirit control. In it, he explained, "With the subject matter of this book, I was wholly uninformed, not knowing even the first word until my hand was moved and wrote it. When written I have often found the sentiment to contradict the convictions of my own mind. This has led me sometimes to suggest amendments, but I have uniformly been unfortunate in that respect."

The book written through Hammond turned out to be authored by the spirit of Thomas Paine. Hammond was troubled, he said, when he discovered this because his beliefs were at odds with Paine's religious infidelity. But then Hammond learned that Paine's postmortem beliefs were different from those he had held while still in the flesh. Namely, he had come to believe in an immortal soul and had realized the error of atheism. The book, in fact, was a narrative of the pilgrimage of Paine's soul after death, as he grew and learned and moved higher and higher—a pilgrim's progress.

That book, *Light from the Spirit World* (and two sequels), sold well, but many readers were skeptical of its content. Methodist minister William Henry Ferris, for example, portrayed the book as a veiled Universalist effort at propaganda. He wrote,

> Mr. Hammond is a lapsed Universalist preacher, and the whole effort of the book is to prove Universalism, by taking one of the vilest men earth ever tenanted, and making him the *superior and teacher* of all *orthodox* in the spirit-world, and then sending him back as a missionary to reform this. . . . If the author of that miserable book is so pressed with the difficulties of Universalism as to resort to this nude trick to sustain it, he is to be pitied.

A correspondent to John Mather Austin, editor of the Universalist newspaper *The Christian Ambassador,* from Auburn, New

York, wrote to ask whether the book was indeed by the Charles Hammond who was the Universalist minister in Rochester. Austin replied, "Br. Hammond has always sustained an unblemished reputation in our midst; for which reason we the more regret that he has published a work which will bring his reputation for veracity into so great a peril."

Hammond also received proverbs and aphorisms from the spirits, which he automatically wrote down on small slips of paper. He collected them and sent them to Samuel Brittan, who published them in *The Spiritual Telegraph*. More than one Universalist preacher had now begun composing the notes for his sermons in a similar way: by cultivating a trance state and then hovering over a blank paper, pen in hand, waiting for the spirit to move him. Some preachers began to deliver their sermons as impromptu trance lectures while in a state of semiconscious automatism, lending themselves to the spirits as their inspired instruments.

When the Davenport boys came to Rochester in the summer of 1857 to give public exhibitions before large audiences, Hammond took part in their demonstrations. Onstage, he entered their specially made, locked "spirit cabinet" with them. After the boys had been bound to chairs and gagged inside the cabinet, he asked them test questions in the dark and received answers from disembodied voices. When the stage lights brightened again and the cabinet was opened, the audience saw the boys, still bound and gagged inside.

Hammond left his pastorate but stayed in Rochester in full pursuit of a new fellowship and a new revelation. He continued to be a strong believer in spiritualism until he died from tuberculosis in 1859.

Those upon whom the spirits descended did not always welcome the experience. Benjamin Scovil Hobbs, pastor of the Universalist Society in South Bainbridge, New York, "became deranged in his mind" and was "removed to the Lunatic Asylum at Utica," according to Thomas Whittemore. Hobbs, as described by an informant of Whittemore, was "a sanguine believer in the reality of the 'spiritual manifestations," and "his mind in its wanderings, [ran] continually on that subject."

Hobbs had begun preaching in Walton, New York, in 1844 and was then granted fellowship by the Chenango Universalist Association in 1847. He became secretary of the group the following year, when he moved to Upper Lisle. He moved again to South Bainbridge in 1849. Then, at the annual meeting of the Chenango association in 1852, he offered the association his letter of resignation, which was accepted. A few years later, however, he was residing in Webster, New York, near Rochester, back in fellowship and serving as pastor of the Universalist Society there.

Even so, Hobbs was still having problems with his ministry. During his preaching, he found himself falling into trance and losing consciousness. Spirits took possession of his vocal cords and his hands, as he described to John Austin of *The Christian Ambassador:*

> My speech was first controlled while in the solemn act of prayer. And then I again was compelled to speak in a manner that, as before, led me to think it spiritual, and others to think me strangely diseased, if not partially insane. . . . I was obliged, in spite of all my *efforts* to prevent it, to exhibit the character of the speaking medium in full, by addressing an audience on two different occasions, and going through the strangest ordeals.

Hobbs, like Hammond, began to write under the control of the "strange spirit-power." He did not doubt that spirits were using him as their instrument, but he regarded it as a disaster. This was clear not only from his description to Austin but also from what he wrote to Brittan at *The Spiritual Age.* At the onset of his peculiar preaching experiences, he told Brittan that he had

> commenced discoursing on the text, when, to my utter horror and mortification, *my mouth was suddenly closed, and for a time I could not utter a word.* . . . again powerless, in a *terrible grasp,* from which I in vain sought for release; and to add to my consternation, I was compelled, in spite of all my efforts, to speak the words, *"Spirits have power on the earth."*

Hobbs explained that he had not set aside or gone beyond Universalism and that he did not wish to separate from fellowship. Perhaps he felt he had to say this, in light of the New York Universalist Association's active disciplining of its ministers for advocating spiritualism. Charles Cravens, the founder and pastor of the Le Roy Universalist Society in Genesee County, near Rochester, had recently turned to spiritualism, much to the consternation of some of the members of his society, and he had been dropped from fellowship. Hobbs wrote,

> And now, brethren—brethren in the ministry—what shall I say more in relation to this matter? Shall I say, like some others, that I have found a purer faith? This I can not do; for it must be a man of keen sight indeed that can discern in "Modern Spiritualism" a purer faith than that contained in the Gospel of Christ.... Must I then, take my leave, and withdraw from your ranks? This it would pain me greatly to do, and for the present I ask you to bear with me.

Brittan printed Hobbs's letter but wryly commented, "Mr. Hobbs is so unaccustomed to spiritual things, that he seems to regard his spiritual experience as a great calamity—a 'terrible ordeal,' and perhaps the greatest that human nature can endure. He addresses his 'brethren in the ministry' rather beseechingly, as though he apprehended a theological decapitation on account of the occurrence of what he can not prevent." Brittan pointed out, "If he is really doomed to feel the weight of an ecclesiastical arm already smitten with a palsy, he will not be the first man that has suffered in this way. We hope he will be encouraged by many illustrious examples of magnanimity under similar or greater trials." Nevertheless, Hobbs's mental problems exemplified why some people resisted spiritualism—not because of theological, philosophical, political, or social issues but simply because they had a reasonable fear of following, encouraging, or even becoming people who heard voices, saw visions, and were guided by psychic forces outside their conscious volition.

Hobbs spent almost the next decade trying unsuccessfully to reconcile his experiences with organized Universalism. He finally separated from the denomination and advertised his services as an itinerant spiritualist lecturer. He declared, "My *trial-ordeal*, protracted through more than twelve years, has stripped me of the last vestige of earthly goods, and it is only in the deeps of poverty and much trial that I can march through even an open gate."

Spirits Preach Universal Salvation

THE REVEREND JOHN AUSTIN DID NOT DISCOUNT the spiritual rappings out of hand. He had been pastor of the First Universalist Church in Auburn, New York, from 1844 to 1851, when he gave up his pastorate to take over editorship of *The Christian Ambassador*. By the summer of 1850, Auburn had from fifty to one hundred mediums in different stages of development. During that entire year, Austin visited clairvoyant mediums around the city, including Eliza Ann Benedict, a member of his own church. She was the medium for the group of Christian spiritualists who would soon recruit Thomas Lake Harris to be the head of their Apostolic Circle.

Austin's experience with spirit contact had been mixed. Sometimes, a medium would give correct answers, but sometimes, he or she could be fooled. And even when the answers were correct, Austin could not convince himself that the explanation was intervening spirits. In fact, the messages reflected Universalist doctrine, even when they were given through non-Universalist mediums.

From trance medium Warren Boynton, for example, Austin received affirmation of the doctrine of universal salvation. Austin wrote in his journal,

> Mr. Boynton is a Methodist, yet while in this mesmeric sleep (of the genuineness of which there can be no doubt) and under the entire influence of the spirit, as he insists, he corroborated the general doctrines of Universalism—declared that my preaching as a whole is true—and urged me to continue to proclaim my sentiments to the world. I am sure I cannot fathom this subject. There certainly must be something important in it.

On another occasion, Austin took visiting Boston Universalist minister Charles Spear (whose brother John had reviewed Andrew Jackson Davis's book with unbounded praise) to a séance in

Auburn with Benedict and her Apostolic Circle. Spear reported their experiences to the readers of his newspaper, *The Prisoner's Friend:*

> The audience were told that that evening was devoted mainly to conversation with St. Paul. A great many questions were asked. Two we remember very distinctly. Is there a future judgment? No, was the reply. Will all men be saved? Yes, was the response. But some one in another part of the room said, not as Universalists believe. This man, who was probably an opponent of that doctrine, was evidently in an unhappy frame from the state of the answer.

Spear was skeptical and, like Austin, dissatisfied with how the spirits performed. He wrote,

> There was one thing, especially, that seemed to contradict all our ideas about the spiritual world, which was, that every question must be put in the most simple form. Our own view has always been that when the spirit enters upon its career, that the whole soul becomes enlarged, and its conceptions perfectly clear. It seemed strange, therefore, that questions which mortals could easily understand could not be comprehended by a spirit.

Universalists were encouraged that the spirits, by and large, added their testimony in favor of the doctrine of universal salvation. But the spirits were not unanimous. Those trying to dampen the enthusiasm of their fellow Universalists for spiritualism seized upon this inconsistency. Sylvanus Cobb, for example, attempted to show that much of what was preached by the spirits from out of the mouths of entranced mediums was the result of the mediums' own beliefs. He was able to find a few mediums whose spirits advocated "the old theology." He also cited as evidence the experience of Universalist minister John Nichols, from Dudley, Massachusetts, who had evidently been able to change the testimony of the spirits on the question of salvation.

Nichols had attended a séance with a Methodist family, in which the daughter acted as the medium. Her spirits had referred to Professor John Webster, the Harvard chemist who had been convicted and hanged for murder, declaring that he would never "progress to a state of holiness and happiness" and that he and others would be "forever miserable." The family had looked at Nichols with an air of triumph, "as if they would say, 'you see that Universalism is down.'" Nichols, however, "believed that his faith in Universalism was stronger than the faith of the whole family against it," and he pressed the young medium for more information. Soon, he "obtained from what claimed to be Dr. [Benjamin] Franklin, concerning Prof. Webster, that he was not positively miserable, but was in a lower degree of happiness; and that he would advance in due time, through successive spheres, to perfect bliss; and that all men would ultimately become holy and happy."

According to Davis's *Philosophy of Spiritual Intercourse*, Benjamin Franklin was often the spirit with whom the earliest mediums were in contact, as he had continued experimenting with electricity in the afterlife and had thus been the inventor of the "spiritual telegraph." Nichols, like Cobb, doubted that much of what appeared at séances was the work of spirits of the deceased. He believed the phenomena could be better explained as the result of the clairvoyant's mind acting on matter at a distance.

Dolphus Skinner, a Universalist minister from Utica, New York, who was unsympathetic to spiritualism, also wrote to Cobb. He asked Cobb to publish his correspondence with George Washington Hyatt, a member of John Mather Austin's Universalist church in Auburn, "a goodly number of the members" of which, according to Hyatt, were believers in spiritualism. Hyatt had written to Skinner at *The Christian Ambassador* of New York in order to describe the revelations that were occurring through the spirit circle around Eliza Benedict in Auburn. Skinner had little patience with spiritualistic phenomena. He wrote,

We incline to think departed spirits find higher employment that that of doing up young ladies' hair, shifting their hair combs, moving finger rings, adjusting dresses, playing guitars, over-turning or violently moving tables, chairs, &c., and furthermore, if they choose to do such things for their own amusement or the instruction and edification of mortals, they would be quite as likely to do them in the light as in the dark.

In response to a letter from Hyatt, Skinner pointed out that the spirits changed their answers, depending on with whom they were communicating. The Fox family, he wrote, had been Methodists, and "when the spirit was inquired of, whether Universalism was true, and requested, if so, to rap three times, it made no answer. It was then requested, if Methodism was true, to rap three times, and an affirmative answer, *rap, rap, rap!* was given." Nevertheless, "now Br. Hayatt [sic] and several Universalists at Auburn get answers favorable to Universalism, and are fully confident that God is converting the world, and doing wonders for our faith through this new and wonderful agency." The Apostolic Circle at Auburn—which included Hyatt as well as Eliza Benedict and her husband, Daniel, and others from the Universalist Society—published a transcript of the spirits' exegesis on various Bible passages. The spirits began with a partialist doctrine but seeing that their auditors had made spiritual progress, "now taught Universal salvation."

On the subject of the vagaries of spirits' messages, Whittemore published, as an arch rejoinder to Universalists inclined to spiritualism, a message reported from the spirit of the recently deceased Hosea Ballou, who had opposed spiritualism. Ballou's spirit was supposed to have said, "I have offered up my petition in the presence of you all, that you may see and know that my views of life and immortality have not been changed."

As the years went by, Austin was less willing to tolerate spiritualism. He encouraged clergy who had declared themselves spiritualists to dissolve their bonds with Universalism. In 1858, he published a notice in *The Christian Ambassador* that Universalist minister Justin Parsons Averill, from Battle Creek, Michigan, had been converted to spiritualism. Austin wrote, "He will, of course, dissolve his connection with the Universalist organization."

That December, Austin published a brief report that Averill had turned the entire Universalist Society of Battle Creek, along with a Hicksite Quaker meeting, into an Independent Church of "Spiritualists, or 'Progressionists,'" who were "independent men, unshackled by creeds, unawed by priests or denominational bulls." Austin commented, "Alas for Battle Creek! Wait five years for the fruit of all this! If religious desolation and rampant infidelity do not predominate in the place, within that time, we shall be most happily mistaken."

Spiritualists felt otherwise. Brittan wrote of Averill,

> While other ministers were balancing the truth against their old dogmas and the prospect of a living, and were ready to kick the beam if the former was likely to be too weighty for the latter, he left these venerable dogmas to their appropriate keepers, and trusting to Providence and his own muscles for a subsistence, he declared himself free from all arbitrary authorities and sectarian shackles.

The Detective of Toeology

SOME UNIVERSALIST CLERGY UNDERTOOK TO EXPOSE deceptions they encountered while investigating the rappings. Daniel Mason Knapen of Randolph, Massachusetts, upbraided spiritualist believers for their credulity and preached on the improbability of their claims. He went further, however, using his mechanical expertise to expose the frauds of several local mediums, at least one of whom had been stealing jewelry and other valuables from those who attended his séances. Knapen had a special claim on his readers' attention: He had just moved to Randolph after serving as pastor for a year or so in Southold, New York, Fishbough's and Ingalls's previous Universalist Society. Knapen had also served there earlier, from 1844 to 1845.

Another Universalist clergy, Charles Chauncey Burr, went on tour to speak against spiritualism and tried to expose its adherents and practitioners as "weak, insane, deluded creatures and fit subjects for the lunatic asylum." Born in 1817, Burr had been pastor of Universalist Societies in Somerset, Bowdinham, and Portland, Maine. He edited *The Universalist Palladium* in Portland from 1839 to 1841. By the time the spiritual rappings began, he had given up his pastoral duties and was making his living in Elmira, New York, editing the popular literary and political journal *The Nineteenth Century.*

As a sideline, Burr became a traveling mesmerist and phrenological lecturer, conducting "experiments with mind," often accompanied by his brother, Heman. The Burr brothers traveled the same lecture circuit as other mesmeric experimenters, such as John Bovee Dods. "Some expect the gentlemen to raise the dead, and to cast out devils," wrote one observer of the exhibition, "others that they are the very devils that should be cast out." In their demonstrations, the Burrs placed willing members of the audience in trance on stage. The mesmerized volunteers

> would be assured that they were all drunk and would forthwith personate a drunken carouse, or that a peach tree overhung their heads, and they would commence pocketing imaginary peaches, or that a boat was floating before them in the river into which they might step. . . . After a great variety of such scenes, Mr. Burr declaimed a piece of poetry (Longfellow's "Excelsior"), while his subjects looked on and fancied the scene, and finally knelt down and wept over the corpse which he depicted.

Another experimenter with mesmerism, Joseph Rodes Buchanan, faulted Burr's public exhibitions as "the practice of delusion and falsehood" upon "passively impressible" subjects. For Buchanan, treating mesmeric subjects from the audience in this way went against his "internal sense of truth and honor." He explained how he treated his mesmeric subjects in a more high-minded way:

> The respect that I feel for my fellow-beings engaged in the pursuit of knowledge, is not pleased in thus reducing them to puppets, played upon by a word. All the noblest and purest sentiments cluster around the scene of my experimental investigations, and I would fain exalt the agents of such pursuits to angelic intelligence and purity, rather than reduce them to the level of the mere automaton controlled by puerile hallucinations.

Burr was also interested in the role of inspiration in literary genius. He was a friend of Edgar Allan Poe and in his journal, *The Nineteenth Century,* became an early and passionate advocate of Poe's works. Burr also experimented in self-induced trance and wrote poems "under the influence," a couple of which he sent to Brittan for publication in *The Univercoelum and Spiritual Philosopher.*

After the rappings began in Rochester, Burr was swept into accepting them as real. For a while, he was "pained by a kind of half belief" that a deceased brother, "a young man of the finest taste and of high poetical genius, had so far forgotten the natural dignity and delicacy of his character as to come back to commune with [him] by making most vulgar noises, rattling about under chairs and tables, and kicking over light-stands and bureaus in the dark, to excite [his] wonder and horror." He later concluded, however, that the rappings had a material basis, not a spiritual one, and that many of what were represented as genuine communications by the spirits were fraudulent. As a result, he took to the lecture circuit again, this time to denounce mediums. He also published an exposé, *Knocks for the Knockings,* in which he purported to show that one could produce the rapping sounds by surreptitiously cracking and snapping one's toe joints.

Burr had mixed results with his audiences. Some people believed that he had demolished the "humbug," but spiritualists often complained that the sounds that Burr made did not resemble the real rappings and that his demonstrations were simplistic and overwrought. One spiritualist wrote,

> He proved to the satisfaction of some that the sounds were produced by the toes, the tables moved by the hands, and the music made by a suck instrument in the mouth—all were convinced that this was his brother's *modus operandi.* (Heman Burr was the rapper.) Mr. Burr asserted that this toe-ology has sent many of earth's lovely children to the suicides' grave; dethroned mighty minds; and sent giant intellects to the rayless regions of idiocy. Rather a poor compliment to those "giant geniuses!" unable to detect one medium in toe snapping, when Mr. Burr has detected forty-seven.

Spiritualists also accused Burr of fraud—namely, of colluding with selected members of the audience in setting up demonstrations of what is known today as *mentalism.* He would show how to guess names by noticing changes in another person's expression during a series of raps that signified possible answers (in the same way that horses can be trained to stomp out the answers to arithmetic questions). Burr was prosecuted for slander twice by spiritualist mediums, one of whom was the eldest Fox sister, Leah. Burr had found a distant relative of the Foxes and solicited from her a deposition that the girls had confided in her that they produced the rappings by cracking their toe and ankle joints. Spiritualists said that the relative's sworn statement was filled with provable falsehoods, but many people accepted it as the real explanation of the Fox sisters' powers.

Burning in the Sunbeams

WHILE JOHN AUSTIN PUBLISHED HIS DOUBTS about spiritualism in *The Christian Ambassador,* another Universalist clergy, Uriah Clark, also settled in Auburn, New York, and published a spiritualist newspaper, *The Spiritual Clarion,* beginning in 1856.

Clark was born in 1818 in Bedford, New York, to a family of devout Methodists. He later remembered revival seasons in which his childhood became a "reign of terror" and visions of "perpetual horror and suspense" in fear that "the day of grace" might have already passed. "The idea of endless punishment," he wrote, "was a living presence . . . burning in the sunbeams, flashing in the lightning, and peopling all the universe with symbols of indescribable terror."

By 1838, Clark had left home to work for his older brother in New York City and had also converted to Universalism. He began preparing himself for the ministry in 1840 and entered the Clinton Liberal Institute, in Clinton, New York, where he was a pupil of Thomas Sawyer. Clark served Universalist societies in Canandaigua, Buffalo, and Lockport, New York; in Philadelphia, Pennsylvania; in Providence, Rhode Island; and in Chicopee and Lowell, Massachusetts. His younger brother also became a Universalist minister.

While ministering in Canandaigua in 1843, Clark began experimenting with mesmerism from the pulpit, it would seem, with his congregation. During his first try, ten or twelve people "yielded their wills" to him and "exhibited almost every phase of psychological phenomena." He found himself in possession of a "healing power," which he began to use among the faithful. He later wrote,

> The tax on my healing power was so great . . . and so many persons called on me for aid, I became at first enfeebled and then alarmed. Orthodox neighbors said I was aided by Beelzebub; I was pointed out on the street as a wizard; some of my ministerial

brethren grew anxious for my reputation, and the committee of my society in Canandaigua waited on me with counsel to desist from all psychological practice. I left the place, and, like Jonah, fled to escape from the sick and suffering who were calling for my aid.

When controversy arose in the denomination about Andrew Jackson Davis's *The Principles of Nature* and Samuel Byron Brittan's *The Univercoelum and Spiritual Philosopher,* Clark opposed the rationalists because of what he regarded as their tendencies to infidelity and even immorality. But in the spring of 1854, Brittan announced in *The Spiritual Telegraph* that Clark had "virtually dissolved his former connection" with Universalism "by adopting a more sublime, living, and spiritual faith."

Sylvanus Cobb immediately wrote to Brittan and accused him of deliberately misrepresenting the facts of Clark's separation from Universalism. The Universalists, Cobb said, had withdrawn Clark's letter of fellowship, not the other way around. He hinted that the reason for their action involved a scandal concerning Clark, about which Brittan then declared ignorance. Clark responded with letters in *The Spiritual Telegraph,* professing his innocence of any wrongdoing and protesting what he saw as the unjust treatment he had received at the hands of the Universalist association that had disfellowshipped him.

When Clark embraced spiritualism, he returned to his mesmeric healing practice, as well. He also became adept in the practices of psychometry and clairvoyance and was "able to read persons at a distance, and telegraph to them"—from Rochester to Albion, New York, for example, from Glens Falls to Buffalo and from Brooklyn to St. Louis. He found himself drained of energy after each session. He wrote,

> Sometimes I feel the spiritual mission so oppressive and overwhelming with responsibilities, I would shrink back and call on Heaven to spare me this never-ending field whitening for harvest. But "woe is me" as thousands exclaim, if I face not the heat and

burden and battle of this dawning day of celestial glory. Bear on, ye pioneers of opening heavens, and unborn millions may yet bless your mission!

Clark saw his turn to spiritualism as further progress along the path that had led him away from the Calvinistic God of his childhood and toward the loving God of Universalism. Spiritualist mediums often experienced a pervasive divine love that tasted of universal salvation. Mary Jane Hendee, author of *The Heavenly Spheres, Character of Residents in Each, and Their Occupations* and *The Social Life of Heavenly Spheres*, had such an experience in church one day:

> As she knelt in prayer, a wondrous power seemed to possess her, and all was light. The church appeared transparent; she could perceive no walls; and her friends seemed divested of their natural bodies, and were as if glorified with spiritual raiment, so angelic was their appearance. It was to her an ecstasy of joy and peace. She loved everybody; there was no sin; all was good, and God was love, pervading all things.

An encounter with the spirits could lead one to Universalism (and not just out of institutional Universalism to something perceived as beyond it). The autobiography of homeopathic physician and devoted spiritualist Julia Smith makes this clear. Smith was advised by a host of spirits—including the spirit of her father, Jesse Norcross—who guided her medical diagnoses and prescriptions. She also acted as their vocal instrument, making it possible for her deceased father to tell his story through her. He wrote through her in her autobiography, "Many years before I had promised my wife that if I died first, I would come and tell her if my belief in Universal Salvation was true or false. And if she passed away first, she also was to come (if permitted to return, which she did not believe), and tell me if there was a Hell for unfortunate spirits."

As it happened, Smith's father died first in 1851, and his spirit materialized in the presence of his children. Then they heard disembodied raps from the drum he had sometimes played to amuse them. Smith's mother, a Methodist, sent for Universalist minister Linus Everett for advice. "He proved worthy of her confidence," wrote Smith (now in her own voice), "for in less than two years she had changed her bigotry and uncharitable belief, for a faith in an Universal God, who is amply able to take care of his children, and gave her testimony, by being sprinkled, and joined the Universalist Church in Salem."

One spiritualist tract, published in opposition to a Methodist preacher's sermons against spiritualism, took issue with the preacher's doctrines of a patriarchal God, the Trinity, the Atonement, Original Sin, and endless misery. In opposition, the spiritualist offered his own religion's view:

> Now let me portray to you the idea of the Divine being, as taught by the spirit world. First, that God is the great ocean of life, love and wisdom of the universe, pervading and permeating the whole realm of nature, physical, spiritual and celestial, in whom we live, move and have our being; that this God is parent, yes, father and mother of all life, intelligence and wisdom, and of all created things; that this being rules the universe with wise, just and immutable laws, which will do justice, ultimately to all created things and beings; and that man, the crowning work and masterpiece of creation is a spark and emanation from Deity, a responsible and progressive being, capable to rule the world and subdue the elements thereof, and do all that you have represented him of being capable of doing, and vastly more too.

The spiritualist belief that the spirits were not horrifying spooks but comforting heralds of joy sat well with the optimistic Universalists, who already believed that all beings progressed into holiness and salvation after death under the guidance of an all-merciful and loving providence. Here, the influential role of the early Universalist leaders of spiritualism is most evident.

In many other times and places, contacting the spirits of the dead or traveling in spirit to the land of the dead was regarded as a

terrifying experience and the spirit world itself as "a source of re-
pulsions and an object of dread." Therefore, it was necessary to establish taboos and restrictions "so as to render them harmless or
nugatory." But *modern Spiritualism,* as a coherent movement, was a
departure from this. What appealed to Universalists about spiritualism (and they may have been largely responsible for it) was its ca-
pacity to take the terror out of what lay beyond death.

No matter how weird or uncanny the séance was, it was now an
exciting revelation of ultimate benignity and happiness, rather
than ultimate terror, punishment, or oblivion. As Clark wrote,
"This revelation has been with a power, a might, that if divested of
its almost universal benevolence had been a terror to the very soul;
the hair of the very bravest had stood on end, and his chilled blood
had crept back upon his heart, at the sights and sounds of its inexplicable phenomena."

Clark and his wife, Eliza, became popular itinerant lecturers on
spiritualism. They both developed into trance mediums, with
Uriah providing inspired sermons and Eliza extemporized poems.
He sent reports of their travels to Brittan, who published them in
The Spiritual Telegraph. In June 1855, he wrote from Buffalo that
they had spoken in the Universalist church at Glens Falls, New
York,

> the first Universalist church I have occupied since openly labor-
> ing in the spiritual field, though I do not expect it will be the last
> I shall occupy; for the Universalist sect, in spite of its conservative
> leaders, is in the line of progress, and there are now between 20
> and 50 of its churches in this State alone, which are wholly or in
> the main favorable to spiritualism, and some of them are waiting
> for spiritual pastors.

In 1850, New York had 200 Universalist societies, 180 Universalist
meeting houses, and 134 Universalist preachers.

Itinerant spiritualist lecturers found that local Universalist pulpits were sometimes open to them and sometimes closed. Andrew Jackson Davis, for example, occupied the Universalist pulpit at Natick, Massachusetts, giving spiritualist lectures. Trance lecturer Charlotte Tuttle spoke at the Universalist churches on Long Island, New York. The convention of the New York State Spiritualists' Association met one year in the Universalist church in Leroy. But trance medium Frank White was refused the Universalist Society's pulpit in Lansing, Michigan, and spiritualist traveling lecturer George Atkins reported varying receptions from Universalist pastors from one day to the next and from one Cape Cod town to the next. Yet the Universalist Society in Willimantic, Connecticut, was simply superceded by a spiritualist society, continuing its regular Sabbath meetings and classes for children.

A spiritualist society, such as the one in Dover, Maine, might use the local Universalist church for its regularly scheduled weekly meetings. A Universalist minister might even share the officiating at a funeral with a spiritualist medium, who would, at some point in the service, voice a message from the spirit of the deceased. A local Universalist church, however, such as the First Universalist Church of Farmington, Michigan, might decide not to let the local spiritualist society use the building at all. (The Farmington society later relented, however.)

Even if a spiritualist lecturer was allowed to speak in a Universalist church, he or she might have to confront an unsympathetic or hostile minister. One Universalist minister allowed a spiritualist lecturer to use the church for his talk but then challenged him to imbibe some arsenic, quoting from the Bible, "If they drink any deadly thing, it shall not hurt them" (Mark 16:18). The lecturer said he was willing, having understood the challenge as a bluff.

Despite all these contacts, however, devoted Vermont spiritualist and ex-Universalist Nathaniel Randall wrote to oppose any

nominal linking of spiritualism to his previous denomination—
especially the suggestion that spiritualism might be called a "wing"
of Universalism. His objections were colored by having been
spurned by his ex-congregation. He wrote,

> Spiritualism is a part of the same Humanitary tree but the latter
> and purer flower—the more interior blossom—the exhalations
> and refinement of Universalism. One, after feeding upon Spiritu-
> alism could not go back to Universalism any more than Univer-
> salism could go back to Calvinism.... Spiritualists have discarded
> Book and Priest authority as final; they call for free discussion
> every where. Universalists have shut up their churches against
> Spiritualists (but open them freely to sects more bigoted than
> themselves) [and] allow no convert from Universalism to Spiri-
> tualism to speak in their meetings (I have experienced the truth
> of this myself within a short time).

Ex-Universalist Austen Simmons also remembered that time.
He wrote, "When first an effort was made to open a meeting-house
in Vermont for Spiritualism," it failed. "A Universalist society held
the door fast, even against the wishes of the share-holders and paying members."

Clark lectured for a while in and around New York City and
served as the New York correspondent for the Boston-based *The
New England Spiritualist.* He promoted himself as "seer, psycogra-
pher, and lecturer," offering "thorough delineations of the spiritual,
physical, etc., nature, conditions and wants, with advice, $5 to per-
sons present; $10 in advance to persons sending by mail; refunded
in case of failure." He and Eliza had moved to Auburn by the autumn of 1856, where they had begun *The Spiritual Clarion.* From
their newspaper office, beginning in 1857 and continuing through
1862, they also published *The Spiritualist Register,* listing lecturers
and mediums around the country. They had copied the idea from
The Universalist Register that had been published annually at Utica,

New York, since 1839. In 1863, Clark published *A Plain Guide to Spiritualism: A Handbook for Skeptics, Inquirers, Clergymen, Believers, Lecturers, Mediums, Editors, and All Who Need a Thorough Guide to the Phenomena, Science, Philosophy, Religion and Reforms of Modern Spiritualism.*

By 1866, Clark had opened the Institute for Invalids and Students in Greenwood, Massachusetts, not far from Boston. During the summers, a band of spiritualists met on the grounds of this rural spa. From this group, the idea developed to organize a camp meeting for spiritualists, the first of which was held at Pierpont Grove between the towns of Malden and Melrose, Massachusetts, in the late summer of 1866. Three thousand people came. These so-called grove meetings grew in size over the years and were held in many places around the country, becoming an important part of the American spiritualist movement.

A few years after the Clarks helped organize the first grove meeting, Stephens Jones, editor of the spiritualist newspaper *The Religio-Philosophical Journal,* included Uriah Clark in a group of spiritualists and ex-ministers who had been infected with the free-love philosophy and had abandoned their wives for new partners. In 1873, however, Jones wrote that Clark had "gone back to an Evangelic church" and was again a preacher.

In fact, by 1871, Clark had taken up lecturing with a new wife, Julia, denouncing spiritualism and asserting that "the only means of salvation is through the blood of Christ." The spiritualist editor of *The Stoneham Amateur* attended one of their lectures and described Clark as "once a prominent member in the Universalist ranks, also formerly a well known spiritualist." In the lecture, he reported, Clark "claimed by his experience that they tended to licentiousness and were entirely devoid of saving grace, and that all who profess to follow its teachings were atheists and licentious" and that "ninety-nine per cent of the manifestations were a cheat, which any can produce." Asked about the other one percent, Clark said, "It has been taken from the Bible and history, for they fully set forth spiritual communication between the spiritual and this world."

The following day, the Clarks put on a séance to demonstrate fraudulent techniques for producing spiritualist phenomena. The spiritualists in the audience found it "ludicrous" and "disgusting," and the editor of *The Stoneham Amateur,* Edward Whittier, concluded his account with this comment: "We really hope that Uriah Clark will see the evil course he is pursuing, and repent sincerely and become a truer and better man, not, however, that he is desired in the spiritual ranks, but for his own good."

Do Planets Go Back?

Two of John Austin's former classmates, who had become pillars of the Universalist ministry, eventually left Universalism and embraced spiritualism. They were James Martin Peebles and Jacob Henry Harter.

Peebles was born in 1822 in Whitingham, Vermont, but his family moved west into New York State, where they converted to Universalism. He attended the Oxford Academy in the town of Oxford, in Chenango County, where John Austin and Jacob Harter were among his classmates.

Harter was born in 1820. His family, of German descent, had been part of the Dutch Reformed Church of German Flats in Herkimer County, New York. By the time young Jacob entered Oxford Academy, he was one of many in the area who had converted to Methodism as the result of two years of revival preaching.

When young Peebles met Harter at the academy, Jacob had his Bible "clutched to his chest," yet Peebles succeeded in converting him to Universalism. The two remained close friends throughout their lives. After finishing at the Oxford Academy, Harter attended the Clinton Liberal Institute and then entered the Universalist ministry in fellowship with the Cayuga, New York, Universalist Association. After several years, Austin offered him (and he accepted) the position of general agent and head of the business department of *The Christian Ambassador* in Auburn, New York.

Peebles also became a Universalist minister, preaching in the Finger Lakes region of New York. His first permanent settlement was with the Universalist Society in Kellogsville, and then he had charge of two other societies at Genoa and Mottvile. He received his letter of fellowship from the Cayuga Universalist Association in 1844 and was ordained in 1846, with Harter offering the prayer during the service and Austin the sermon. From 1853 through

1855, Peebles was pastor of the Universalist church at Elmira, New York. He married Mary Conkey, a teacher at the Clinton Liberal Institute.

Peebles underwent a crisis of spirit in Elmira—or perhaps a crisis of the spirits. He attended séances, and the experience changed him. He wrote long letters to his friend Harter and wondered, "Were the spirits burning up his theological rubbish?" He gave up his pastorate in Elmira and moved to the Universalist Society of Baltimore, Maryland. But in less than a year, he resigned amid rumors of his conversion to spiritualism. Samuel Byron Brittan wrote of him,

> These [spiritualist] discoveries enlarged and spiritualized the views of Mr. Peebles and greatly modified his style of preaching. He was warned that the theology of Universalism was not sufficiently elastic to admit of such expansion. True, the clergy were ostensibly very liberal, and always ready to open their pulpits to any orthodox divine over whom they might expect to obtain an advantage in controversy. But in respect to any views more enlightened and progressive than their own, the accredited leaders of the denomination were as intolerant as the Calvinists.

In 1856, Peebles returned to New York State, and in 1857, he quit the ministry, much to his friend Harter's distress. Peebles felt that the Universalist establishment had become a hindrance to progress and that, as a spiritualist, he could now say to Harter, "We have some old fogy Universalists among us, who treat Spiritualists just as the Orthodox have treated us!" Peebles's spiritualist testimony would ever after be colored by his unhappy treatment by the Universalist establishment. "We bid Universalism, as interpreted by its better and broader-souled exponents Godspeed," he wrote, "but this little picayunish sectarian Universalism, that says, 'Thus far and no farther,' is only comparable to Martha's representation of Lazarus's body, four days dead. We believe in Universalism still, as a faith . . . but add to faith *knowledge.*"

After leaving the Universalist ministry, Peebles was at first uncertain about what to do. But when he read *The Christian Ambassador*'s notice of the conversion to spiritualism of Universalist minister Justin Averill, he and his wife, Mary, traveled to Battle Creek, Michigan. She had developed into a painter whose brush was guided by the spirits. When they arrived, Averill arranged to have Peebles help him minister to his First Free Church. The Peebleses settled there, although James began to tour as a spiritualist lecturer.

Peebles still corresponded with his friend Harter, who wrote him from *The Christian Ambassador* office with his wish that he would come back into fellowship with the Universalists, back to "the old Cayuga Association." To this request, Peebles replied, "Do Planets Go Back?" Their correspondence had an effect that Harter had not intended. As Peebles had converted Harter to Universalism when they were boys, so now he led Harter's way into spiritualism. Harter, too, resigned his letter of Universalist fellowship and emerged as "a well-skilled officer in the army of Spiritual Reformers."

Harter continued to live in Auburn but began a new career as a spiritualist lecturer and preacher of "the gospel of angel ministry." Although he became well known, his financial needs were not being met. Before Christmas in 1873, for example, acknowledging "his circumstances and conditions," he asked the readers of *The Religio-Philosophical Journal* to donate "presents in money, provisions or other valuables" to him and his family.

Nevertheless, Harter's career as a spiritualist was a long one. In an 1880 letter to *The Religio-Philosophical Journal*, he responded to a note by Peebles to the paper that had facetiously recommended forming an ecclesiastical committee of (ex-) Universalist ministers to vet the doctrinal correctness of new clergy. Harter referred to himself in the letter as "the pastor of Jacob's branch of the Church of the Divine Fragments, located wherever a fragment of humanity can be found." No longer having clerical credentials from the

Universalists, he had made up the title for himself and, tongue in cheek, presented it to the chaplain at the state prison at Auburn in order to be allowed to minister to the inmates. That summer, he was one of the speakers at a huge spiritualist camp meeting at Lake Pleasant, Massachusetts. He told those assembled there, "I was once a member of the Dutch Reformed Church; then I changed to the Methodist; then I moved forward to the Universalist; my last jump was into Spiritualism. I sing hosannas of praise for Spiritualism. It is a glorious religion."

Peebles also enjoyed a long career as a lecturer, writer, spiritual medium, and physician. He traveled to California in 1860 and, while in San Francisco, contributed articles to Alvah C. Edmunds's Universalist paper, *The Star of the Pacific*. This was misinterpreted back East, Peebles later wrote, as his having turned back to Universalism, but as it turned out, Edmunds's editorial policy had been loose. He, too, soon turned to spiritualism and became an itinerant trance lecturer, finally settling in Portland, Oregon.

In the late 1860s, Peebles embarked on the first of five world tours he would make in his long life. While in Cairo, Egypt, on the first trip, he encountered a woman making a living as a soothsayer. She was Helena Blavatsky, who would go on to found the Theosophical Society in 1875. Peebles associated with the society for a while but lost interest when he came to believe that Blavatsky was a fraud and that she and her associates were trying to elevate their new organization by undercutting spiritualism.

Universalists who became spiritualists pointed to episodes in the lives of the early leaders of Universalism in the United States that demonstrated their spiritualist experiences as evidence of the existence of independent, guiding spiritual intelligences. The converts were reminded, for example, that John Murray was led across the Atlantic to the precise place on the coast of New Jersey where Thomas Potter had been led by the spirit to build a church so that some preacher of universal salvation would come and find a place to address an audience.

Some Universalists saw spiritualism as a renewal movement, bringing Universalism back to its nonsectarian, even apostolic roots, to the time of the widespread outpouring of the gifts of the Holy Spirit in the early church. (Universalists explained universal salvation as the common belief among the first Christians.) Peebles wrote, "Modern Spiritualism in many respects is but a revivification of primitive Christianity, with the attending signs, gifts, trances, visions, dreams, prophecies, tongues, healings, &c." But most Universalist leaders denied the similarity between the gifts of the early days of the church and spiritualist phenomena.

Spiritualism's treatment of spiritualist manifestations as similar to biblical wonders made it open to continuing revelations. This moved spiritualism beyond the pale of institutionalized Universalism. Neither ex-Universalist advocates nor current Universalist opponents of spiritualism, therefore, were inclined to describe spiritualism as a mystical, experiential Universalism, although outsiders hostile to both Universalism and spiritualism hinted in that direction. Moreover, those who had become spiritualists from other religious backgrounds (or no religious background at all) did not see themselves as part of a Universalist renewal movement, even if their views, as spiritualists, included the conviction that no soul would be consigned to eternal punishment.

Throughout his long spiritualist career, Peebles pointed to Universalism as an institution that had become fossilized and unable to progress. In 1897, for example, he wrote a long article for *The Philosophical Journal* that began, "I listened to a straight, old-style Universalist sermon to-day. It reminded me of the explorations in Babylon." Yet he described his own beliefs as "Universalist Spiritualism." Part of what he meant by this term was the universal reconciliation of all the world's religions, based on a recognition that they were essentially all manifestations of a spiritual experience of the same thing. He argued this point in his 1869 work on comparative religion, *Seers of the Ages; Embracing Spiritualism, Past and Present; Doctrines Stated and Moral Tendencies*

Defined. He believed that such a *universalism* had outgrown Universalism, like a butterfly emerging from its chrysalis.

Seers of the Ages captured the spirit of the time by seeking a vision of unity within all the various disparate religious beliefs of humankind. Peebles relied on the work of previous writers who had worked toward a similar goal, such as Godfrey Higgins, author of the *Anacalypsis;* Joseph Ernest Renan, author of the *Vie de Jesus;* and Frederick Denison Maurice, author of *The Religions of the World and Their Relations to Christianity.* Joseph Barrett, who wrote the introduction to *Seers of the Ages,* described the work as follows:

> With indefatigable labor, James has gathered rich lore where others saw only alloy. A band of spirits, some of them very ancient, and all lovers of antiquity, desirous of blossoming into life "all things new and old," has directed his mind and his steps adown the sombre walks of the past, amid the brooding silence of buried civilizations. The pyramids had voices for him; the obelisks glared forth a hidden mystery in their inscriptions; rocks and tombs, scepters and swords, dust and ashes all bore traces of oracles that once built kingdoms and empires, all were prints of events readable under the spirit-vision of his guides, aflash with the truth that ministering angels have ever been the arbiters of human destinies.

In other words, the meaning he derived from the dead facts he surveyed came from the whispered inspiration of the spirits. They showed him the true story that lay under the mass of incoherent data. This method was often taken up by writers on comparative religion at the time, as they were stimulated by the conviction that what had been hidden or occult could now be revealed. It was taken up, as well, by Peebles's fellow spiritualists Helena Blavatsky and Henry Olcott, the founders of the Theosophical Society, as they wrote and published the tomes that were meant to rework the findings of archaeologists, historians, philologists, and philosophes into a comprehensive story that revolved around their own revelations. Anticipating Blavatsky's later descriptions of a brotherhood of hidden teachers through the ages, Peebles's *Seers of the Ages* "placed the past wave-eras, with their representative spiritual chieftains, in chronological and systematic order," as Barrett expressed it.

For anyone working under spiritual inspiration, so-called facts may float into the mind from above, ungrounded by mundane evidence but with a rightness of feeling. They operate as magnets, in a sense, attracting bits and pieces of language and history to their unifying core, as in spiritualist Gerald Massey's 1881 *Book of the Beginnings, Containing an Attempt to Recover and Reconstitute the Lost Origins of the Myths and Mysteries, Types and Symbols, Religion and Language, with Egypt for the Mouthpiece and Africa as the Birthplace.* This method would seem to explain some of the more extraordinary historical claims of spiritualists who were working in this genre of synthetic history, such as Matilda Joslyn Gage's 1893 statement in *Woman, Church, and State* that 9 million women were burned as witches in the Middle Ages (in support of her vision of an ancient universal matriarchy) and Kersey Graves's 1875 statement in *The World's Sixteen Crucified Saviors* that Jesus was a Nubian. This historical method resembles constructing a piece of sculpture using found objects. It could produce a long, detailed book, full of notes and obscure quotations, that might turn out to be a "thesaurus of munchausenisms," as one spiritualist reviewer described Blavatsky's *The Secret Doctrine.*

Peebles's conclusions in *Seers of the Ages* were in line with the assertions that spiritualist and occultist writers made repeatedly: All religions were one. Their unity was demonstrated by reducing their differences as unimportant historical appurtenances and by highlighting their core similarities. In Peebles's case, this meant accepting that traditional Christian claims about the historical Jesus were untenable. In *Seers of the Ages,* he accepts that Jesus was a myth invented by the early Christians and that the gospel writers copied the story, with slight changes, from the story of Krishna in *The Bhagavad-Gita* and *The Puranas.*

Insofar as Peebles accepted that Jesus may have been a real person, he was prepared to portray him simply as a man with highly developed mediumistic powers—that is, able to manipulate electromagnetism and to invoke and control spirits, which he used for healing people and to battle the priests of his day. In short, he was a kind of Martin Luther with super powers. Peebles also accepted that Jesus was trained in the mysteries during his travels to Egypt "and perhaps other Asiatic countries" and that he was a "Gymnosophist, a Yogi, a Hierophant," and "a Magus." Jesus' resurrection was his return as an adept spirit, as others have also returned as spirits. All of this, Peebles argued, was covered up by corrupt Jewish and then Roman priests, who wished to control the people and keep from them the truth that each person has spiritual power within him or her. In his book, Peebles resolved all religion, past and present, into spiritualism.

Seers of the Ages, as well as all the similar works that came before it and after it, provides evidence that the fears that were expressed in the Universalist denomination when Andrew Jackson Davis's first book was published were well founded. The historical Jesus had disappeared into a cloud of myth, and the unique truth of the Bible had been replaced by the ever-changing syntheses of visionary revelators, each of whom comprised his or her own authority. But in fact, Peebles's effort was not really so different from the efforts of earlier Universalist efforts to place in a historical context (and thereby demythologize) orthodox Christian doctrines about such matters as Hell, the Devil, the Atonement, and the Trinity. Namely, he argued that these doctrines were mere accretions to Christianity.

In an 1879 newspaper column, Peebles described an occasion on one of his lecture tours in which a Universalist clergy paid him a visit, "confessing himself a Spiritualist and his wife a partial medium." The minister estimated that one-third or more of his parishioners believed in spiritualism. Peebles asked him why he did not call himself a spiritualist and touch on the subject from the pulpit. "'I could not get a living,' was the prompt reply. 'I have four children, and they must be educated. Were I to leave my pulpit and become a traveling lecturer, what would become of my family?'"

In the same newspaper column, Peebles made a further point about the spiritualist underground within Universalism. He noted the recent death of Hannah Robinson Tufts, the widow of businessman Charles Tufts, who had endowed the Universalists' Tufts College. Although both of the Tufts had been spiritualists, wrote Peebles, and Hannah had been a medium, "Universalist clergymen attended the funeral, and Universalist newspapers, in chronicling her good qualities and deep religious convictions, conveniently forgot to state" the fact.

Not long after this, in 1880, Peebles wrote another column, noting that membership in the Universalist denomination had fallen away from its peak. In his view, Universalism had amounted to a "timely and effective protest against the old and hideous dogmas held by Orthodoxy." But it had a single idea, universal salvation, and after that idea had leavened religious thought in society at large, a separate organization could not be sustained. He believed that many of Universalism's leaders, despite having recognized this, had sought to crystallize Universalism into a permanent institution even though it no longer had a reason to exist.

Peebles moved to California. He took up the study of alternative healing, became a physician, and practiced and prescribed well into the 1900s. In fact, he used his own longevity as an advertisement for his medical advice. He died in 1922, just before his one-hundredth birthday.

The Machinery of Spiritual Telegraphy

To write *The Gadarene; or, Spirits in Prison*, a book about the bright and the dark sides of spiritualism, James Martin Peebles collaborated with Joseph Osgood Barrett, another ex-Universalist minister who had become a spiritualist. They had such high regard for each other that Barrett also wrote a long biography of Peebles, *The Spiritual Pilgrim*.

Barrett was born in 1823 in Bangor, Maine, of Universalist parents and trained in botany and forestry, but he vacillated about both his spiritual life and his career. He became interested in mesmerism and experimented with inducing trance in himself. He experienced visions, including one that he regarded as a spiritual consecration, in which he gained the ability to see "the soul of things, the heaven within that is struggling for fit expression." It came to him while he was ill in bed. As he later described in a newspaper article (referring to himself in the third person),

> Feeling spirit hands touching him, he looked up, and lo, a heart pulsing with vigorous life, radiating with musical coruscations, descending gently and lighting upon his breast; there it fluttered a moment in plain sight, and then descended into its proper place in the body, thrilling through and through his whole being, creating a joy which no language is adequate to describe.

As a result of this experience, Barrett trained for the ministry and began preaching. He was welcomed into fellowship and served for years as a minister, but unknown to members of his church, his spirituality turned into spiritualism and he became a medium for the spirits. On one occasion, he dreamed that his church was a bank, a worldly enterprise, which transmuted into something grander, a spiritual telegraph station. Again, he wrote, "Before him was the machinery of spiritual telegraphing, that was really alive, wheel within wheel, self-acting, golden in luster, all in motion, beating as in heart-pulses the 'spirit rappings,' and sending heavenly news along the attached wires, or chords of love-thought, uniting heaven with earth." Overseeing the operation were three angels in white and blue robes, who "explained the conditions requisite to reception of news from the spirits."

Barrett soon found it difficult to conceal his spiritualism from the members of his church. When they discovered it and a few tried to censure him, he accepted the position of pastor in the Universalist Society in Sycamore, Illinois, believing he might leave behind opposition to his beliefs. At first, he again hid his spiritualism from the congregation of his new church, but he eventually felt impelled to preach what he believed, the angelic gospel, from his pulpit, which created a deep division in his congregation. After he declared himself a spiritualist, a citizens committee in Sycamore appointed him chaplain of the city's Fourth of July celebrations, but "the deacons and dignitaries of the Methodist and Congregational churches would not allow the Sunday school children to walk in the procession!"

In the early 1860s, Barrett moved to Madison, Wisconsin, where he took up lecturing, writing, and editing and also worked as a forestry expert. For a few years, he helped edit *The Spiritual Republic,* published in Chicago. During the early days of the Civil War, he tried to secure an appointment as an army chaplain. In the summer of 1864, he attended a Universalist convention in Janesville, Wisconsin. With a few others, he wrote and distributed a platform (without much success), proposing the formation of a new movement of liberal Christians that aimed to unite Universalists, Unitarians, and spiritualists with what he breezily called a "chowdered theology."

One person who joined with Barrett at the Janesville convention was Alexis J. Fishback, another ex-Universalist minister. He had established himself in Jefferson County, Missouri, and spent decades as an itinerant lecturer and debater on behalf of spiritualism. Fishback's debates were enormous spectacles. One of the largest, in which he prevailed, was with Disciples of Christ debater Clark Braden. Toward the end of Fishback's life, however, in 1888, he debated another preacher from the Disciples of Christ, William Henry Boles, and during the course of the week was converted to Boles's brand of Christianity.

Barrett did not retreat from spiritualism, and finally, in 1869, the state committee of the Illinois Convention of Universalists disciplined him and then dropped him from fellowship after twelve years of ministerial work. Barrett's associates included many activists from spiritualism's most socially and politically radical wing. In 1873, with publication of his book *Social Freedom; Marriage: As It Is and As It Should Be,* he became known as an advocate of women's civil, social, and reproductive rights. He and his friend Peebles had both supported Victoria Woodhull in 1872, when as president of the American Association of Spiritualists, she endorsed free love as the fundamental plank of the new social order that the spirits would build upon Earth (although there was much confusion in the spiritualist camp about what *free love* entailed).

The most vocal spiritualist opponent of Woodhull and her free-love philosophy was also an ex-Universalist. He was Stephens Sanborn Jones, editor of *The Religio-Philosophical Journal* of Chicago, one of the two largest circulating spiritualist newspapers of the 1860s and 1870s. (*The Banner of Light* was the other.) Jones was born in 1813 in Barre, Vermont, and later studied and practiced law. In 1838, he moved west, settling with his family in St. Charles, Illinois; there, he opened a successful law practice and became a probate judge. Raised a Universalist, he remained active in the denomination into his adulthood. He was "generally the presiding officer at the state conventions, associations, and representative gatherings of the order during the first fifteen years of their history in the State of Illinois." He was converted to spiritualism, however, upon reading Andrew Jackson Davis's works and during the spread of spirit circles that began with the Fox girls' rappings.

Jones took over editorship of *The Religio-Philosophical Journal* in the spring of 1865. From its pages, he led the charge against the radical free-lovers, whom he believed were tainting the moral purity of spiritualism. The level of vitriol between the pro– and anti–free love factions of spiritualism reached its climax around the time of the 1873 Chicago convention of the American Association of Spiritualists, the organization of which Woodhull had been elected president two years before. At the previous year's convention, Woodhull had accused the famous Brooklyn minister Henry Ward Beecher of having an affair with Elizabeth Tilton, a member of his congregation, a scandal that fascinated the country for several years.

Woodhull's supporters, who were in control of the 1873 convention, attacked Jones and his newspaper from the podium. Delegate Juliet Severance imitated Woodhull's accusation against Beecher at the previous year's convention by accusing Jones *in absentia* of keeping a mistress. He denied it the following week in *The Religio-Philosophical Journal*.

A few years later, in March 1877, William Crawford Pike, an "insane Phrenologist," as one source put it, snuck into *The Religio-Philosophical Journal* office one night in order to blackmail Jones with purported evidence of his sexual infidelities. Pike's rage overtook him, however (or his demands were simply refused), and using the anatomical knowledge he had gained in his phrenological studies, he aimed a pistol at the most lethal spot of Jones's head, his "amative region," and shot and killed him. Pike's wife, Genevieve, was brought to trial along with him as an accessory before the fact based on testimony that she was Jones's paramour. Pike was put away in a mental hospital, and the editorship of *The Religio-Philosophical Journal* passed to Jones's son-in-law, John Curtis Bundy. Although Bundy had been brought up as a Methodist, he had been convinced by his in-laws to continue his spiritual career in the liberal theology of the Universalists, Unitarians, and spiritualists.

Under the editorship of Jones and then Bundy, *The Religio-Philosophical Journal* provided a more skeptical counterweight to *The Banner of Light,* which made little effort to distinguish sincere mediums from deliberate frauds. *The Journal* tried to dampen spiritualist enthusiasm for the more sensationalistic phenomena produced at séances, such as levitation, disembodied voices and noises, spirit materialization, rope escapes, and mind reading. In the 1870s and 1880s, in an attempt to purge the spiritualist movement, the editors devoted some of their attention to investigating séances and exposing fraudulent mediums. They argued for stringent test conditions at séances, and encouraged the development of a more scientific *psychical research.*

The editors' path between skepticism and belief was nevertheless difficult to follow. In 1888, Margaret Fox explained onstage that forty years before, she and her sisters had caused the rappings by cracking their toe joints, and she demonstrated her ability by making the sounds for the audience. Later, she recanted her confession, but *The Religio-Philosophical Journal* reported that even if the confession had been true, the accumulated experiences of spiritualists for the previous decades could not be invalidated by revelations that a few mediums had practiced deceptions.

Spiritualism had been validated for its believers by their own experiences. It offered a personal, intimate gospel: that loved ones had survived death (as would everyone) and that individual progress and happiness were assured. Spiritualists believed that those who had died remained accessible to those still in mortal form and thus able to offer comfort and guidance to them—whether across the parlor table or through the mortal voices of friends, neighbors, or family. It was a well-received gospel, especially during the decades around the Civil War, when so many souls departed so suddenly and violently from their loved ones.

The Annunciation
of the New Age

MANY OF THE UNIVERSALISTS IN THE BOSTON AREA who turned to spiritualism (and those with whom they associated) sensed an approaching biblical millennium, which manifested itself in plans for egalitarian utopias where humans would mingle with angels or become as angels themselves. Thus, spiritualism was not just a means of contacting the spirits of the deceased or of exploring the afterlife. Rather, it meant the opening wide of a gate between a perfect Heaven and an imperfect Earth. This idea provided a link between spiritualism and social reform.

This Earth and All Things Upon It

THE SPIRITS WERE THE SPIRITUALISTS THEMSELVES, one might say, represented in a blessed futurity. A glimpse into the afterlife revealed an alternate, glorified world that contrasted with the present and therefore offered a model for social change. The afterlife was a visualization of a better, more fundamental realm.

The séance was an attempt to materialize that world in the present, not just metaphorically. In order for that vision to be truly expressed in the material world, the visionary had to explore the actual matter of the universe and uncover its natural law. A spiritualist in trance might have to travel to another planet, for example, to examine its geological formation, its flora and fauna, or the social conditions of its inhabitants.

The New England Spiritualists Association, formed in 1854, announced spiritualism's intention to break down the walls between the past and the present, the future and the present, and even this world and other worlds. The association stated, "It is not the future and distant *alone* that the clairvoyants are describing; but the near and the present also. This earth, and all things upon it, are being analysed and unfolded and made of higher use." Thus, spiritualism was linked to the progressive, enlightened, utopian goals of radical social reform.

In the years before Andrew Jackson Davis's revelations and the Fox sisters' rappings, Universalists had prepared themselves, in a roundabout way, for an exploration of the afterlife. Universalism rejected the notion of eternal damnation through appealing to God's love but also to God's justice. Hosea Ballou explained his work *A Treatise on Atonement* by describing it in its subtitle as one "in which the finite nature of sin is argued." God made his ways commensurate with those of his creatures and thereby expressed his love for them. Ballou argued, "As no finite cause can produce an infinite effect, no finite creature can commit an infinite sin." And God could not (or would not) assign an infinite punishment for finite sins.

Spiritualism extended discussion within Universalism of a question that had always been at the core of the denomination's identity: What happened to the soul after death? The answer that Universalism provided—namely, that every soul would achieve salvation—had set it apart from the mainstream Christian churches. Universalism was a revolt against the orthodox doctrine that at least some, if not most, of humankind would be consigned to eternal Hell, to endless misery. Universalists directed their energies to describing the afterlife as universally blessed.

Within Universalism, too, the most intense factional dispute during the first decades of the nineteenth century hinged on varying descriptions of the afterlife of the soul. One faction, the *ultra-Universalists,* held that there was no punishment after death for anyone—that all were brought immediately into salvation. This group was especially identified with influential Universalist clergyman Hosea Ballou and his associates, including Thomas Whittemore.

Their opponents within Universalism held that there was some limited punishment and further development of the soul after death but that all would eventually be restored to God. The proponents of this view were called *restorationists.* The controversy between these two factions led to a schism among denominational leaders in the 1830s. And so when spiritualism emerged in the late 1840s, the same questions about the afterlife that had surfaced in the earlier dispute suddenly came alive again. Some of the same actors in the earlier dispute took to the field of controversy, fortified by new circumstances.

Some Universalists described the orthodox picture of the afterlife as static. They argued that, according to that picture, the individual soul underwent no development or change after death and divine judgment. Souls in damnation spent eternity in the same vat of molten lead, one might say, burning off the same arm over and over again. Infants in Heaven spent eternity standing in the same place, singing in an endless choir the same parts in the same hymns.

But if the afterlife was a place in which nothing changed, then its nature could not be contingent on causes in this life. Universalists found that notion not only inconceivable but also unacceptable. In the afterlife, the soul underwent change, development, and progress. Universalists had argued among themselves about this issue, questioning whether the consequences of one's sins would follow him or her into the afterlife.

Calvinist doctrine, it seemed, had made the afterlife incommensurate with this human world of cause and effect, for nothing a person could do on Earth would affect God's disposition of his or her soul after death. Thus, if God had predetermined the soul to eternal damnation, one could do nothing to change that. Ballou said that God would bring all humans immediately into eternal salvation after death. But was that not merely Calvinist doctrine on its head? Ballou's followers found themselves poised not before eternal damnation but before eternal bliss, irrespective of their own actions. This suggested to some that there was no need to be moral or to make sacrifices in this life.

James Martin Peebles argued against this view, which he referred to as the "'Death and Glory' System of Universalism":

> It puts a Nero and a Knowlton through the grave into the presence of "Him that sitteth upon the throne forever." Glory be unto Death! The body is the sinner, Death the saviour! Admitting the position of these Universalists, is it not true that "Judas, with a cord, Outstript his Lord, and got to heaven first"? Do they not ignore all moral distinctions, so far as the future existence is concerned? ... Reduced to the last logical analysis, it is rotting into Paradise—rotting into robes of glory and the society of angels!

Woodbury Fernald, after leaving the Universalist ministry, expressed the same concern about doing away with the notion of punishment in the afterlife. His concern would bring him all the way back to arguing for the reality of eternal punishment and (a

Swedenborgian) Hell. "I never preached the 'death and glory system,'" he wrote in *The Spirit Messenger*, "and if there is any one truth which mankind now need to be told . . . it is that they must not think lightly of life's duties, or wish too speedily to get away from its sorrows, in view of supreme felicity beyond death."

Ballou's restorationist opponents within Universalism held that the afterlife flowed out of the human life that preceded it. According to this view, causes in this life were joined to effects in the next. Natural law was universal. As long as there was a cause, there would be an effect. All souls would be saved in the end, but one could not automatically escape suffering after death. Continued development, probation, and work would be necessary even after death, at which time one would feel the effects of his or her prior actions.

Universal salvation was an implicit belief of American spiritualists, even those without an explicit Universalist background. So widespread was it that when a spiritualist lecturer or medium suggested that souls might be consigned to Hell, his or her fellow spiritualists drowned out the remark in a sea of countering voices. When one spiritualist made this suggestion in the columns of *The Spiritual Telegraph* in 1854, another spiritualist, Thomas Neibert of Natchez, Mississippi, wrote to Samuel Byron Brittan, editor of the newspaper, to say he had "consulted with Spirits through at least sixty mediums in the South, and not through one of them could he obtain a sanction of the theory of endless evil." This was a remarkable unanimity of opinion among spiritualists in an area of the country not at all known for its embrace of Universalism or of radical egalitarianism.

In contrast, widespread consternation and dismay overtook the spiritualist community over certain revelations of spiritualist medium and lecturer Amanda M. Westbrook Britt Spence and her lecturer and physician husband, Payton Spence. In 1859, they began teaching the "strange theory," as spiritualist writer Emma Hardinge put it, that a large proportion of the human race did not attain to the glory of immortality, and that only certain souls, under conditions which seemed terribly vague and unsatisfactory, survived the shock of death as individualized entities; their spiritual essence being either absorbed in the great ocean of being, or reincarnated in some subsequent state of higher development, etc.

The Spences had come to believe "that few, if any, souls maintained their individuality after death, unless they lived out their rudimental existence in the earth-form, for at least seventy years." Hardinge wrote that this nonimmortality doctrine was troubling to "bereaved parents, whose newly-born hopes of eternal life and unbroken progress" for their deceased children, "this remorseless theory crushed into annihilation."

Hardinge argued that this theory, like the priestly doctrines of old, was based on sheer metaphysical speculation and thus contradicted by the repeated contact that had been made with the spirits of young children. She placed spiritualism into the role of a hard science, in opposition to the Spences' speculative theology. She also placed spiritualism into the role of a reforming and liberalizing religion, in opposition to the traditional idea that some souls could not gain salvation. Hence, the Spences resurrected for a moment the Universalist debate with the orthodox Calvinists about the extent of salvation, which had been generally assumed in spiritualism as having been decided on the Universalist side. The Spences' theory placed spiritualism in question because one of the main aspects of spiritualism that attracted people to it, after all, was assurance about immortal happiness for themselves and their loved ones.

Hardinge also echoed another debate transplanted from Universalism into spiritualism, which centered on the question of retrogression: Would all souls progress into blessedness after death, or would some fall back into a lower state? Spiritualists, in general, answered that retrogression was possible but that it was temporary.

Many Universalists became spiritualists, at least for a time, in all but name. Spiritualist beliefs about the progress of the soul into salvation were close to restorationist beliefs, for spiritualists did not simply affirm that the spirits of the dear departed were contacting the living. Rather, they affirmed that the afterlife was commensurate with this life, that one's actions on Earth affected the conditions of his or her life after death, that a bridge of cause and effect spanned Heaven and Earth, and that Heaven was not exempt from the same impartial providence that guided the rest of the universe according to natural law. Spiritualists also affirmed that Heaven and Earth were both subject to evolution and that the religious forms of humankind were subject to change, as well. Spiritualism therefore presented an especially sharp rationalist challenge to faith, and in response to it, many Universalists wondered how far one could go in questioning the Christian tradition and still remain a Universalist.

Spiritualists revised their understanding of the miraculous events of the Bible, which they believed were in tune with natural law and not unique or ultimately inexplicable. They regarded their own psychic experiences as similar to those of the biblical seers and prophets. By adopting a theory that explained miracles as the manipulation of electrical and magnetic fields, spiritualists portrayed Jesus as having developed and used the same physical, mental, spiritual, and reformatory powers available to people in all times and places.

Swedish seer Emanuel Swedenborg had visualized Heaven not as a static state but as a dynamic field, in which spirits and angels led lives that resembled human lives but sanctified and made glorious. Universalists, too, now tilled the field of Heaven and domesticated it as part of the universe of cause and effect. All the attention they had paid to the nature of the afterlife predisposed them to accept the claims of spiritualism and even to take the lead in shaping the emerging but initially fragmented phenomena into evidence of their own notion of the afterlife. The spiritualists/Universalists connected to the newspaper *The Univercoelum and Spiritual Philosopher* understood the opposition against them in the mainstream

Universalist press to be opposition from ultra-Universalists, so they (the spiritualists) were restorationists of a sort.

Barnabas Hall, a Universalist clergy from Gouverneur, New York, wrote a letter to Brittan at *The Spiritual Telegraph* about his conversion to spiritualism. He described how it had both purified his Universalism and changed his view from ultra-Universalism, which he now saw as irrational absolutism, the negation of cause and effect, and the voiding of human agency in the face of God's omnipotence. He wrote,

> The great error is the doctrine that all our goodness would be given us when we were raised to incorruptibility and immortality. The more revelation I receive from Spirits the more am I confirmed in the belief that my willing mind must acquiesce in the moral government of God, and that I must conform to all the laws which govern me, in order to reach the port of blessedness and peace.

This defined the controversy about spiritualism within the Universalist ranks: Could the supernatural be made part of the natural world or be subject to empirical investigation, as was used to explore the natural world? Restorationists brought Earth to Heaven by extending natural law and causation into the afterlife. If the link was real, however, spiritualists believed that the opposite could also occur: Heaven could be brought to Earth. Radical utopian spiritualism worked on this assumption—that ultimately nothing could prevent transforming Earth into a paradise.

For Universalists fascinated with spiritualism, these issues were echoed in the question of whether retrogression was possible after death. To spiritualists, the core of their new revelations was that "Retrogradation, nor Evil, *as principles,* find no place in the procession of the divine plan and purpose. The soul of man, being the individualized and only personal expression of the essence of the Infinite Soul, is unchangeable, indestructible, and immaculate as its divine original." (Spiritualists' denial of the real existence of evil gave them one reason for believing their philosophy was different from and superior to Swedenborg's.)

In other words, sin and its retrogressive consequences were adventitious to the soul. They were not permanent. However, the progress of the soul occurred in the long run. After death, the soul did not necessarily fly to the highest Heaven or enter into ultimate bliss. It might, *for a time,* stay even or even descend some, depending on the person's life before death.

The spiritualists' belief that the final resolution of one's destiny could occur well beyond the point of death, however, gave their opponents a point of attack. John Stoddard, for example, wrote to Sylvanus Cobb of the spiritualism preached in his town. He paraphrased their teaching:

> We begin our future immortal life exactly where, and as we are, when we leave this life, in all respects, except that we do not then have our material body.... Sin originates in the spirit and its spiritual body, originates in them from their own inherent depravity and tendency to produce temptation and evil volition; the fleshly body and its wants have nothing to do with the production of moral evil. At death, the fleshly body dies, and the spirit with its spiritual body moves out, as a man would move out of a dilapidated dwelling, or as a prisoner will leave his prison house when he is legally discharged.

This was a caricature of most spiritualists' beliefs, but it made its point by describing spiritualists as locating evil and sin within the human spirit, not the flesh. If a person still could sin after having left the body, then sin was not inherent in the flesh. Spirits continued on their way, developing and progressing and not finishing with their trials or their sins, even though they were no longer of the flesh.

To Cobb, this meant that spiritualists who believed this "outdid Calvinism," in his words, because sin would inhere in the spirit. Or one might say, sin would be so pervasive that it would find a place in Heaven. Cobb argued this would "set the spirits of men, even in the spirit world, at work doing evil" and would provide a justification for the false notion that humans were innately depraved.

Stoddard tried to solve the mind/body problem through imagining that the spirit, after discarding the body at death, put on a spiritual body (whatever that was) to await the final consummation of events. He wrote,

> It is common for those who entertain these views to say, "Man is a spirit." But we respectfully ask, Is it not equally true that man is a body as well as a spirit? All will admit that he is so in this life. And are we not taught by the Divine Scriptures, that, in all future, conscious existence, man will as certainly be a body as he will be a spirit? be both, a body and a spirit?

Cobb preferred to locate evil and sin entirely in the flesh and to say that when the spirit was no longer tied to a body, it would not and could not sin. He wrote, "All the wrong we ever willed, or consented to, or committed, was induced by the appetites, passions and circumstances of the animal life, which is not the life that is to be through the resurrection, when this corruption shall put on incorruption, and this mortal shall put on immortality."

Unitarian William Ellery Channing had understood Ballou in his *A Treatise on Atonement* to assume that a soul could not sin after death. Channing concluded that Ballou believed that death (and neither the individual soul nor God) would do the entire work upon the soul necessary for its salvation. Ballou denied this, saying that he believed that a soul could sin after death and that it would be immediately punished as a result. Cobb, however, did not shun even the notion that death does the entire work, since through death, the flesh is abandoned.

Cobb was taking a page from Ballou's argument against retribution in the afterlife. "What a plunge for Universalists to make," Cobb wrote, "to descend back into Calvinism from the murky darkness of which they had risen, and to fall from the glorious Christian hope of a resurrection into a higher and purer and better life, into the old heathen fables of a spirit world of demons and satans."

But the problem with locating sin and evil in the flesh was that it led to an even more ancient heresy, the gnostic one, in which the pure soul is regarded as imprisoned in a degraded body and in an impure world. This was the point of Peebles's jibe at the ultra-Universalists' doctrine of "rotting into Paradise." In fact, spiritualists did see the change at death as an important one—as a glorifying, educating, illuminating, liberating, and upward-tending one. Most of them did not reduce death to a matter of changing one's domicile. Rather, speaking that way comforted the dying and the bereaved and countered the notion that at some point, "the state of all will be unalterably fixed" and that either punishment or happiness will be endless and unchanging.

These terms, by which Universalists debated spiritualism, were detailed and mechanistic in regard to the causal connection between this life and the next. After death, would the soul locate itself near its decaying body? Would it travel somewhere at all? Was the passage at death a change of place or a change of state? If it was a change of state, would the same person persist, or would the new state be something or someone different?

These questions stimulated the original restorationist objection to Ballou by Universalist minister Jacob Wood in his 1817 pamphlet *Brief Essay on the Doctrine of Future Retribution*. The issue of the continuity of the individual in the afterlife was still unsettled in Universalism when spiritualism appeared. Hosea Ballou II struggled with it in the columns of *The Universalist Quarterly and General Review* during the time that Davis was dictating *The Principles of Nature*.

To meet the objection that God's providence required a continuity of cause and effect between this life and the next (an argument drawn from the Enlightenment commitment to science as well as from the desire to preserve the connection between human acts and their consequences in the next life), some presumed the existence of an intermediate state after death. In it, the soul was disciplined and brought to holiness. More importantly, in this state the soul awaited the results of the effects of its earthly actions.

Those effects continued to work themselves out until time was no more, when all souls would be restored to God.

The debate within Universalism about the afterlife typically resolved itself into one approach that was somewhere between an empirical stance, advocated by spiritualists, and a stance that simply referred to faith. This divide remained throughout the second half of the nineteenth century. In 1891, the Reverend Thomas Woodrow, pastor of the Universalist church in Marshalltown, Iowa, wrote to the spiritualist newspaper *The Religio-Philosophical Journal,*

> I am engaged by a congregation here in this city to preach to them the hope of immortality and furnish them all the consolation possible in that line, and having learned that many intelligent men claim that the facts of psychology furnished proof of what I am engaged to preach, it occurred to me to look at those facts to see if their claim is true and this has caused some of my congregation to make complaints against me.

Woodrow was sharpening his sarcasm here. By the following month, editor John Curtis Bundy had announced that Woodrow was

> open to engagement to lecture for any spiritualist camp this season. Some of his clerical brethren criticized him for attending such a camp two years ago and *The Journal* half suspects that his purpose in again visiting some camp is to show that he proposes to be free to do as he thinks best regardless of the fears and prejudices of his Universalist contemporaries.

The Communion of Saints

THE SINGULAR EVENTS HERALDED BY THE FOX SISTERS' RAPPINGS and the results that attended upon the spirit circles that began afterward convinced spiritualists that angels and spirits were mixing with humans. Heavenly and Earthly boundaries—even the physical limits of what was possible—had begun to shift. The golden light of the millennium approached, the great turning point in human history. Reforms of all kinds were not only possible but also necessary and expected. If a cause in the earthly life could have an effect in the heavenly life, then conversely, a spirit could bring about an effect on Earth.

Spiritualists were derided for mixing the spiritual and the material, for thinking "when the soul shuffled off its mortal coil," it "placed its neck into another one." But their impulse to mix the spiritual and the material was, in a sense, the result of their enthusiastic adoption of the universality of natural law.

Ironically, spiritualism, which argued for the universal application of causality, was criticized by scientists on the grounds that the laws of nature are constant. For example, gravitation could not be set aside because of a few reports of tables levitating. To complete the irony, pointed out the spiritualists, some of these scientists also attended church. There, not only did they hear that God had parted the seas for Moses and that Jesus had changed water to wine, but they approved these things based on reports thousands of years old, rather than through the testimony of their own senses.

Samuel Byron Brittan complained,

> We have intimated that our science demeans itself in a very unscientific manner. It has nothing whatever to say against the spiritual experience of the ancient Jews. It neither disputes the facts nor discredits their spiritual origin. But modern facts of

analogous character, and obviously depending on the same general laws, it utterly discards, while it treats those who certify to their occurrence, with marked displeasure.

For these church-going scientists, what relation did spirit have to matter? What effective relationship did Heaven have to Earth? Or did religion have to science? Or did God have to them?

Ralph Waldo Emerson's comments on spiritualism raised these questions for spiritualists. He believed that all of spiritualism was derived from Emanuel Swedenborg, whom he thought was a genius but a misguided one, given his belief that the specific imagery of his experiences—the angels, their clothes, their language, their behavior, all the details of Heaven and Hell—were literally true, not just inspired fictions. Emerson's realm of the spirit, in contrast, was abstract, impersonal, general, and "elevated in tone." He wrote, "The Spirit which is holy is reserved, taciturn, and deals in laws. The rumors of ghosts and hobgoblins gossip and tell fortunes. The teachings of the high Spirit are abstemious, and, in regard to particulars, negative."

Emerson objected to mixing the high and the low, to finding the holy in "rat-hole revelations" or in "midnight fumblings over mahogany." He wrote, "One of the demure disciples of the rat-tat-too the other day, remarked that 'this, like every other communication from the spirit world, began very low.'" This raised the question of class distinction between the Unitarian-trained Emerson and the lower- and middle-class Universalist enthusiasts of spiritualism. As one spiritualist asked (or as the spirits asked through their mediums), "Why do spirits select men of no acknowledged respectability if they wish to improve *respectable* society?" And then answered, "Why was Jesus born in a manger, and crucified on a tree by *respectable* society? And not God in his infinite wisdom ever shamed the false and selfish pretensions of the would-be-great by choosing the base things of this world to confound the mighty?"

Edwin Whipple, Emerson's friend, wrote of him,

He was specially indignant at the idea of women adopting spiritism as a profession, and engaging to furnish all people with news of their deceased friends at a shilling a head. The enormous vulgarity of the whole thing impressed him painfully, especially when he was told that some of his own friends paid even the slightest attention to the revelations, as he phrased it, of those seamstresses turned into sibyls, who charged a pistareen a spasm!

Emerson's colleague Theodore Parker was no public spiritual-ist. But before he died in 1860, he had become an interested investi-gator of spiritualism and an admirer of the open-ended nature of its revelations. He talked about "every man bearing within 'lively oracles,' the present witness of his God." In addition, he wrote, "The Spiritualists are the only sect that looks forward, and has new fire on its hearth; they alone emancipate themselves from the Bible and the theology of the church, while they also seek to keep the pre-cious truths of the Bible, and all the good things of the church." He predicted that the number of followers would increase quickly in the years and centuries ahead.

Spiritualists returned his compliment. *The Washington Evening Star* reported in January 1858,

At a recent meeting of Spiritualists in Dodworth's Hall [in New York City], a prominent professor of the faith opened by saying it was customary in religious assemblies to read a portion of divine truth; and that he would begin the exercises of the occasion by reading *a portion of divine truth according to Theodore Parker.* He accordingly read an extract from one of Mr. Parker's discourses.

The eldest Fox sister, Leah, wrote in her memoirs that Parker had attended her séances several times and that she remembered his "beaming, kindly face." According to her, Parker "fearlessly, frankly, and honestly announced to his friends that he was a be-liever in Spiritualism."

During the last couple of years of Parker's preaching, in 1858 and 1859, when he was still estranged from the Unitarian establishment because of his radicalism, Boston's spiritualist newspaper, *The Banner of Light*, published long reports of his weekly sermons at the Music Hall and the Melodeon. The newspaper also printed the sermons of the Reverend Edwin Hubbell Chapin, a very popular preacher and Universalist-trained minister serving a Unitarian congregation. Even though spiritualists accepted Chapin as a fellow believer, he modulated his publicly expressed beliefs with an eye toward remaining within the bounds of what was acceptable— explaining, for example, that "the dead are near us and our communion with them intimate" but describing mortals' perception of the immortal spirits as being based on memories and on living among their works that remain in the world.

Chapin's public expressions of belief, according to James Martin Peebles, represented the stage of "Universalism just blooming into Spiritualism—faith smiling at its first glimpse of knowledge." Peebles saw the same emergent spiritualism in the writings of Unitarian minister George Hughes Hepworth, whose mother had been a spiritualist medium. Hepworth wrote, "Nothing is more evident to my mind than that the world longs to believe and needs to believe something of this kind" and then, "Yes, I do believe in this possible communion with all my heart."

Establishing the causal connection between this life and the afterlife (and mixing the high and the low, Heaven and Earth) provided a foundation for practical social and political reform work. Emerson's Unitarian colleague turned spiritualist, the Reverend John Pierpont, responded to objections to spiritualism that were couched as objections to having the exalted divine involved in the lowly happenings at séances or in the gritty particulars of the world. He pointed out that the Lord's Prayer itself asks the high creator and governor in Heaven to arrange the causal chains of the vast universe so that bread will be delivered daily to the devout soul who utters the prayer.

Brittan's publishing partner, Charles Partridge, wrote that spiritualists were best suited to lead the reform movement because they had the widest perspective. They were deliberately creedless (in part, a reaction to the sanctions against the Universalist clergy who had become spiritualists) and therefore, he claimed, not biased "hobby-riders," or unbalanced pursuers of a single idea. More important, having explored the afterlife and talked with spirits, they understood better than anyone the consequences that attended an ill-spent or ill-managed life. Regardless of whether his claim really applied to individual spiritualists, the spiritualist conventions, camp meetings, lectures, and societies during the last half of the nineteenth century functioned as a venue in which progressive activists in all branches of reform came together.

Pierpont was not the only Unitarian clergy who become a committed spiritualist and lectured and worked for the cause. Harvard-trained Allen Putnam and Herman Snow were both well-known spiritualist leaders. Leah Fox described a highly successful séance she conducted at a home in Somerville, just outside Boston, in which fifteen Unitarian clergy participated; the most enthusiastic among them was James Freeman Clarke. At the end of the demonstration, one participant laid his hand on the shoulder of Lydia Child's brother, the Reverend Dr. Convers Francis from Harvard, and declared that the display was the proof for which they had all been waiting "from time immemorial."

Thomas Wentworth Higginson converted to spiritualism after he investigated Harvard Divinity School's expulsion of one of its students, Frederick L. H. Willis, for conducting séances. Higginson managed to embarrass the school in print for having entrapped a reluctant Willis into trying to contact the spirits for the benefit of a calculating member of Harvard's science faculty and for having dismissed Willis without a full hearing. Willis eventually became minister of a church in Coldwater, Michigan, but it was a spiritualist, rather than a Unitarian, church. And Higginson took up lecturing on behalf of spiritualism.

Even so, Unitarianism, more than Universalism, was comfortable with a far more secular view than could be reconciled with a belief in discarnate spirits. Many Unitarians shared the materialist skepticism of Emerson's Harvard-trained protégé, the Reverend Moncure Conway, about séances and spirit contact and read with approval his scathing commentary on the occasion of Margaret Fox's public recantation of spiritualism.

Nevertheless, Unitarians who did become spiritualists were better able than Universalists to retain membership in their churches because they tended to regard spiritualism in a different light than their Universalist colleagues. Unitarians were more hypothetical, noncommittal, and tentative about spirit contact than were Universalists. John Curtis Bundy, editor of *The Religio-Philosophical Journal*, wrote,

> In most Unitarian churches there are Spiritualists, more than is supposed, for in too many cases they hold their views in reserve with a polite timidity which might as well be called moral cowardice. Many of their ministers have their own thoughts and experiences on this subject, held usually in quiet reserve or giving new cast and tinge to their discourses. Spiritualism does not pass well enough in polite society yet to be admissible in Unitarian circles.

Universalists often treated the spirits in literal terms—as either true or false, as cither what they presented themselves to be or as delusions. Unitarians, on the other hand, often treated the spirits as tropes or figures. They were rather less concerned with whether the revelations that mediums received came from independent, disembodied spirits or from some hidden portion of their minds. Unitarians were therefore better able to avoid confronting their fellow church members with direct claims about the reality of the spirits. Unitarians' spirits were susceptible to fading into insubstantiality between quotation marks.

Amory Dwight Mayo, for example, who was trained by Hosea Ballou but pastor of a succession of Unitarian churches, spoke about spiritualism as a kind of enthusiastic, folkloric myth that countered the materialism of the age. To him, it was spirituality for the masses—the common person's fable that nevertheless pointed, in a simplistic way, to the central Christian truth of immortality, dramatized by the séance. He wrote,

> Spiritualism is a natural awakening of the American masses to the doctrine of the immortal life taught by Jesus. The materialism of our society has brought the popular faith in immortality to a very low ebb; while the evangelical church has so caricatured the sublime idea by its doctrines of probation, judgment, heaven and hell, that the people have begun to feel this part of their religious belief slipping from them. The natural recoil from these influences has produced that outbreak of mingled fanaticism and piety which some mistake for a new gospel; yet, all that a rational Spiritualist believes of the future life and communion of souls was taught by Jesus, and has been believed by spiritually-minded people for eighteen centuries.

Minot Judson Savage, pastor of Boston's Church of the Unity, devoted years to investigating spiritualism and writing favorably about it. Yet he never committed himself to it in writing or from the pulpit, always hedging his words with the conditional "if it is true." Also in line with a Unitarian vagueness (as Universalists saw it), Savage argued that if one became convinced of the truth of spiritualism, he or she would not be called to do anything differently at all. Spiritualism, he believed, could offer no guidance or impetus to action—social, political, or personal. All it could offer was a blessed feeling of assurance about immortality, or what had previously been only a matter of faith.

A few thousand spiritualists and social radicals gathered in 1858 in Rutland, Vermont, at the Free Convention and spent much of their time debating whether spiritualism was a disastrous distraction for the social and political reform movements of the time or whether it supported, aided, and justified them. Trance speakers opened the convention. The first, young Nellie Temple, scanned the large crowd from the platform and declaimed, "Too often has the question been sent forth, 'Who can you spiritualists count, but infidels and Universalists?'"

The convention did not reach a consensus on the relationship, if any, between spiritualism and reform work. Some of the speakers thought that spiritualism distracted people from working on the tangible problems of the world. Many others, however, defended spiritualism as the basis of all reforms, especially those meant to ensure the freedom of individuals. Humans had rights, it was said, because their lives transcended the mundane.

Spiritualism kept reform efforts directed toward the most exalted ends. Even the effort to abolish slavery was a step toward the universal liberation from every form of human bondage, including the old theology of predestination and endless misery. As spiritualist physician Heman Storer told the crowd at the convention,

> The fact that children are torn from their parents and sold on the auction-block has been introduced here as one of the greatest wrongs and injured that can be inflicted on humanity. But what is that, compared with the idea that children are taken from their parents, and are, for all eternity, consigned to hell, and separated from those nearest and dearest to them?

How spiritualists thought about the link between the spiritual and the material, the abstract and the particular, affected not only how they thought about practical activism but also how they thought about spiritualism. Thomas Starr King, trained to the Universalist ministry, served Unitarian churches. Spiritualists saw him as manifesting the same Unitarian indefiniteness that depicted spiritualism, even when in a positive light, as an abstract philosophy that would not necessarily have any implications for one's behavior. Under these terms, one could hold on to a spiritualist philosophy conceived as a form of antimaterialism, progressivism, and visionary mysticism—and still maintain one's church membership. One could separate oneself from a popular but error-filled version of spiritualism while still describing oneself as a spiritualist. One might not even mention the many séances he or she had attended.

King privately consulted mediums who put him in contact with the spirit of his father but never mentioned it in public or endorsed spiritualism. To the incipient spiritualists in his congregation, his well-publicized sermons, especially after he moved to San Francisco in 1860, recommended spiritualism in everything but name. He praised the inner voices and holy monitions that opened people to the divine. When the spiritualists in his congregation approached him on the subject, King told them, "Though he had not come to California as a *spiritual lecturer,* he was thoroughly convinced that under favorable circumstances spirits did communicate with mortals."

King once spoke explicitly about spiritualism in a sermon and thrilled the spiritualists who heard him, assimilating the inexplicability of spirits to transcendentalist wonderment at the exalted mysteries of the physical world and exalting much of what they believed about inspiration. He said, for example,

> Is the statement that there is an enduring spirit within us, entirely distinct from the corporeal organization, and which the cessation of the heart liberates to a higher mode of existence, any more startling than the statement that a drop of water, which may tremble and glisten on the tip of the finger, seemingly the most feeble thing in nature, from which the tiniest flower gently nurses its strength while it hangs upon its leaf, which a sunbeam may dissipate, contains within its tiny globe electric energy enough to charge eight hundred thousand Leyden jars, energy enough to split a cathedral as though it were a toy? And so that, of every cup of water we drink, each atom is a thunder storm?

But King also disappointed the spiritualists in his audiences with his sarcasm about specific claims of contacting the dead.

Unlike Unitarian clergy, many Universalist clergy opposed the spiritualist interest of their colleagues not as a low form of superstition but as a secular rationalism, because spiritualists revised the status of the Bible and other received truths, based on their practical investigations. For example, Universalist minister George Truesdell Flanders, while serving as a pastor in Brooklyn, New York, was one of a few distinguished members of the audience at the Davenport brothers' popular exhibitions at the Cooper Institute in New York City who was chosen to serve on an oversight committee of skeptics for the performances. Even into the 1880s, Flanders was a proponent of hewing to the Bible and wrote that Samuel Byron Brittan, William Fishbough, Thomas Lake Harris, and Andrew Jackson Davis had led the rationalist challenge to Universalism.

Spiritualists, as rationalists, believed that just as the afterlife was not static but dynamic, so, too, scriptural truth was not plenary and unique to a far past but part of a developing, universal revelation. Uriah Clark wrote,

> With a genuine Universalism, in its broadest, truest, eclectic sense, I have no conflict, and if you accept Universalism in this sense, you have the "more sublime, living, and spiritual faith" I recognize as taught by the higher spiritual manifestations of all ages, including the present. But ... conservative Universalism would insist on clinging to the Spirit-revelations of the Bible as the only and all-sufficient ground of faith, and would dash out all hope founded on modern manifestations claimed to be spiritual.

This formed the Universalist/spiritualist controversy with institutional Universalism. To mainstream Universalists, spiritualists demeaned Christianity because they upheld spiritualistic phenomena and present-day visionaries, seers, and prophets as equivalent to those described in the Bible. As Clark put it, spiritualists accepted "all the genuine manifestations recorded in the Bible, and corresponding manifestations in all ages and among all nations, including the present." But this meant that they also accepted that the manifestations described in the Bible were not more significant than those unfolding in the present. That is, a levitating table was like the Burning Bush, and Moses and Jesus were mediums.

Hosea Ballou himself had rejected miracles and been an eager participant in a detailed rereading of the history of Christianity in order to highlight what he considered the original message of universal salvation held by the first Christians but later declared heterodox by the Church. Spiritualists made the connection between this rereading of the history of Christian doctrine and coming to a new understanding of Jesus as an exemplary human who had developed in himself the same powers all humans have.

Spiritualists were intensely interested in the Apocrypha, which they believed the early Church had suppressed in order to convey the impression that the canonized versions of biblical events were unique and unquestionable. They thought their conservative, former denominational brethren had grasped the dead husk of religion but had missed its living essence. Spiritualism was more sublime than Universalism "in opening the heavens of celestial intercourse as a reality," according to Clark.

Another Universalist minister who became a spiritualist and was censured for it, George Washington Gage, from Louisville, Kentucky, wrote to the Universalist newspaper *The Star in the West* in order to make a similar point to his former Universalist colleagues. He wrote, "If you repeat the question heretofore asked by you, 'Wherein is Spiritualism superior to Universalism,' I will at present only answer that whereas we have believed in immortality and the spirit-world, now we *know* it."

Spiritualists' emphasis on direct personal experience of a reality beyond convention led to their assumption that all religions had a single, universal core. They investigated other religions not with the goal of a biblical apologist (such as proving the dispersal of peoples after Eden or after Babel) but with the goal of proving the religions all spiritualistic at heart. In this sense, the millennium, or new era, that spiritualists anticipated was one that required only the discovery of a bridge between Heaven and Earth that had always been there but had been hidden. Spiritualism's attempt to bring cause and effect over that bridge into the afterlife was part of a single rationalizing effort that rejected the idea that God would suspend natural law.

The suspension of natural law was implied by the ultra-Universalist view of Ballou. (William Ellery Channing, at least, had argued this.) Namely, Ballou denied that the person after death, although persisting, would experience any effects of his or her previous sins. As Thomas Whittemore described that view in 1853,

> The Universalist denomination for the last twenty-five years has been growing into the belief that sin cannot exist in the resurrection state; that the power or source of temptation is in the flesh, or the body; and as we can feel neither hunger, thirst, lust, or any other appetite that leads us to sin, when the body is thrown off, the reign of sin will be arrested at death. In the life beyond the grave, there will be no sin.

This doctrinal conflict within Universalism provided the context for Brittan's description of what spiritualists, in general, believed. Some spiritualists argued that spiritualism should be defined in the most minimal way, as the belief that spirits communicate with humans. Their argument, however, was an attempt to count as many people as possible as spiritualists. It was also more of a nod toward the principle of respecting the integrity of individuals' beliefs and remaining suspicious of dogma than a true description of the beliefs that spiritualists shared.

In fact, most spiritualists shared quite an extensive belief system, even if under the principle of independence they would not commit themselves to it as a creed. To an outsider's eye, it was Universalistic and restorationist. In an 1861 survey article, "The History of Modern Spiritualism," Brittan did not label it that way, but his description of spiritualist belief made it evident: Spiritualists believe in one God, a spirit, who is the spirit of love, "the indwelling Soul of the Universe," from whom all things proceed. "With some exceptions," he wrote, "the Spiritualists believe that Man is immortal by virtue of what may be denominated the *universal incarnation;* or the existence of the Divine Life in the spirit, soul, and body of every man, and the consequent indestructibility of our spiritual constitution." All the human faculties are good but can be perverted. Brittan described the result:

> Most Spiritualists believe that the abuse of the faculties must necessarily involve consequences that reach forward into the immortal state of being. . . . However, the almost universal opinion doubtless is, that the tendency of all souls—if we regard their existence *as a whole*—is forever upward toward the Divine Source and Centre of all life . . . and very few, if any, are disposed to admit that death fixes the moral state or establishes the general condition of any one.

Brittan was also still a "universalist" in assessing the Christian revelation and scriptures as one variation on the great universal religious expression of humankind. He wrote,

> While Spiritualists generally admit that the original Source of all true inspiration is immeasurable and infallible, they yet regard its mortal channels and mundane receptacles, in every age and country, as subject (in varying degrees) to the same finite limitations. . . . Thus each one of the contributors to the Bible—not less than the authors of other books held sacred—has left his own mental and moral likeness on his portion of what is denominated "the infallible word of God." From a calm and rational analysis of the book, its contents are believed to be of a mixed character and unequal value.

The biblical miracles and apostolic gifts of the early days of the Christian church were episodes in the ongoing, universal history of spiritualistic manifestations. Brittan wrote, "They are believed to have required the exercise of essentially the same occult powers that have often been mysteriously displayed in the presence of modern Spiritualists and their opposers. Such extraordinary phenomena are ascribed to the application and operation of existing spiritual forces and natural laws."

Burning Out the Rubbish

IF SPIRITUALISTS OFTEN UNDERSTOOD THEIR EXPERIENCES as a universal and timeless natural religion that simply needed to be realized, they also often understood spirit contact as a historically unique dispensation by which Heaven and its inhabitants were flowing down to Earth. The difference was a matter of intensity and clarity. Effective help from the spirits would be given to those struggling down below. Divine help was now available to reform the world, including plans for utopias and mechanical inventions that would mix Heaven and Earth, spirit and matter. If binding miracles and the supernatural to natural cause and effect demoted Heaven, it also made it possible to think that Earth might be made more like Heaven. And so reformers could feel encouraged that the angels would help them along the way. As it happened, reformers working for the elevation of women in society were particularly heartened.

Some have believed that spiritualism was simply a mental disorder or a coping mechanism for weak souls grieving over the deaths of loved ones and unable to face reality. Whatever may be the truth about any individual spiritualist, spiritualism as a whole presented a comprehensive challenge to institutional religion and to the social institutions of society, which spiritualists meant to change for the better. Spiritualists gave voice to an enlightened progressivism and were among the era's strongest proponents of the liberation of all people from oppressive bonds and limitations. Spiritualism was simultaneously idealistic, liberal, and anarchic. (Karl Marx and his colleagues recognized that it could not become part of the disciplined force they believed would be needed to carry out a revolution.)

Some people believed that spiritualism was simply a woman's religion, but in fact, it was an integral part of the reform movement and both men and women were spiritualists. Nevertheless, spiritualism did help feminize religion. Andrew Jackson Davis propagated the Swedenborgian notion that the Godhead was a union of the male principle of wisdom and the female principle of nature, and Thomas Lake Harris described a "divine one-in-twain" that encompassed both male and female principles.

Spiritualists generally believed that sexuality was the instrument through which the universe would achieve its evolutionary goal, but in order for that to occur, women had to be elevated as men's co-equals in vision, in power, and in authority. This provided spiritualism with an agenda for political and social reform. Spiritualists believed that women would lead humankind into a new era through the liberation of their sensitive powers. Insofar as it was male power that was ensconced in the Bible and enshrined in traditional Christian doctrine, spiritualism undermined that power and offered an alternative.

Most of the Universalist clergy who turned to spiritualism had daughters or wives who were also active with the spirits. Many of these women became trance mediums and drew their fathers or husbands toward spiritualism. Commonly, a wife or a daughter took the role of oracle and her husband or father the role of exegete—that is, writer and public lecturer. With others, the social roles were reversed: The wife became the public figure and the breadwinner, through lecturing or healing, and the husband followed along as her booking agent or business manager.

On the one hand, the passivity of trance mediums who vacated their bodies and left them to the control of spirits drew criticism that spiritualism was "effeminating" and "unmanly," as Ralph Waldo Emerson put it. On the other hand, becoming trance speakers and mediums had ambivalent consequences for women. It may have made them passive, but it also liberated them and gave them power. Women could assume authority they did not have otherwise by becoming trance mediums for spirits who had possessed authority when living.

To put the issue of power in gothic terms, spiritualism was an upwelling fountain from the dark, underground realm of the feminine into the light of the everyday. As such, it was something that the fathers thought they had to quell. Spiritualism provided plenty of ideological support for women's rights. After the Civil War, it was closely linked to the women's movement, particularly to the struggle for reproductive rights, but this link merely elaborated what was present in spiritualism from its birth a dozen years earlier.

Despite that, even spiritualism had a gender-based division of labor. Spiritualistic experience often first appeared among pubescent girls and spread through the rest of the community. Spiritualists said this was because females were more sensitive than males to subtle impressions and the whisperings of spirits. Thus, females were more likely to become mediums. Through trance mediumship, as well as through lecturing and writing, both single and married women came into positions of independent influence and leadership within the spiritualist community.

Uriah Clark's annual *The Spiritualist Register* was not a complete listing of all the "workers in the field of Spiritualism." The careers of many spiritualists were in constant flux and not captured in any annual collection of names. Also, many people in the movement were reluctant to allow their identities to be published. Nevertheless, Clark's listing showed a division between public lecturers, including both trance and normal lecturers, who promoted the ideas of spiritualism, and mediums and clairvoyants, who most often worked in their own or in others' homes, conducting spirit circles and healings.

Although public lecturers were often women, they were more often men. But in the roles of mediums and clairvoyants, women far outnumbered men. Social pressures kept women at home and sent men out as itinerant lecturers and preachers. Spiritualism created new opportunities: Women could now be private consultants and, through the tradition of midwifery, healers. The 1870 Boston city directory listed different categories of physicians. The listing in one of these categories, "Clairvoyant Physicians," consisted of all women. And almost all of them were also listed in another business category: "Mediums."

Focusing on the Universalist clergy who became spiritualists reveals the mutual influence that Universalism and spiritualism had on each other. Universalist authorities felt forced to react to their clerical colleagues who had turned to spiritualism, even when they might have ignored the spiritualist beliefs and practices of laypeople. Focusing on clergy, however, may obscure an important fact about spiritualism: It was not just another denomination or sect but in part an alternative form of spirituality to what was available in the traditional churches. The characteristics that made spiritualism what it was were therefore well suited to the advancement of women as religious authorities and as independent actors in society.

Universalist women who became famous for other accomplishments sometimes grew into devoted spiritualists. Mary Ashton Rice Livermore, Frances Dana Barker Gage, Matilda Joslyn Gage, and Alice and Phoebe Cary, for example, all became progressive spiritualists, who believed that the spirits were aiding the other reforms of the age. (A list of Unitarians would include, among others, Lydia Maria Child and Lucy Stone.) These women's fame did not rest on their spiritualism but on their other activities and writings. Nevertheless, their belief in the spirits must be understood in order to appreciate how extensively spiritualism played its part in the religious ferment of the time. The career of Universalist and spiritualist medium, lecturer, and activist Frances Brown demonstrates how spiritualism and women's rights were intertwined.

Hannah Frances Morrill was born around 1816 in Salisbury Village (which later became Franklin), Merrimack County, New Hampshire. With thousands of other young women from the hills of New England, she left home and traveled down the Merrimack River to Lowell, Massachusetts, to work in the textile mills there. In Lowell, she became a member of the Universalist church and taught children in the Sabbath school. Universalism was being preached among the mill workers, and Morrill had come to reject the doctrine of endless misery and to accept that of universal salvation as a means to envision a radically reformed world. In August 1836, she married John Brown, from Vermont.

In Lowell at that time, Thomas Baldwin Thayer was pastor of the First Universalist Society, and Abel Thomas was pastor of the Second Universalist. Together, they formed *improvement circles* for the young members of their churches. These circles became writing workshops for developing talent and resulted in the publishing of the well-regarded *The Lowell Offering,* beginning in 1840, a journal that astounded its readers because all of its contributors were young mill women. Morrill was probably a member of these improvement circles and developed her writing skills and her political sensibility there, although it does not appear that she was a contributor to *The Lowell Offering.* By that time, she had also become a public advocate for the rights of women.

Around 1848, Hannah Frances Brown's husband decided to pursue business in the Western Reserve and the Browns moved to Cleveland, Ohio, where he opened a tobacconist shop. From Cleveland, Brown was a regular correspondent for Sylvanus Cobb's *The Christian Freeman and Family Visiter,* and she remained one until 1853. She also wrote many letters to Universalist friends back East, including the Reverend Edwin Chapin. Her marriage was not going well, and having been brought West increased her sense of isolation and constriction.

In 1850, Brown visited her family and friends back in New Hampshire. During a revival season in 1838, they had become members of the Congregational church, and she felt estranged from them as a result. Her yearning for a higher and independent life burst out in her column in *The Christian Freeman.* She wrote,

> If I were only a preacher! I mean if I had a *right* to preach, and could preach, I would not contend about forms and creeds.... My mission, with God's blessing, should be, to make war with the evils that attend man all his life long; to cry aloud against the abominations that make desolate this beautiful earth of God's;

and to clear away some of the mud and rubbish that impede mortals' progress to happiness.

Brown struggled to obtain a divorce from her husband. She also became interested in the burgeoning phenomenon of spiritualism. On a trip back East, she wrote to Cobb's paper,

> In company with some of your enfranchised spirits, I shall turn from heaven to revisit the places and people that will forever be dear to my memory. Who knows but I may be one of the favored few sent to earth to "knock" out the thoughts and things that have place in the spirit land? If I take the trouble to visit your sanctum, let none but friends listen to my revelations, for I would not be interrogated, and then reported "an imposter" to the world.

Brown attended Joel Tiffany's series of lectures in 1851 in the Prospect Street Universalist Church in Cleveland. Tiffany was the lawyer who had brought suit against Chauncey Burr on behalf of Leah Fox. He had come to believe that the Foxes were being libeled and had done his own investigations into spiritualism, which resulted in his conversion. His lectures, in turn, converted Brown as well as Massachusetts abolitionist and women's rights activist George Bradburn, who had trained for the Universalist ministry and served in Nantucket, Massachusetts. He had moved to Cleveland to help Joshua Reed Giddings as an editor of *The True Democrat.*

To Cobb's readers, Brown had promised to report who was occupying the pulpit of the Universalist Society in Cleveland. She demurred from referring to the uninspiring pastor, the Reverend Gibbs, however, and instead, tongue in cheek, named Tiffany. She wrote,

> What his creed is, I know not, and, to me, it matters not, so long as I know that he repudiates the doctrine of total depravity and endless misery. Do not understand me that Mr. Tiffany is the pastor of the Universalist Society. They neither hire nor pay him; and but few of them hear his lectures. He lectures to large congregations gathered from all churches and from the world's people.

Tiffany's lectures gave a detailed treatment of Jesus as a highly developed medium, wielding magnetic powers. By the following year, the Universalist Society of Cleveland no longer existed.

Brown saw spiritualism as the widest and most practical foundation for the reform movement. "To me, the spirits' teachings are sublime, glorious," she wrote. "They remove the partition walls that the Infidel and the religious bigot have built; they are filling the great gulfs dug by Pharisees and hypocrites; teaching man to regard man as a brother, without respect to color or grade, and God as a universal Father." She attended a lecture by Andrew Jackson Davis in Cleveland and wrote to Cobb that Davis was "scattering firebrands in this spiritual wilderness. They may burn out the rubbish; but I must be excused from hoping and wishing, lest Br. Cobb lose a subscriber thereby."

A divorce was granted Brown in 1856 or a little later, and she became a full-time social activist in the causes of women's rights and spiritualism. She began her own radical newspaper in Cleveland, *The Agitator*, which she published from 1858 to 1860, and she ventured onto the lecture circuit as a powerful speaker. Along with other social radicals and spiritualists from Cleveland, Brown became associated with the Berlin Heights free-love community nearby, although she did not move there. She did, however, lecture two thousand eager souls who attended a socialist convention there in the summer of 1859. Spiritualist lecturer Warren Chase sent a letter to *The Banner of Light* about it. "The cause of woman and man, of God and the angels," he wrote, "was nobly and ably vindicated by our sister of the Cleveland Agitator, and I know it had an effect, for I saw the crowd drink the thoughts as they flowed from her heart and head."

Brown was "a woman of decided free love tendencies," according to Stephens Jones, editor of *The Religio-Philosophical Journal*. However, William Denton, spiritualist lecturer and editor of *The Vanguard*, described her as "a high-minded, eloquent defender of woman's rights, and a glorious woman she is, whose fame and worth will shine brighter and brighter on the historic page that records the heroic virtues of illustrious women, when the names of those who get up resolutions for a time-serving, ignorant and bigoted market, will be forgotten forever." She was part of the most radical wing of the movement to place women in control of their own bodies, to allow them to decide when and by whom to have children. She often spoke of marriage as degradation and legalized slavery and prostitution. For her, spiritualism was a reform and liberation movement with a special mission for women.

At a spiritualist convention at Ravenna, Ohio, in August 1857, one woman in the audience objected to the speeches, including Brown's. These speeches advocated

> what some call Free-love, that is, that each man and woman has
> an inalienable right to judge and decide in relation to their own
> conjugal relations, and that it is nobody's business but their
> own. That they themselves are to judge or ought to judge of the
> reasonableness and propriety of such relation for themselves,
> and of everything pertaining to it and its conclusions; and that
> others have no business to judge and decide their matters for
> them.

The audience member objected that this was supposed to be a convention devoted to spiritualism and that spiritualism "had nothing to do with woman's rights." Brown took issue with this, "declaring that if Spiritualism was not calculated to elevate woman, improve her condition and exalt her to the enjoyment of her God-given rights, she wished to have nothing to do with it."

Brown published two books of literature for children and sentimental fiction while she was editing *The Agitator*. These, she published under the name *Frances Brown*, rather than *Hannah* or *H. F. M. Brown*, perhaps because of the notoriety she had earned under those names as a social radical (and perhaps therefore as someone whose writings would not be perceived as appropriate for children). In 1861, she also published *The False and True Marriage: The Reason and Results*, a work of radical social critique, using the name *H. F. M. Brown*. In it, she did not mention her own marital difficulties.

In 1863, Brown moved to Chicago and worked with spiritualist Moses Hull, first in editing *The Religio-Philosophical Journal* (before it was sold to Stevens Jones) and then in editing *The Spiritual Republic*. At the same time, she also was a regular correspondent for A. J. Davis's New York–based newspaper *The Herald of Progress*. Brown also received a license to conduct marriage ceremonies as an agent of the Religio-Philosophical Society, which she and Joseph Barrett and Stephens Jones founded in Chicago in 1863. The society granted her a letter of fellowship, and she traveled as an itinerant minister, conducting marriages and reporting them in *The Religio-Philosophical Journal*. Brown was a friend of spiritualists and radical activists Milo and Elizabeth Townsend. They inspired her to establish a new form for the marriage ceremony by describing the ceremony of abolitionists Stephen Symonds Foster and Abby Kelley, which had been performed at the Townsend home in 1845. The ceremony Brown developed emphasized women's essential integrity and independence, even within marriage.

Brown began *The Lyceum Banner* for spiritualists' children in 1867. In that same year, she was made the general agent for the Religio-Philosophical Society and then for the American Association of Spiritualists. She toured the West, lecturing in California, Utah, and Oregon. In 1870 and 1871, she served as president of the American Association of Spiritualists, helping turn its focus to women's rights, especially reproductive rights, before Victoria Woodhull took over as president in 1872.

Brown then moved to California, lecturing and organizing for women's rights and spiritualism. In addition, she continued to write for children and to organize the children's educational organizations of spiritualism, called *children's lyceums*. She helped found a spiritualist colony and successful children's lyceum in Santa Barbara. In 1879, the year in which she passed away, she still had her eyes set on the dawn of a new era. She wrote,

> Young America wearies of the old, and strikes out for nooks where ferns and violets are fresh with dew. Who wonders? We of larger growth tire of dull sermons. I am confident that our

need is new thoughts, new inspirations. Let us deal less in methods and books, and go to the heart of the child; learn his needs
and the varied avenues to the soul; bring out the angel, and the
demon will forsake the field.

To Brown, spiritualism was a field of opportunity, through
which the world could be made better. Her Religio-Philosophical
Society made it possible for other women to enter the ministry and
preach at a time when opportunities in the mainstream denominations were few. It provided the credentials for spiritualist women to
demand recognition for their pastoral work.

A good example is the career of Ella Elvira Gibson. She was
born in 1821 in Winchendon, Massachusetts. For several years, she
was a member of the Methodist church, but after a profound sickness, "she experienced an entire change in her religious views" to
embrace a love that was convinced of humans' innate goodness and
of the ultimate salvation of all.

As an adult, Gibson lived in Barre, Massachusetts, where she
wrote and published some of her poetry. In the early 1850s, she became a devoted spiritualist and then a trance lecturer, advertising
in the spiritualist registers her willingness to travel and speak all
over the East. Under "spirit influence," for example, working
"through her organism," Gibson delivered lectures in 1856 and
1857 in the Universalist church in Belfast, Maine (John Dods's and
Luke Rand's previous platform) on the subject of humanitarianism. (Actually, she spoke on the "origin of mind, and soul marriage" and how certain combinations of spiritual natures between
men and women could produce elevated human offspring.)

Shortly before the beginning of the Civil War, Gibson married
John Hobart, another traveling spiritualist lecturer, and they moved
to Darien, Wisconsin. At the outbreak of hostilities, Ella Hobart
worked to organize ladies' aid societies for the soldiers. Both she
and her husband, however, had joined the Religio-Philosophical
Society, and they were made ministers. As a consequence, John
Hobart was given a commission as chaplain in the Eighth Wiscon-

sin Infantry, and he served from 1862 through the end of the war. This unit also informally used the services of Joseph O. Barrett, who wrote a popular pamphlet after the war on "Old Abe," the eagle mascot of the so-called Live Eagle Regiment of the Eighth Wisconsin.

Ella Hobart, as a minister of the Religio-Philosophical Society, was drawn into chaplaincy work with her husband and then worked independently. In 1864, the First Wisconsin Heavy Artillery elected her their chaplain, making her the first woman chaplain in the U.S. Army. She served for several months in that position, until Secretary of War Edwin Stanton disallowed her position, not because she was a spiritualist but because he did not wish to set a precedent for women serving in the military. It took until 2002 for the U.S. Congress to award Ella E. G. Hobart an officer's commission retroactively as captain for her services as chaplain.

After the Civil War, Hobart continued to lecture and write and to progress further into radicalism and free thought. In the 1870s, she published a book entitled *The Godly Women of the Bible*, written, she explained, "by an ungodly woman of the 19th century." In that book, she wrote, "Christianity is an insult to the wisdom of the nineteenth century. To place before its progress and development a leader, ruler, king, savior, god, whose knowledge was less than a modern five-year-old school girl, is an outrage upon humanity."

Many spiritualists, in fact, were not only proponents of women's equality with men but advocates of women's superiority over men, based partly on women's apparent ease in becoming mediums (which displayed their direct access to spiritual power). As one woman medium put it, "Women . . . are perfect, they are the purest of God's creatures; they have an interior power that is calculated to set all things right." She anticipated a "Woman's Kingdom," in which women would naturally assume the reins of power. The spirits, unfettered by mere earthly custom and contingency, could suggest the most radical changes to society.

The Hierophant of Hopedale

ADIN BALLOU, THE MOST FAMOUS UNIVERSALIST REFORMER to become a public advocate of spiritualism, was born in 1803 into a Baptist farm family in Cumberland, Rhode Island. After converting to Universalism as an adult and entering the ministry, he became disenchanted with and then cut his ties with the denomination because of its factional infighting. In 1842, he set up a practical Christian commune, named Hopedale, in the town of Milford, west of Boston. He intended it to be a refuge for so-called Christian *perfectionists,* who hoped to achieve a reformed society on Earth—that is, a society that would embrace nonresistance, which meant both nonviolence and noncooperation with the corrupt civil powers of the world. Around 1850, spiritualism became entwined with his reform goals.

Like many other Universalists, Ballou conceived of spiritualism as a form of rationality. He wrote,

> I am a Spiritualist because I regard Spiritualism as a great help in the promulgation of free discussion. There are thousands of questions on the subject of religion, science and philosophy, which must be discussed, but could never be solved by any method mankind possessed prior to the birth of modern Spiritualism.... Man's eternal destiny was a mere fancy; the essential religious truths were mere baseless whims. The time has come when religion and reason must be married.

Ballou's point seemed to be that the realm of ultimate questions—Is the soul immortal? What happens to the person after death? Is there an afterlife? What is it like?—was one about which the living had little knowledge. Materialists and scientists, on one side, had blocked investigation of that realm by declaring it nonexistent, and clergy, on the other side, had blocked investigation of it with warnings and images of eternal punishment and reward. But why could not the intrepid explorer see if the territory on the other side of mortality could be surveyed?

Ballou believed that spiritualism was the place where ultimate things were being investigated. Spiritualism provided more than just a way for the bereaved to cope with their losses. In spiritualism, the realm of the ultimate was opened. Spiritualism pointed to the border between life and death and to a higher realm by way of the most hidden paths in the mind.

This was an answer to the transcendentalists' efforts to divest religion of its supernatural and otherworldly trappings and to read the natural world as the seat of the religious sentiment and the human mind as the temple of mysteries. As Ballou's friend, Unitarian minister George Ripley, put it, "Let the study of theology commence with the study of human consciousness."

In that sense, it was appropriate for Samuel Byron Brittan to wonder whether spiritualism had a real connection to Christianity. He also wondered whether spiritualists ought to have a religion at all, whether spiritualism was itself a religion, and whether spiritualism's intent was to "trample religion underfoot." He thought it was perhaps more a science than a religion, but however its followers described it, they did not wish it to become a mere sect. Brittan wrote, "We have no disposition to identify the spiritual movement with any existing form or modification of Sectarism. Nor is it the object of those most interested in the Spiritual Philosophy to establish a *new* sect."

By the summer of 1851, Ballou was leading his Hopedale congregation in Sabbath services that were directed by the spirits, according to one visitor to the community, who described the experience to the editor of *The Anti-Slavery Bugle*. She wrote of Ballou,

> Last Sunday, he preached a most excellent and effective sermon from a text proposed to him through the "rappings," while they were heard in response all over the house, by every one present, and twice a large heavy desk near where he stood was moved. . . .

He closed with a beautiful application, and he opened his arms with an ineffable expression of love and kindness, and a smile that was in itself a benediction, and pronounced the blessing in a simple, heart-felt manner, and with clear, wide open eyes.

Other clergy visiting Hopedale around this time also gave sermons with spirit assistance. Universalist minister John Murray Spear went further still. He went into trance, and with the blood drained from his face and turned away from the audience toward the wall, he acted as the mouthpiece of exalted spirits who delivered homilies on Gospel passages, such as one by Benjamin Franklin's spirit on Isaiah 11:10: "And his rest shall be glorious."

"Fortunately," Ballou wrote, "our people are too free minded and familiar with strange things, to be startled by such developments." He admitted that he "read in various countenances skepticism enough to save the place from the utterly overwhelming scorn of the wise and prudent." But he also added, "Some may be thought silly fools, for believing too much; but others, I wot of, are in danger of becoming learned and wicked fools by a bigoted, pertinacious, irrational and persecuting skepticism."

Ballou's attitude toward spiritualism was to thread a way between unreasoning skepticism and unreasoning belief. He walked a line between the Sadducees, the materialists and atheists who did not believe in angels and the afterlife, and the Pharisees, the religionists who did believe in them but who forbade spiritual intercourse with them as purely demonic and evil. Summing up the criticisms lodged against spiritualism, he said, "The Alpha of these objections was—It is all a humbug! The Omega is—It is all of the devil!"

Ballou had his own experiences that confirmed spiritualism. As a boy, he had awakened one night to find the spirit of his deceased older brother, Cyrus, standing at the foot of his bed. Cyrus's spirit encouraged him to enter the ministry. Later in his life, at Hopedale, in February 1852, his precious and brilliant son, Adin Augustus, who was studying for the ministry, suddenly died from typhoid fever. Ballou was devastated, but within hours, Elizabeth Reed, a medium in the Hopedale Community, began receiving messages from his dead son. John Murray Spear, while in trance, also received from the spirit of Adin Augustus Ballou the outline of a speech on the text "Love one another," which he delivered to the community.

Receiving these messages of consolation from his son firmly guided Ballou into spiritualism. That autumn, he organized and presided over a spiritualist convention in Worcester, Massachusetts. Ballou, the "hierophant of Hopedale," as *The New York Times* editor Henry Raymond called him, served as president of the convention. According to Raymond, he was "full of the spirit, and bubbling to pour his ounce-vial of inspiration into the common stock." Spear was one of the vice-presidents of the convention, as was Ebenezer Daggott Draper, the "sharp and industrious" operator from Hopedale, who would eventually buy out the struggling utopian community and turn it into a company town for the manufacture of textile machinery. For the Worcester convention, Raymond proposed, "Let us have a commission—*de lunatico inquirendo*, if you please—to hold solemn inquest upon these Worcester eccentrics, to learn whether there be method in their madness."

Ballou's community became a center of spiritualist activity. From there, Hopedale communicants published the newspaper *The Radical Spiritualist*. At the height of his public participation in spiritualism, Ballou recorded that on twenty Sundays of the year, he performed services at Hopedale, but on twenty-three Sundays, he performed services for a society of spiritualists in Milford. Yet he believed that all was not well with spiritualism. He was concerned that spiritualists often discarded Christianity and became infidels, leaving them prey to errant and lower spirits. Nevertheless, many mediums for whom Christianity was merely a stage took his own son as their spirit guide.

No Eternity So Dark

THE MOST FAMOUS AMONG THOSE INDIVIDUALS who claimed to have communicated with the spirit of Adin Ballou's son was the beautiful medium and trance lecturer Cora L. V. Scott. She was born in 1840 in the town of Cuba in Alleghany County, New York. In 1850, her family moved to Hopedale to join Ballou's community. They spent a few months there before the Scotts decided to move to Jefferson County, Wisconsin, to help establish a branch of the Hopedale community. Before they left, however (according to Scott's biographies), while the child Cora was picking flowers in the field one day, she met the young Adin Augustus Ballou, then eighteen years old.

As the story goes, when Ballou died, his spirit visited young Cora Scott, then at her new home in rural Wisconsin, before she could have known about his death. This began a life-long relationship between Scott and her spirit guide. By the time she was in her early teens, she had begun to deliver trance lectures that he dictated. He spoke through this wonder child at great length on whatever subjects that committees from her audiences proposed. In 1886, in giving a summary of Scott's life thus far, the spiritualist newspaper *The Carrier Dove* printed a narrative that she submitted as if it had been a story told about her (and through her) by the spirit of Adin Augustus Ballou.

Cora L. V. Scott became the nineteenth century's most famous trance lecturer, conducting a long career of public exhibition and propaganda for the spirits with the spirit of Adin Augustus Ballou by her side. She picked up other spirit guides along the way, including an Indian maiden named Ouina. Others were the spirits of famous politicians. For instance, she once received a message from the spirit of Abraham Lincoln that was meant for Woodrow Wilson and his cabinet. Universalists, in particular, who had turned to spiritualism would have been interested in *psychopathy*, discourses she received in trance from the spirit of Universalist physician Benjamin Rush.

Scott's love life was controversial. Her full name, with all her husbands' names added, was Cora L. V. Scott Hatch Daniels Tappan Richmond. Nonetheless, she became pastor of the First Society of Spiritualists in Chicago and helped found the National Spiritualist Association of Churches, also serving as its first vice president. In 1893, she made a presentation on spiritualism to the World's Parliament of Religions.

Scott's spirits did not teach explicitly Universalist doctrine, but those who heard their messages sometimes called them *Universalist*. On one occasion, her spirits responded through her, "We are not aware, precisely, what are the views entertained by Universalists, upon this subject. But, most certainly, it is our opinion, whether it be Universalism or the belief of any other class of men. It is certainly our fixed belief." Then her spirits, in effect, placed themselves in the restorationist camp, opposing the ultra-Universalists. She said,

> Not with Universalists would we proclaim that all men, after death, are to be instantly placed in the enjoyment of perfect purity and happiness, however little they may be developed in their spiritual natures. But we will say that there can be no eternity so dark, no torment so dreadful, no hell so strong, no devil so infinite, that in God's infinity he cannot snatch his children away from them.

On one occasion, the Reverend Thomas Sawyer attended a trance lecture that Scott gave, and he rose from the audience to debate with her (or her controlling spirit) over the reality of angel and spirit communications. The accounts following the incident faulted Sawyer for his "unchivalrous" disruption of the proceedings and were divided about who had the better of the other in the exchange. At one point, Scott, in trance, faced off against both the Reverend Sawyer and the Reverend Cyrus Fay. When they accused her of necromancy and other practices forbidden in the Bible, Scott scored a debate point when she said, "The witch, the wizard, the necromancer, thou shalt not consult. We do not, in modern Spiritualism, believe in holding intercourse with the dead, but with the living."

Henry James went to see one of Scott's trance lectures and probably used the experience to help build the composite fictional figure of medium Ada T. P. Foat in his novel *The Bostonians*. The fictional name, however, more nearly resembles that of another female medium and trance lecturer of the time, Ada Lenora Hoyt Foye. She was born in Boston about 1833 and also spent time in Chicago and San Francisco. She, too, was raised a Universalist. Samuel Clemens, better known as Mark Twain, attended one of Ada Foye's public séances in the Nevada Territory, where she contacted the spirit of deceased Universalist minister Thomas Jefferson Smith (who had died a confirmed spiritualist at his home in Ridgeway, New York). Clemens published a humorously biting account of his experience hearing about the afterlife progress of the minister's spirit.

Adin Augustus Ballou's father carefully disassociated himself from the public spectacles of spiritualism by the early 1870s, although he and his family took some interest in the messages from the spirit of his son through Scott. Adin Ballou's daughter, Abbie Heywood, wrote to Scott's biographer, "The discourses and messages which have purported to come from my brother, as the central control, through Cora, have always had an unusual interest for us, some of them containing passages so strikingly like himself as to need no other confirmation of their origin."

Adin Ballou found himself publicly at odds, however, with many spiritualists because, as he put it, he "adhered inflexibly to Jesus Christ" as his "religious Lord and Master, superior to all spirits or spirit-mediums of ancient or modern times, and maintained that His expositions of truth and righteousness were divinely authoritative." He criticized not only those spiritualists who had cut their ties with Christianity but also those who, as he saw it, had left sense and morality behind once they went into trance. Ballou kept his ties to Christianity and traditional morality strong, but the entire question was framed within a larger debate that was paralleled by the Universalists' own debate over their ties to mainstream Christianity.

A sign of how former Universalists framed this debate within spiritualism is that for several months during 1856 and 1857, the spiritualist community in New York City split in two, with some advocating a "Christian" spiritualism and some a minimally defined, bare spiritualism. Each faction had its own meeting hall: Academy Hall for the Christian spiritualists and Dodworth's Hall for those "in favor of nothing in particular, and everything in general." Nevertheless, each group was under the guidance of an ex-Universalist minister: Thomas Lake Harris at Academy Hall and Russell Perkins Ambler at Dodworth's. Between them, they represented, at the time, the entire range of opinion on the subject.

Laboring for the New Era

INSTITUTIONAL UNIVERSALISM WAS SKEPTICAL of other millennial or enthusiastic movements, whether William Miller's Adventist expectations of the second coming or Charles Grandison Finney's theory and practice of revivals. This might suggest that as a group, Universalists who were drawn to spiritualism would have been interested only in its rationalist aspect, but the evidence does not support that. Ex-Universalist ministers had some extraordinarily idiosyncratic and strange adventures in spiritualism. The strangeness came from their vivid belief that the effective gap between Heaven and Earth had been closed, that spirits were now able to act in this world, and that humans were now able to walk into the dawn of a revolutionized world.

John Murray Spear was born in Boston to members of John Murray's First Universalist Society. He and his brother, Charles, were trained as artisans—Charles as a printer and John as a shoemaker—but after finishing their apprenticeships, they both decided to become ministers. They studied with Hosea Ballou II at his home in Roxbury, Massachusetts. John followed his brother to Cape Cod, where Charles had become pastor in Brewster, Massachusetts, while John served the nearby Barnstable Universalist Society. (John Dods was the Universalist pastor at Provincetown at the time.) John next settled as the pastor in New Bedford, Massachusetts, and then served in Weymouth.

During these years, John Spear developed into a radical reformer. A Garrisonian abolitionist, he was an active leader and speaker for the Massachusetts and the New England Anti-Slavery Societies and a co-founder of the New England Non-Resistance Society (with his brother Charles, William Lloyd Garrison, and Adin Ballou, among others). Spear was one of a few lecturers hired by the Massachusetts Anti-Slavery Society to conduct more than one hundred antislavery meetings throughout the state in order to ignite enthusiasm for the cause.

One of Spear's church members in New Bedford was Nathan Johnson, the gentleman with whom Frederick Douglass lived when he settled in the city after his escape from slavery. In his church one day, Spear found Douglass debating with members of his congregation. They were arguing for universal salvation, and Douglass was arguing for the existence of eternal punishment. Spear was much impressed with Douglass's abilities and encouraged him to become a public speaker.

While in New Bedford, Spear also gained notoriety by precipitating the legal emancipation of a young slave woman whose owner, visiting the city, had brought her along from Virginia. And while in Weymouth, Spear divided his time between pastoral duties and activism in the causes of temperance and the abolition of slavery. In 1844, while he was on an antislavery lecture tour, he was attacked outside the Portland, Maine, city hall. He received a concussion and nearly died, but his friends nursed him back to health.

The following spring, in 1845, Spear left his pastorate at Weymouth and moved to Boston to help his brother Charles promote the abolition of the death penalty and the reform of prison conditions and to help him edit his newspaper, *The Prisoner's Friend*. Within a couple of years, however, Spear was on his own again, serving as an independent agent of philanthropic donors and tending to the needs of the indicted, prosecuted, imprisoned, and paroled. Although he worked by collecting sympathizers' donations, he felt that by remaining independent from all organizations and societies, he could focus on individuals' needs in a way that no bureaucrat could. He tried to assess the needs of each moment and to bend his efforts to meet them. Often, he did not know at the beginning of the day where he would be led or where he would spend the night. His philanthropic wanderings, guided not by reasoned calculation or deliberate missionizing but by intuition, left him with a heightened sensitivity toward subtle promptings of the spirit.

Spear also seems to have experimented with inducing mesmeric trance in himself during this time. His friend and fellow abolitionist, Theodore K. Taylor (who had been the Universalist minister in Cape Cod, Sippican, and Randolph when Spear was in Barnstable and New Bedford), had given up the ministry and moved to Boston to open a clinic as a "botanic physician and medical electrician." Taylor advertised in *The Prisoner's Friend*, offering diagnoses from a "first-rate clairvoyant," perhaps Spear. The diagnostic procedure employed by physicians who used clairvoyants in their work was oddly akin to that later developed for psychoanalysis but with a twist: The doctor would be seated in a chair in his office and take notes from what was being said by a person lying on a couch. But that person would be the entranced clairvoyant, diagnosing the condition of a third person, the patient, who would be seated nearby, facing the doctor.

Spear was also well acquainted with Universalist minister Russell Perkins Ambler. Ambler was born in 1827 in Danbury, Connecticut, and was a student of Thomas Sawyer. He served as pastor of the First Universalist Society of Albany, New York, from 1847 to 1848 and then moved to Springfield, Massachusetts. But after reading Andrew Jackson Davis's *The Principles of Nature* and investigating the Fox sisters' rappings, he resigned his pastorate and the active ministry and began publishing a spiritualist newspaper, *The Spirit Messenger and Harmonial Guide*.

In an early issue, Ambler described the ideal of the objectless, wandering holy one. Spear, who wrote that he was a regular reader of Ambler's journal, would have seen himself mirrored there. "He is placed in a position where the soul is moved and the actions governed by the most pure and disinterested motives," wrote Ambler. "The Reformer should be regarded as an instrument in the hands of angels and of God, to impel man onward to an exalted destiny." Ambler, too, began touring as a trance lecturer and medium, settling at various times in Cleveland, Ohio; St. Louis, Missouri; and then New York City. There, he set up an office on Broadway for those seeking contact with the spirits or the clairvoyant treatment of a medical problem.

Spear's itinerant life became more focused. He would be guided by intuition to someone suffering from illness and would be directed to pass his hand over the affected spot in order to bring the individual relief. In these missions, he also consecrated various people, often seemingly at random, to the goals and activities of the spirits. In a trance, Spear would place his hand upon the individual's head and endow him or her with a name. James Martin Peebles, for example, became the Elucidator, and Semantha Mettler became Charity. In this way, Spear came to enlist many other spiritualists in his spirit-guided reform projects, including Universalist ministers Daniel F. Goddard from Boston and David J. Mandell from Athol Depot, Massachusetts.

Another of Spear's Boston-area associates in spiritualism was John Prince, who had been preacher at the Universalist Society of Beverly, Massachusetts, and pastor of the Second Universalist Society of Danvers, Massachusetts, replacing John Austin there. A large portion of Prince's society in Danvers considered his preaching to be too provocative, however, and he resigned.

Prince was an uncompromising abolitionist. He worked with Spear in the New England Anti-Slavery Society and in trying to bring the Universalist leadership toward an explicit abolitionist stand. By 1851, Prince was ministering to a congregation in Meredith Bridge, New Hampshire. Spear visited him there while on a mission connected to his prison reform work. Spear had not yet headed off into spiritualism, but together, they visited a clairvoyant medium, who received messages for each of them. Prince received a message from his deceased aunt. Spear received one message from his deceased infant son, Henry Wright Spear; one from his brother Charles's recently deceased wife, Frances; and one from abolitionist Nathaniel Peabody Rogers, who said he had found peace in the next life. The experience fortified both Prince and Spear in their belief in spiritualism.

By 1855, Prince was in Essex, Massachusetts, serving as a member of the state legislature but also speaking on behalf of spiritualism, which he saw as a source of new religious vitality in an ossified religious landscape. He had been among the pioneers of higher criticism and comparative religion among Universalists. In 1846, he had published *Eight Historical and Critical Lectures on the Bible,* an overview of the Bible that relied on naturalistic explanations for miracles. "While all religious sects and systems, at their commencement," he now wrote, "are largely imbued with spirituality and life, in process of time the spirit departs, and they degenerate into lifeless formality." He continued, "What is now needed is not so much a destruction of existing institutions and the rearing of new, as an infusion of vitality into what we have. This, Spiritualism, by its demonstrations and its living energies in the soul, is calculated to give."

Spiritualists explained the phenomena produced at spirit circles as pieces of evidence that could be gathered and investigated rationally. Spirits appeared as empirical proof of the persistence of a person after death. Many within liberal religion could not accept a complete separation of the natural and the supernatural. Spiritualists saw the séance as the point of intersection between Heaven and Earth but also as a tool for propagating religion among atheists and materialists and for fortifying the religious sentiment of believers in the face of an assault by the prevailing materialism. For this reason, liberal Universalists were tempted to understand the new dispensation of spirit contact as an affirmative answer to their prayer "Can these dry bones live?"

Adherents to less liberal denominations, or materialists, were more likely to propose different explanations for spiritualistic phenomena (which included levitation, trance speaking, clairvoyance, automatic writing, materializations of objects, mysterious sounds, and messages from unearthly intelligences). Even if one set aside the instances of fraud and delusion (the most common materialist explanation for spiritualistic phenomena) and accepted them as real, he or she still did not have to conclude that the immortality of the soul had been proved. The spirits contacted may not have been the spirits of the deceased but perhaps lying and deceiving demons of the air (the conservative religious explanation), or they may have been creations of the telepathic or electromagnetic powers of the spirit medium at the center of the séance. But the fact that virtually all spiritualists accepted these phenomena as the spirits of the deceased, bringing tidings of their happy careers after death, underscores how far the idea of universal salvation had spread through American culture by the midnineteenth century.

Before modern Spiritualism defined itself, the forms of the manifestations were volatile and their interpretations protean. For the first few years, spirits sometimes manifested themselves in their human mediums through shakings, speaking in tongues, and so on—similar to what appeared in revival meetings. That similarity rapidly diminished. At first, the spirits had sometimes appeared as heralds of the second advent of Christ, ready to shake apart the world.

Mother Ann Lee's spirit and those of other deceased Shaker elders possessed young people in Shaker communities across the United States, teaching revivified Shaker doctrines a full ten years before modern spiritualism began. Rochester Quaker abolitionist Isaac Post and other Quakers, steeped in the expectation of receiving "the New Light" within, obtained messages from the spirits of George Fox and Elias Hicks. In addition, spiritualists pointed out that even Methodist founder John Wesley's family had been visited by mysterious sounds and premonitions of spirits.

Soon after modern Spiritualism began, however, the various spiritualist phenomena and their interpretations largely resolved themselves into a system of beliefs and practices that were consonant with the many Universalists who came to the forefront of the movement. Methodists may have been receptive to personal visions, to being possessed by the spirit or powers, but these entities were not necessarily human-like nor were they necessarily benevolent. And Swedenborgians were not part of modern spiritualism, partly because spiritualism would not allow Emanuel Swedenborg's eternal Hell or his ultimately existent evil into their cosmology and metaphysics.

The particular Protestant filter through which most spiritualists made sense of their experiences is clear from the account given by Frances Hyer, a Wisconsin native, after encountering a variant form of spiritualism in New Orleans, where she had moved with her husband, Nathaniel. Hyer was horrified when she found that a young Protestant woman, under the direction of spirits, had fitted out a séance room "with all the paraphernalia of a Catholic Church," including images "calculated to strike the soul with horror," such as "that terrible picture of Christ hanging on the cross." The wooden altar was "studded with brass nails, and the forms of innumerable crosses gleam[ed] upon the senses till it [seemed] that the insensate wood [was] writhing with agony." During the séance, the medium actualized "a set of low and ignorant spirits" who "wrought upon" four young teenagers, who were "held in this condition by threats, blows and frequent penance" involving "kneeling, making repeated passes over people who were sick, repeating the Lord's Prayer or the Catholic creed many times" or "to drink some nauseous mixture which was ready prepared for the occasion." Hyer, spiritualist and medium, believed the scene reeked of all that was repugnant, low, and superstitious in Roman Catholicism. Members of the liberal New England denominations, steeped in dissent from Catholicism, were likely to consider spiritualism not as a retreat to magic and superstitious "priestcraft" but as a further departure from it into a free, rational philosophy.

Not long after John Spear began attending séances, he became a speaking medium himself. At first, he found his hand compelled to draw wonderful nonrepresentational drawings and then messages, some on his own body. Soon, however, exalted spirits began to control his voice, and he delivered trance lectures, sermons, and messages. A series of lectures given through Spear in Boston and in Lynn, Massachusetts, from the spirit of John Murray was attended by other Universalist ministers and others. Sylvanus Cobb came but wrote, "There was nothing in the whole process that could suggest the interposition of any foreign agency."

Murray's spirit explained through Spear that the spirits of those who died found joy and emancipation. The spirit foretold a new harmony on Earth, a new influence of wisdom, the appearance of new teachers, new social arrangements and institutions, and the manifestation of "wonderful, mysterious powers; approaching . . . almost into the neighborhood of the miraculous." But the spirit told his audience that they were "in bondage to custom."

That had to end. Instead, the world was to prepare for the dawn of a new light, a light that "shall be a revealer of things which are now concealed" and that would reveal all things *"as they are!"* The spirit then consecrated Spear to the mission, using him, as it were, as an entranced instrument to personate Murray speaking to the normal inhabitant of the body he was using. Murray said to Spear (and through Spear),

> Your back life is all open before us, and it is seen that you have earnestly desired to receive and declare the truth; and you are to consecrate yourself, more perfectly than before, in the advancement of the new light, which now just begins to dawn upon the world. [Mr. Spear here struck his foot violently.] That foot, my young friend, is to go up and down on your earth; and as you need strength, so shall that foot, as I now press it, receive the aid you need. And these hands [here the speaker's hands were raised] are to work, work, *work,* as you shall find labor to do; and there shall be given you that strength which you at all times need.

Not too long afterward, Spear's hand was moved to write an announcement by a group of twelve spirits of people who had been famous while living on Earth, such as Benjamin Rush and Benjamin Franklin. They had decided to form an association in the spirit world for accomplishing philanthropic work on Earth. They called themselves the Association of Beneficents and decided to use Spear as their agent and communicator to people on Earth. Spear now began delivering trance lectures from Rush on medicine and from Thomas Jefferson on the evils of slavery and the need to free the slaves by taking up arms and replacing the present government with a true democracy. The Hopedale press published the *Twelve Discourses on Government* from the spirit of Jefferson, and Adin Ballou wrote a positive introduction to it.

Spear headed to western New York to investigate a mineral spring whose waters, he became convinced, had extraordinary healing powers. On the way back to Boston, he stopped in Rochester and visited Charles Hammond, who had already published the pilgrimage stories from the spirit of Thomas Paine. Seated at a table together and entranced simultaneously, Spear and Hammond received a joint dictation from a universal congress or general assembly of spirits, who said they had formed seven associations for philanthropic purposes on Earth. Each association adopted one realm of human endeavor and took its name accordingly. Spear and Hammond pronounced the names in turn, "in strophe and antistrophe": Electricizers, Elementizers, Educationizers, Governmentizers, Healthfulizers, and Agriculturalizers.

Each group would begin delivering specific plans through Spear for the thorough reformation of human society. He was able to find a coterie of associates to work on each set of plans. If the spirits were real, they thought, would they not use their energies to help those they had left behind? Would they not deliver up the treasures of Heaven to those on Earth? Spear and his associates were convinced that the spirits would act as servants to the reform of human society and would insert themselves into the particulars of the world. They would instruct humans on very specific ways to reorder their lives. They would chastise those who held slaves, those who drank liquor, and those who smoked tobacco. They would deliver detailed plans for new machines, new architecture, and new political institutions. They would tell people where to dig for water, where to look for misplaced valuables, and even which dangerous rail lines to avoid.

Nevertheless, the example of Spear provided a caution against assuming an easy relationship between an interest in worldly reform and spiritualism, for the spirits also directed him to curtail his previous reform activities. "Mr. S. used to visit prisons," wrote a reporter, "and to take a great interest in the prisoners, but now the spirits impelled him to shun such places." Spear himself believed that his reform work was in no way diminished by spiritualism but rather made larger and exerted in other fields than in prison reform.

As soon as the Association of Electricizers made themselves known to Spear, they began delivering instructions from their leader, the spirit of Benjamin Franklin, for a variety of inventions. Each of these inventions found a team of Spear's followers who attempted its construction—without success.

The most notorious planned invention was the "New Motor," which Spear and friends constructed over the spring and summer of 1854 at High Rock Tower in Lynn, across the water from Boston. It was to collect atmospheric energy in order to provide power to all the machines of the age. In that way, it was also a perpetual motion machine. As the motor was built, however, the projectors' expectations expanded, and they came to understand it in alchemical and even eschatological terms as a living machine and a magical microcosm, "God's Last, Best Gift to Mankind," "The Great Spiritual Revelation of the Age," and "The Electrical Infant."

The "New Motive Power" project was the construction of a mechanical analog of an ideal, new person: a sensitive medium, acting under a new motive, channeling divine energy as an automatic philanthropist to all who would need it. It was not just a universal machine but also something capable of reproduction. "It is not only capable of performing any kind of labor," wrote one mocking commentator, "but it is capable of reproducing itself. It 'throws off' from itself small machines after its own pattern, and those 'in turn throw off a multitude of other little ones,' so that the number of machines may increase correspondingly with the population."

Many people were scandalized by it. Perhaps they heard rumors of how it would be made functional. Those working on the project were instructed by the spirits to collect a series of energies from various kinds of people and to impart them to the machine.

The scandal increased when one of Spear's associates became convinced under trance that she would become the Mary of the new dispensation. (A couple of later sources identified the associate as Semantha Mettler, but it was almost certainly Sarah Jane Emery Newton, a Boston medium and wife of spiritualist writer Alonzo Eliot Newton.) She was impressed to visit the machine. When she came into contact with it, her energies flowed into the still, motionless mechanism. When they did, she went into (false) labor pains.

After two hours, those in attendance were sure they perceived movement in the machine. They announced to the world the news that *"the thing moves,"* and the Madonna stayed close to the machine for several weeks, "in a relation to the machine perfectly analogous to nursing," as one of Spear's followers put it. Simon Hewitt announced,

> The time of deliverance has come at last, and henceforward the career of humanity is upward and onward—a mighty, a noble, and a Godlike career. All the revelations of Spiritualism heretofore, all the control of spirits over mortals, and the instruction and discipline they have given us, have only paved the way, as it were, for the advent of a great practical movement, such as the world little dreams of, though it has long deeply yearned for it and agonized and groaned away its life because it did not come sooner.

Samuel Byron Brittan, however, sitting at the editor's desk of *The Spiritual Telegraph,* was skeptical and attributed the machine's perceived small movements to the effects of accumulated static electricity. Amid the public derision and outcry over the claims about the machine and its ultimate failure, Adin Ballou wrote an article about it in *The Practical Christian.* He said that spiritualism does not justify reliance on "some wonderful and unparalleled event to be brought about mainly by spirits for the regeneration and harmonization of the world." True spiritualism, he said, had to be careful not to discourage attempts to improve the human condition through ordinary means. People should not wait to act until the spirits prepared the way with a miracle nor should they follow blindly the monitions that come from spirits. "Are we not all spirits before God," he wrote, "and responsible to him for our conduct? Have we any right to become the mere tools of any fellow-spirit, in or out of the flesh?"

Nevertheless, like nearly all his fellow spiritualists, even Brittan seems to have been ambivalent about whether spirits always left ordinary means to mortals. He was not just interested in the philosophical aspects of spiritualism. He eagerly collected and published evidence on quite banal spiritualistic phenomena: spirits levitating leaves of tobacco, cooking and serving pancakes, producing accordion music without an instrument, and materializing cigars, pumpkin seeds, coins, and silver candle molds and floating them in the air or sneaking them in and out of people's pockets.

Spear and his group of associates, however, did not see themselves as passive tools of the spirits. The spirits helped those who helped themselves, they might have said. They had expended thousands of dollars and months of time in their experiment, after all, in order to make real what had been given to them in fragments and images. Was that so different from the experience of any inventor—or any reform activist, for that matter?

The group disassembled the New Motor late in 1854 and moved it to a farm near Randolph in western New York State. A mob of locals broke into the shed where it had been reassembled and tore it apart. Spear wrote to *The Spiritual Telegraph* to announce that "the electrical motor" had been "mobbed." His words bring into high relief the fact that he regarded spirit invention as a reform movement, just like the movement to abolish slavery. He wrote,

> The little mechanism has been assailed, torn asunder and trampled beneath the feet of man. But if this effort to use electricity as a motive power fails at this time, I am persuaded that in the coming future, when man becomes more intelligent and more fully unfolded, he will be able to command this element with greater ease and with more economy than he now does steam.

Spear and his associates, linking spiritualism to the reform movements of the time, were the first to call for organizing associations of spiritualists, both on the local and the national levels. They issued a call for a national convention, for example, in the summer of 1854. Their vision of spiritualism as a reform movement (they called it *practical spiritualism*) also guided them to purchase a hotel in Boston, which spiritualist and Hopedale alumnus Herman Snow had operated as Harmony Hall and which they renamed the Fountain House. They ran it as a hotel for spiritualist travelers seeking accommodations, similar to the temperance hotels of the day. It was also an urban commune and headquarters at which spiritualists could meet, organize, publish, and conduct séances and give lectures. And it was a training ground and networking venue for mediums, where they could concentrate on developing their psychic gifts.

After the debacle of the New Motor, Spear and his associates, still under the guidance of spirits, headed out to the mineral spring in western New York State that he had earlier visited. The group bought land nearby, south of Jamestown in Kiantone, and constructed a tiny settlement. They elaborated plans for more inventions, including a modification of the New Motor that would turn it into a "thinking machine" that would receive, store, and transmit thoughts. They also envisioned an intercontinental telepathic transmitter, powered by a corps of sensitized, uniformed mediums installed in male/female pairs (send and receive) in high towers (like rune-encrusted obelisks), which would compete with the telegraphic service that was soon to be provided by the completion of the "monopolistic" transatlantic cable. They called it the *soul-blending telegraph*.

Spear was not the only medium involved in these plans. Hannah Frances Brown was one of his closest associates. She experimented with a device she called a *pschycosmon* that she placed lightly on her lap. Touching it with her fingers, she entered a trance in which she contacted the spirits of Frances Wright, Hiram Abiff

(the mythical Masonic figure), and Thomas Paine, who were surrounded by rainbows "of the seven magnetisms." These spirits told
Brown that the device, made of copper and zinc and various semi-
precious stones, was a kind of observatory, "containing all the magnetisms," which could be enlarged so that one could climb inside it
and there sit in a "metallic chair" and take notes on the cosmos.
"My spiritual eyes were then opened," she wrote after a long session
with the device, "and I saw how earth from chaos came forth; how
man was developed. The immortal germ seemed at first like a grain
of mustard seed. I saw it germinate, break its clay fetters, and come
forth, a God in miniature."

And like the New Motor, the device represented the new
human, the elevated race, a temple that needed to be constructed.
The spirit of Fannie Wright told Brown, "Some of the best materi-
als for that temple are those bound by law and by custom, and must
be loosed." By this, she meant the marriage institution. "It would
shock the strong of heart to know the plans and purposes of the
spirits." Brown wrote, "I expressed a wish to know the future. For a
single moment the veil was lifted, and I was awed by the strange
changes among my friends. 'This is five years in the future,' was
whispered, and the curtain fell."

The pschycosmon would attract the "specific magnetisms" of
the stars in Orion, where resided the spirits who were humans'
closest kin. These spirits already possessed their own pschycos-
mons and were waiting for humans on Earth to begin constructing
and using their own. The pschycosmon could be enlarged still further as an outdoor amphitheater in the ground, in which people
could gather, focus their psychic powers, be focused upon, and
make interplanetary contact. Some efforts to excavate the land for
this purpose were made at Kiantone between 1856 and 1858.

Spear and his group also worked on an iron-hulled electric
ship that was to be powered and guided by male/female pairs of
mediums on board, ensconced abed in something like a combination stateroom, engine room, and bridge. The mental energies of

the mediums, acting as "a bark launched on a shoreless and fathomless ocean," would be wired to a version of the New Motor to provide the ship's guidance system. Spirit was "the living channel of the inflowing universe," said Spear's spirits, and the "self-moving entity—the mighty inner ocean, whose ever moving tides set upward and high, but never ebb—whose silent undulations move suns and systems, from and to eternities!"

The members of the group also outlined a vague plan for levitating vehicles that were to be powered by electromagnetic energy amplified by mediums. And they anticipated establishing a network of mediums who would wear wired caps that would amplify and direct their thoughts across the country in order to share stock price information instantaneously.

The spirits instructed them in other projects, as well. Shortly before the Civil War, the spirits issued a directive to Spear's followers to undertake a river expedition during the winter on a borrowed flatboat down the Allegheny, Ohio, and Mississippi Rivers. The group gave it a try in order to set up a cooperative commercial network as the backbone of a new society, in case some of their visions of an impending crisis turned out to be true. They spent much time and money floating to New Orleans, where they recruited a few people to their cause but failed to establish any sort of effective network.

For Spear and his followers, belief that the world was progressing and that providence wished and worked for the happiness of all people made it plausible for them to accept or to seek a spiritual source for technological inventions to improve the everyday human lot. Working from the same belief, Amanda Theodocia Jones, from East Bloomfield in upstate New York, received from spirits and in dreams the successful and patentable ideas for several inventions, including, in 1873, the vacuum canning of fruits and vegetables, a process that revolutionized the food industry. She proudly traced her spiritual lineage back to her great-grandfather, Seth Jones, an early Universalist preacher, who was active in Massachusetts and

New York and was known for his mastery of the "Prayer of Faith," by which he brought rain down from the clouds. He had impressed Amanda's father, Henry Jones, with the idea of universal salvation, and that each person "would roam from star to star to learn of God, and perhaps find at last that 'Central Sun,' from which all glory and all law emanate."

Amanda Jones leaned more toward her father's Universalism than her mother's Methodism, she wrote, although she believed she inherited her maternal kin's susceptibility to visions. Both of her parents, however, had become spiritualists not long after the rappings began in Rochester. "They had emerged from Calvinistic mazes, and, in the sanctitude of home, had broken bread with angels." When Jones became a trance medium, her spirit guides gave her poems but also discoursed on social reform and the remaking of society at large. She thirsted for a reform mission and was surprised when the spirits revealed to her that her social mission was to be the inventor (with their help) of a number of processes and devices that would enrich human life.

Another successful inventor working with spirits was William Francis Channing, son of William Ellery Channing. William Francis was a physician and experimented with the application of electricity to the body for medical treatment. His cosmology was

> the material universe, with its majestic movements of suns, stars, planets, light, heat, winds, tides, seasons, is thus a mechanism, actuated ever by the infinite Power, shaped and guided by the infinite Wisdom, animated by the infinite Love. The power which went forth at creation established the universe, with all its beauty and capacity, by the intelligent combination of outward parts.

He was guided by the ancient doctrine of microcosm and macrocosm, the "highest philosophy," as he called it, "that society, in its form of organization, is human, and that it presents in its progressive development continually higher analogies with the laws of individual being." In other words, the body politic was really a *body*.

On that conviction, Channing speculated soon after the invention of the telegraph that its wires could serve as a nerve system for a geographical region. But the ordinary telegraph was linear and could only relay messages back and forth, so he envisioned a complete system of circuits, spread out and composed like the human nervous system. Some of those circuits would carry messages in to a central intelligence, and others would carry commands back out to the extremities and cause mechanical actions "at a distance" (for example, the ringing of alarm bells). Based on these ideas, Channing invented and installed throughout Boston the first municipal fire alarm telegraph system. Herman Snow later wrote that Channing spent time at spirit circles in Boston receiving guidance on its design. Clearly, Spear was not alone at the time in seeking help from the spirits in technological innovation.

Simon Crosby Hewitt was an intimate spiritualist associate of Spear. He was born in 1816 in Sutton, Massachusetts. His father, Nathan Hewitt, had worked as a mechanic in a textile mill but died when Simon was not yet three years old, leaving his mother with six children to raise. Simon Hewitt, too, became a mill mechanic but then left that work and studied for the Universalist ministry. He was installed as the first settled pastor at the Wrentham, Massachusetts, Universalist Society and served there from 1840 to 1843. During this time, he also married a sea captain's daughter, Delight Peck.

Hewitt was both an abolitionist and a temperance advocate. After reading Albert Brisbane's exposition of Charles Fourier's *The Social Destiny of Man,* he became an enthusiastic Fourierist, lecturing in public on Fourier's ideal of *association* (that is, an overarching force that would naturally bind all things together and, when unhindered by selfish, individual actions, would reorganize human society into socialistic structures in which all people could live happily). During the summer of 1844, while established at the Universalist Society at Dighton, Massachusetts, the Fall River Mechanics Association hired Hewitt as a traveling lecturer. In accepting this position, he became the nation's first itinerant labor organizer.

Taking leave from his pastorate, he traveled throughout eastern Massachusetts, Rhode Island, and Connecticut. He was a brilliant and forceful speaker and helped working men and women form local organizations and elect delegates to the fall convention at which the New England Workingmen's Association was founded.

A remarkable number of Universalist ministers who were involved in the radical labor movement in New England during the 1840s turned up as spiritualists in the 1850s. Newton graduate William S. Bell, for example, who had followed Spear, after several years, to the pulpit of the New Bedford Universalist Society, resigned his position and declared himself to occupy "a broad and independent platform," upon which he declared his adherence to spiritualism. Bell remained a lecturer on spiritualism and labor rights until he further progressed into the movements of free thought and philosophical materialism.

In Hewitt's case, the connection between spiritualism and labor activism can be seen in his notion that the reorganization of the means of industrial production, most especially the human labor required, would establish the visible pattern of the kingdom of God on Earth. The correct arrangement of the pieces of society, in other words, would animate or enliven the whole. In this way, Earth and Heaven could be brought into a close correspondence. A bridge would be established, joining socialist plans for rearranging the parts of society into a utopia to the spiritualist assumption that the spirits of Heaven could be found walking and talking among the inhabitants of Earth.

Hewitt served as pastor in Rockport, Massachusetts, in 1848, at the Sandy Bay Universalist Society, and over the next few years, he served in West Amesbury, Salem, and Cambridgeport. His wife, Delight, was an active reformer, as well, attending the First National Convention on Woman's Rights in Worcester, Massachusetts, in 1850. During this time, Hewitt also associated himself with the Hopedale community, spending considerable time there and sometimes preaching and lecturing.

In 1852, Hewitt was one of a group of people present during the series of trance lectures given through Spear from the spirit of John Murray. Hewitt edited these messages, and when he found the Universalist newspapers reluctant to print them all, he found a publisher to issue them collected in a book, *Messages from the Superior State*. He also decided to begin a newspaper that the spirits, especially those communicating through Spear, could use to propagate their messages. Hewitt edited and published the newspaper *The New Era; or, Heaven Opened to Man* in Boston and Hopedale from 1852 to 1854.

Both Hewitt and his wife found solace at séances in contact with the spirit of their daughter Flora, who had died in infancy. They joined with other of Spear's Boston associates to issue a call for a national convention of spiritualists. The call was steeped in the language of radical and millennial reform:

> We entertain the conviction that the new, wide-spread spiritual movement of the age is to ultimate in something more than the production of startling phenomena, more than the demonstration of immortality and the opening of pleasant intercourse with friends who have passed on to the spiritual realm—namely, *in the institution of practical measures for the physical, social, and spiritual elevation and progress of humanity*, and the impartation of superior wisdom that shall secure success.... In short, we look to nothing less than the complete inauguration of the kingdom of Heaven on earth.

Again, the question of the miraculous was raised. Spiritualists were progressive rationalists, who disdained the miracles of Bible, which were traditionally understood as unique revelations of divine power outside natural law. On the other hand, spiritualists saw unprecedented revelations unfolding all around them.

Doubters saw a promiscuous multiplication of miracles, as if a wonder existed in every nook and cranny. "Men of very ordinary qualifications," wrote one skeptic, referring to Spear, "are selected by the Spirits to travel, and anoint 'silly women' to open the eyes of the blind, and in the case of Mrs. Mettler, of Hartford, to 'walk on the elements' and 'to raise the dead,' all by the power of man." What had been banished by the rationalistic rejection of miracles had seemingly been welcomed in by the back door:

> "Miracles shall be wrought by the Spirits," say they, through Mr. Hammond, and John M. Spear commissions men and women to go forth and "heal the sick, and raise the dead." Verily, this is a "new era," for man apes the power of the Almighty. . . . Many of these devout believers in Mr. Spear's movements, and we believe Mr. Spear himself, once doubted the miracles of the New Testament . . . but now they are able to swallow these human miracles without gulping. It is hard to believe that Jesus, by the power of God, walked on the water, but perfectly easy to believe that Mrs. Mettler, of Hartford, is to do the same by the power of John M. Spear!

Spear believed his experience was no different than that of the prophets in earlier ages. Events seemed to foreshadow what was coming to pass. Even delirious visions that Spear had dreamed after being attacked in Portland years before were now revealed as omens, as explained by his friend Alonzo Newton, editor of *The New-England Spiritualist*:

> Mr. John M. Spear, of this city, several years ago, during a severe illness which he suffered at Portland, Me., fell into a peculiar psychological condition, which would now be recognized as trance; while in that condition he had a vision, in which, among other things, he saw himself standing in the parlour of his hostess, clothed in a garb of different color and style from that which he was then in the habit of wearing, and addressing a company of people. *Nine years afterwards*, he (having in the meantime become a spiritualist and a medium,) addressed, under spiritual influence, a company of people assembled in the identical apartment, himself occupying precisely the position, and being clothed as seen in the vision. The vision was not recalled until after this had transpired. We were among the persons present at

the time, and heard the confirmation from the lips of the lady of the house to whom the vision had been narrated on its occurrence. *Query*: If the above narrations were to be found in the Bible, would they not be considered by religious people, as not only worthy of all credence, but as indicative of something highly important to mankind?

What was being revealed through Spear was of biblical importance, or tantamount to what was revealed through the gospel writers. Andrew Jackson Davis made this clear to a large Boston audience at the Melodeon:

> Suppose, instead of being St. John, we should say, it was John M. Spear, of Boston—that he was requested by his brethren to write an account of something that occurred sixty-three years ago in the State of Massachusetts. He feels a little solicitude about it, but says, "I will do so if you fast and pray." He puts his pencil in his hand, and his hand and paper on the table; he commences to write, instead of speaking. The portals of his soul are opened— his hand becomes the hand of an angel, and he writes, "In the beginning," etc., etc.
>
> St. Jerome has given us his testimony, that St. John wrote his gospel in the manner and method, and after a certain principle, which is identical in every respect [with that through] which John M. Spear has been impressed to speak hundreds of times. Call it what you will, the experience of St. John comes under the same explanation which that of John M. Spear will receive.

In 1855, during the time Hewitt was editing *The New Era,* his friend Paulina Wright Davis asked him to publish for a time her newspaper, *The Una,* one of the first, if not the first, newspapers devoted to women's rights. For a while, subscribers to either of the newspapers received a free subscription to the other. After *The New Era* folded, Hewitt temporarily served as a co-editor of another spiritualist newspaper, *The New England Spiritualist,* also published in Boston.

Hewitt was an enthusiastic participant in Spear's spirit-directed projects, including the construction of the New Motor, in which his mechanical skills took a leading role, but to no ultimate effect. Hewitt was also an enthusiastic proponent of the spirits' announced intentions to reform human social arrangements, especially the institution of marriage, on the argument that it deprived women of their individual rights. According to then-current notions about heredity, the traditional marriage arrangement tended to degrade the human race through forcing unwanted progeny on women.

Particular spirit directives also set Hewitt to work designing buildings that incorporated natural, organic lines and that represented, in some ways, the form of the human body. Such buildings, the spirits told him, would foster the conditions that their residents would need in order to "elevate the Race." For a few years, he designed *Homes of Harmony,* the plans for which he advertised through the mail. He also forwarded samples of the plans to British socialist Robert Owen, who, having become a spiritualist himself, published them in his *Millennial Gazette* and announced the commencement of a new age on Earth. Beginning in 1856, the designs were used, very loosely, to construct a small cluster of buildings at the utopian community that Spear's associates had built near Kiantone.

By June 1857, Hewitt's mind was spiraling into elaborate cosmic visions, in which, as he later described in an article called "The Picture Gallery of the Universe," the universe was revealed as a hall of mirrors. His visions crystallized into a conviction that an immense cosmic change was about to occur: The sun would give birth to a new planet. New types of animals would emerge. Through war, the old civilization would die, and a new one would be reborn from a remnant he believed would be gathered at Kiantone. He advertised in *The Spiritual Telegraph* to lecture on the great coming crisis. In addition, he went on a speaking tour, during which he spoke

at a spiritualist convention in Buffalo, New York, and told the assembled crowd that spirits were fructifying Earth by inseminating
sensitive women.

In 1858, Hewitt planned another speaking tour, but he "left his
ailing wife in a water-cure establishment in Ohio," wrote a spiritualist critic, "and went off on the lecture tour with another woman,
and sent his wife a letter, telling her he had found his 'affinity' in
someone else, and that she should cease to regard him as her husband.'" Hewitt's new "affinity," however, soon left him. In 1860, *The
Spiritualist Register* reported him residing in Battle Creek, Michigan. After this move, his trail became too faint to follow, but he was
no longer associated with Spear's core group of followers. His wife,
Delight, divorced him and remarried, going to live in Salem with
her sons Henry Channing Hewitt and Starr Hewitt.

John Allen, another of Spear's associates, was born in 1814 in
Leyden, Massachusetts. As a young man, he studied for the Universalist ministry in Malden with Sylvanus Cobb and then served as a
minister for ten years. His pastoral settlements included Rockport,
Watertown, and Sterling, Massachusetts.

Allen was a Garrisonian abolitionist and nonresistant. He agi-
tated for an end to the death penalty, for the reform of prison conditions, for temperance, and for women's rights. He participated in
the Chardon Street Convention of Universal reformers in Boston
in 1840. He also worked, with little success, for an institutional response against slavery from Universalist organizations. Allen's in-
sistence on preaching about social problems, especially slavery and
alcohol, created opposition to him within his congregations. His
society in Watertown, for example, prohibited him from speaking
in the church building except to conduct Sabbath services. Shortly
afterward, he resigned his pastorate and left the Universalist ministry to devote all his energies to social reform.

Allen became an acquaintance of Albert Brisbane and through
him a student of Fourier. He joined a succession of associations,
serving in 1844 on the business committee for a convention of

associationists held in Clinton Hall in New York and as secretary of the New-England Fourier Society when George Ripley was its president. The same year, Allen helped found the New England Workingmen's Association, and from 1845 to 1846, he published its newspaper, *The Voice of Industry*, from Boston. He then joined the Brook Farm Community, lectured on Fourierism, and until Brook Farm dissolved, helped George Ripley, Charles Dana, William Henry Channing, and John Orvis edit its newspaper, *The Harbinger*.

After Allen's first wife died, he married Ellen Lazarus from Long Island, New York. She was the sister of radical reformer Marx Edgeworth Lazarus, whom he had known through his work in Fourierism. With his new wife, Allen moved to Cincinnati, Ohio, where he founded a Church of Humanity. While there, he visited with John Wattles's Cincinnati Brotherhood, a few miles away on the Ohio River. He bought land down the river, at Patriot, Indiana, and moved his family there in order to devote his energies to growing and hybridizing grapes and other fruit.

In 1854, Allen read Fourier disciple Victor Considérant's *Au Texas*, which proposed establishment of a new utopian commune, and in 1855, he moved with other hopeful settlers to Considérant's new colony, La Reunion, near Dallas, Texas, to try to establish a settlement based on Fourier's socialist principles. When the colony failed the next year, Allen returned to his family and his Indiana home.

Allen's interest in spiritualism had grown during the 1850s. He had been in Cincinnati in 1848, lecturing on labor and social reform, while Thomas Lake Harris was lecturing on Davis's harmonial philosophy. By 1854, with his former associate from Brook Farm, John Orvis of Boston, Allen became involved in the spirit-guided projects of his previous fellow minister and activist John Spear, who was focused on the reproductive elevation of the human race through spirit contact. To provide a model and a stimulus for the reform of the social institution of marriage, Spear,

Allen, and others, including Hannah Frances M. Brown, took over a secret spiritualist fraternal society, the Order of the Patriarchs, and dedicated its innermost coterie to the principles of free love.

Convinced now that spiritualism was the "one grand lever of social reform," Allen moved to New York City to try to establish a spiritualist newspaper, but his effort failed. His family then took him back to their farm in Indiana, but his health gave out and he died there in October 1858. Afterward, his spirit delivered the message that he had been frustrated during his life in trying to "raise harmoniac fruit" in an "age of discord." The year after his death, Allen's wife sold the Indiana property to other Spear associates, who established a short-lived utopian spiritualist settlement there. They called it Mount Alpheus after one of their financial benefactors, Ohio abolitionist and spiritualist Alpheus Cowles. There, for a while before the Civil War, they raised grapes and strawberries by the banks of the river and envisioned plans for a new society.

Amen, Saith My Soul

JESSE BABCOCK FERGUSON WAS ANOTHER ASSOCIATE of John Spear. Born in 1819 and raised in the South, he became a preacher for the Church of Christ, the noncreedal and Bible-only sect headed by Alexander Campbell. Beginning in 1846, Ferguson served as pastor of the Nashville Church of Christ (Andrew Johnson was a member of his congregation), and through his editorship of *The Christian Magazine* and his powerful preaching throughout the region, his influence came to rival Campbell's. Ferguson was also a popular orator throughout the South on political topics, for he was a Southern partisan and a defender of the "God-appointed relation of master and slave."

Around 1851, however, Ferguson's religious views began to change, and he became an enthusiastic proponent of universal salvation. "Eternal doom or damnation," he preached, "is a hideous fable of a barbarous age; a dream of the fanatic, a tool of the designing, and a curse to all who receive it." He preached that there was a "future Spiritual life to all human beings that death cannot destroy" and that "future Spiritual life is progressive to all souls." In a second chance after death, this life's inequalities, such as were embodied in slavery, would be reconciled. Ferguson preached both Universalist and Unitarian doctrines from his pulpit, and he retained the vigorous support of the overwhelming majority of his congregation through the early 1850s, despite heated criticism from Campbell and others in the Church of Christ, who attempted to oust him.

Around 1854, Ferguson let it be known that his evolving religious views, which he summarized as "One God, one race, one destiny," had been stimulated by messages he received in séances from the spirit of William Ellery Channing through trance mediums, including his wife, Lucinda, and daughter, Virginia. Influenced by the spirit of Channing, he declared, "I hail, with delight and satisfaction, the dawning of an era of liberty of conscience and liberty of thought. Man is no longer to be led; but he is to walk forth in the light of day."

Spiritualist Joseph Rodes Buchanan later pointed out that even in 1844, Ferguson had been an advanced thinker and prophet about the advent of spiritualism. Buchanan quoted Ferguson:

> We would say that from the invisible world there will be such a manifestation of the saints that the veil of flesh and sense will be rent away, and the connection will be permanent. The cherubim, or "living creatures," will appear upon the earth. The angels of God will ascend and descend as Jacob saw, and as Jesus promised, and the tabernacles for which Peter asked on the Mount of Glory will be granted to all.

Ferguson's spiritualist millennium was not the clarification of a perennial philosophy but an apocalypse-rending history.

Another ex-Campbellite convert to Universalism, the Reverend Charles Francis Rollin Shehane, of Georgia, visited Ferguson and participated in a few séances, in which Lucinda Ferguson acted as a speaking medium. Shehane gave his conclusions about spiritualism in a letter to John Crawford Burress, the editor of *The Universalist Herald:*

> If it be a delusion, it is one of the most singular upon earth. It converts atheists into devout worshippers of God—infidels into Christians—and, in a word, makes man a better and happier being. Like the stone which the eastern monarch saw in his vision, it is, I think, destined to crush all theological or pragmatical barriers and false governments, and bring the down-trodden from the depths of despondency to the bright mansions where angelic hosts tune their harps of "lucid gold." Amen, saith my soul, the frowns and sneers of an ignorant world to the contrary notwithstanding.

Thomas Lake Harris, on his lecture tour of the West, spoke from the pulpit of Ferguson's Nashville church. Spear also visited, his controlling spirits recruiting Ferguson to their cause.

Even when the Church of Christ finally succeeded in relieving Ferguson of his Nashville pastorate, he continued to gain renown throughout the South as an orator and exhorter of the South to rally itself to fend off the impending Northern aggression. After the Civil War began, he made his way to England to lay the groundwork for an international congress that would adjudicate the differences between the North and South. He then lobbied in both Washington, D.C., and Richmond, Virginia, for a truce that would allow such an international congress to intervene, but he found little support for the idea.

After the Civil War, Ferguson went to New York City in the hope of obtaining a pastorate in Brooklyn, but while he was there, he happened to see the Davenport boys give a sensational "spirit cabinet" performance at the Cooper Institute. He was so impressed by what he regarded as demonstrations of spirit activity that he allowed himself to be recruited to join their entourage for a tour they were about to undertake to England and Europe. Ferguson's job was to begin the shows with religious lectures on spiritualism and to provide an entrée into respectable society, so that the Davenports might demonstrate their rope untying and other phenomena to upper-class homes abroad. The tour was accompanied by plenty of controversy, including challenges that suggested that the Davenports used simple conjuring tricks to produce their effects. Ferguson's reputation for integrity, which he had built during his previous trip to England, suffered as a result.

Spear was also in London at the time. He convinced Ferguson to quit the Davenports' tour on the grounds that the shows were demeaning to spiritualism. Ferguson wished to return to the United States because he was also worried about the fate of the South, as Congress confronted his former congregation member, Andrew Johnson. Ferguson sailed back and made his way to Washington, D.C. There, he lobbied for Johnson, who had succeeded Abraham Lincoln as president, and delivered to Johnson a packet of messages from Spear's spirit guides. Returning home to Nashville, Ferguson found that real estate investments he had made some years back had been profitable. He retired a wealthy man and made plans to begin a utopian spiritualist settlement in the Tennessee countryside. He grew sick, however, and died in September 1870.

Ferguson was not the only Universalist minister from the South who became a pilgrim into spiritualism. Lewis Feuilleteau Wilson Andrews was another. Andrews was the son of a well-known minister of the Old School Presbyterian Church and raised in Kentucky, Ohio, and Pennsylvania. He trained for the ministry but did not feel the call, and so he transferred his studies to law and then to medicine, practicing as a licensed doctor for years in western Pennsylvania.

At the age of twenty-seven, Andrews heard a traveling Universalist preacher speak and was converted to the doctrine of the "restitution of all things." He became a minister of Universalism and an itinerating evangelist of its gospel in both the North and the South. He also published a book that became popular throughout the Universalist denomination, *The Two Opinions, or, Salvation and Damnation*. Settling in Columbus, Georgia, in 1843, Andrews began a weekly political newspaper, *The Muscogee Democrat,* and then he moved to Macon, where he began publishing *The Evangelical Christian* in 1847 and *The Georgia Citizen* in 1850. He was a social reformer, advocating the abolition of capital punishment, the adoption of eclectic treatments by allopathic medical practitioners, and a liberal although eccentric politics.

While presiding over the Universalist Society in Macon, however, Andrews, along with members of his family, became an enthusiastic spiritualist and the organizer of a small but devoted band of spiritualists. These were mostly "estimable ladies, unsustained by male relations or sympathizers," who met in spiritual circles and invited mediums and lecturers from the North to visit. Andrews even began publishing another newspaper, *The Christian Spiritualist.*

It was a brave act. Spiritualism was widely regarded in the South as a threat. It was tainted as a Northern variety of fanaticism and as a leading wedge for all kinds of social and political radicalisms. Just before the beginning of the Civil War, Andrews ceased publication of *The Christian Spiritualist,* and in 1863, he began *The Macon Daily Confederate*. Nevertheless, he finished the war an avowed Universalist, a nonproselytizing spiritualist, and a loyal son of the South.

Women's Power Over the Future of the Race

JOHN SPEAR AND HIS ASSOCIATES WERE DEEPLY INVOLVED in the social reform that established the deepest relationship to spiritualism, the women's movement. Spiritualism offered women a means of gaining autonomy and religious authority. It also provided a rationale for elevating women as particularly sensitive mediums, through which spirits could manifest in the world. For that to happen, however, women had to be free to allow their minds to guide their bodies and to allow their affections to guide their sexual relations. That freedom would give birth to a new era. And if sexual relations were guided by deep affection, rather than loveless marriage contracts, the healthful energy exchanged, they believed, would ensure that the new generation would be elevated in mind and body. This was only possible if women were emancipated and allowed to follow their "spiritual monitions."

Lois Waisbrooker, one of the nineteenth century's most radical women's rights advocates, converted to spiritualism in 1856. She was born Adeline Eliza Nichols in 1826 in the town of Catherine in Schuyler County, New York. (The name *Waisbrooker* came from a failed second marriage.) At the age of twenty-eight, she adopted *Lois* as her *nom de plume* and, as she put it, "discarded my baptismal name, as I have since discarded Christianity in all its forms." The name change reflected a new personality within her, one that would speak through her and that she first learned to contact through attending séances. Among her written works was *The Occult Forces of Sex*, which looked at the ways in which society linked money and sex. She believed she had received this book, acting as a medium, from the spirits of Alexander and William Von Humboldt, poet Felicia Hemans, and Lady Mary Wortley Montague.

Waisbrooker became a leading agitator for socialism, labor reform, and women's rights. She wrote a regular column,"The Way I
See It," in the spiritualist newspaper *The Banner of Light,* and she
edited the anarchist newspaper *Lucifer* while its regular editor,
Moses Harman, was serving a jail sentence for obscenity for printing information about birth control. Waisbrooker also published
her own radical newspaper, *Clothed with the Sun,* in the utopian
colony of Home on Puget Sound in Washington State. She, too, was
prosecuted for sending obscene material through the mail because
her newspaper discussed sex. She advocated a sexual magic
through which women would retain, increase, and transmute their
sexual power by refusing coitus with men, a subject she treated in
her essay "From Generation to Regeneration; or, A Plain Guide to
Naturalism" and in her utopian fantasy *A Sex Revolution.*

Toward the end of her life, Waisbrooker wrote that she traced
her road to spiritualism back to her maternal grandfather, Thomas
Reed, who was "among the first Universalists in the country." She
wrote, "It was my talks with my grandfather in the summer of his
eighty-first year, which helped to break me from the bondage of
church teachings."

Spear and his associates turned their spiritualist brotherhood,
the Order of the Patriarchs, to the breeding of a new order of humans, who would be created out of the ideal sexual matchings of
mediums who had opened themselves up to the noblest spirits of
the past. These spirits would imprint themselves into the bodies
of the women in the order and take flesh again. This phenomenon
would bring about a true communion of saints, as women gave
birth to children whose spirits were the distilled spirits of the best
of the race. These sexual matchings were not countenanced by any
worldly marriage contract, and they were secret to all but the innermost circle of the organization.

The Order of the Patriarchs had an outer circle and an inner
one. The outer circle gained membership based on the propagation
of the blandest and most unexceptionable reformist principles.
One member wrote later that he had witnessed as many as one

hundred new members join in a day. When the practices and principles of the order's innermost initiates were revealed, however, its membership disappeared overnight amid public recrimination. Spear and his colleagues came to believe, in retrospect, that many of the things the spirits directed them to do were intended to purify and humble them in the crucible of failure and foolishness.

Although the Order of the Patriarchs could no longer suit the purposes of Spear and his cohorts, they did not abandon their sexual radicalism. In fact, they gained a reputation as the foremost exponents of the theory and practice of free love. Adin Ballou wrote a warning in *The Practical Christian* that some Boston spiritualists (referring to Spear and his associates) were making a terrible mistake. He wrote that a medium from his Hopedale colony had perceived that low spirits were just then waiting for the opportunity to contact susceptible mortals so that they could materialize in this world. He wrote,

> Mediums will be seen exchanging its significant congenialities, fondlings, caresses and *indescribabilities*. They will receive revelations from high pretending spirits cautiously instructing them that the sexual communion of congenitals will greatly sanctify them for the reception of angelic ministrations. Wives and husbands will be rendered miserable, alienated, parted, and their families broken up. There will be spiritual matches, carnal degradations, and all the ultimate wretchedness thence inevitably resulting.

Spear's wife was neither a social radical nor a spiritualist. The woman whom he described as his "affinity," however, was Caroline Hinckley. She had grown up in his Universalist Society in Barnstable, Massachusetts, and become a Garrisonian abolitionist, women's rights activist, and spiritualist. In 1858, she and Spear had a child—or as they were more inclined to believe, the spirits had a child through them—creating another public scandal. The boy was neither a spirit child nor (apparently) the first of a new race of humans.

Spear's associates continued to experiment with sexual genera-tion, convinced that sexual concatenations could generate noble children. In addition, they pursued novel ideas in the "experi-menters," including ideas for mechanical inventions. In a way, they simply continued their quest for a so-called Electrical Infant by other means. They meant to generate progress itself.

To carry out their project, they formed another organization to succeed the defunct Order of the Patriarchs. The spirits named it the Sacred Order of Unionists. Like the previous organization, it had two groups of practices and two groups of members: one pub-lic and one secret. The esoteric circle constructed private and elab-orate moving *tableaux* using their own bodies, which were meant to stimulate mechanical invention and to organize the process of innovation. In them, for example, entranced participants would play the roles of the parts of a sewing machine in action.

The participants' purpose was to receive mental impressions of patentable ideas for the machine. Their methods, the spirits told them, would ensure that the novel mechanical designs would be balanced between male and female energies, unlike the designs of other machines of the day, which were the results of male, projec-tive energies. Their research was done in secret, not only to protect the ideas but also because they were conducted in the nude. The re-searchers culminated their investigations in sexual activity in order to increase their sensitivity to impressions from the spirit world.

Another occult practice the Sacred Order of Unionists pio-neered in their shop was the development of the powers of clair-voyant travel. The researchers would, as they believed, leave their bodies, send their spirits to Russia, and watch iron craftsmen per-forming burnishing processes, thereby learning their well-kept in-dustrial secrets. Their machine shop back in the United States was adjoined to a large bedroom, in which the astral travelers would incubate their ideas in dreams.

In all, the group's efforts bore little fruit, although in light of their production of spirit-directed dramatic *tableaux,* their efforts can best be regarded as "modelizing" inventions (as Spear's spirits called it). They practiced something like performance art, a theater of the imagination that they hoped would somehow be realized in the material world. Their research and development shop was meant to bring the process of invention and creation itself under control through stimulating and harnessing dream imagery.

They were perhaps inspired by the experience of Elias Howe. He had solved the essential problem in the invention of the sewing machine (namely, the placement of the thread hole in the needle near the tip and the consequent lock-stick, abandoning the imitation of stitching by human hands) in a dream, in which he was chased through the jungle by natives who pointed their spears at him, spears whose tips were perforated. (Howe's dream became well known through the publicity surrounding the patent disputes in which he was later engaged.) Spear and his associates approached Howe several times in the hope of striking a deal with him but were unsuccessful.

After the Civil War, Spear and his new wife, Caroline (he had finally divorced his first wife), continued their spiritualist activities, with Spear giving lectures, conducting séances, performing psychic healings, and giving psychometric character readings. But they also devoted themselves to activism for the causes of women's rights and labor and social reform. Spear helped found a chapter of the International Workingmen's Association in San Francisco; he and Caroline helped organize Victoria Woodhull's Equal Rights Party; and Caroline, for a while, served as corresponding secretary of the National Woman Suffrage Association.

During these years, the radical wing of the spiritualist movement identified itself with the issues of women's reproductive rights and alternative medicine. Some spiritualists also developed a raft of spirit-inspired theories of human reproduction that were antiegalitarian and racist in the narrowest sense, as evident, for example, in the 1876 work of James Martin Peebles, *Conflict between Darwinism and Spiritualism; or, Do All Tribes and Races Constitute One Human Species? Did Man Originate from Indians, Apes, and Gorillas? Are Animals Immortal?* These theories often focused on mistaken notions of protecting blood purity, as described, for example, in Peebles's *Vaccination a Curse and a Menace to Personal Liberty, with Statistics Showing Its Dangers and Criminality,* published in 1900.

All these theories accepted the idea of evolution but treated it as French naturalist Jean-Baptiste Lamarck had done, as a fearfully fluid process in which the mental and spiritual factors acquired by a single individual could be passed to his or her offspring. Maintaining the distinctions between species (or making sure the race did not degrade) was exceedingly difficult under these assumptions.

This was the dark, reverse side of the reformist notion that the human race was highly malleable and open to benevolent influence, even to the extent that the embryo could be physically and mentally shaped in the womb through the mother's thoughts, which could be *daguerreotyped* onto the child. Woman, it was said, was the narrow gate through which the future of the race would pass. Through this mechanism, what had been regarded as the immutable destiny of each person, set through original sin, the "sins of the fathers," could now be modified and even improved. Those sins—understood now as the parents' benighted or ignorant practices, which imprinted their images onto the embryonic mind and body of their child—could be dissipated through moral and social reform that was guided by elevated spirits.

Those who kept the radical free-love torch lit, even after Woodhull's disastrous scandal during her presidency of the American Association of Spiritualists, called a convention in Vineland, New Jersey, in 1874. The proceedings were reported in *The Religio-Philosophical Journal:*

> The "faithful," true to the instincts of their animal natures and the baptism of "free love," according to the gospel of Woodhull, being assembled together "with one accord in one place," did then and there declare to the world what is fair to presume they "knew after experience," as the best and only means of inaugurating a revolution through the enchanting galvanized doctrine of "social freedom."

The reporter focused his sights on Spear, Woodhull, and free-love spiritualist agitator Moses Hull, who had publicly announced his extramarital affairs as healthful and holy. The reporter wrote, "And behold there was present 'him who is first in the holy trinity,' even John M., whose surname is Spear." Spear was "first in this work being moved by the spirit" and the "most conspicuous in this congress of reformers as he is the best known, being one of the first to openly advocate the free love doctrine, having compassed sea and land to disseminate a theory 'conceived in sin and brought forth in iniquity.'" The reporter explained, "The Holy Trinity is supposed to be made up of John M. [Spear], Victoria [Woodhull] and Moses [Hull]." Spear offered a resolution to the small gathering to mark their sympathy with and support for Woodhull, hoping that she would "yet pursue her agitative work, believing as we do, that in the future she will be classed with the most eminent reformers and benefactors of mankind."

Even at this late date, more than twenty years after Spear received his "commission" from the spirits, some of his Universalist associates from his earlier days continued to become believers in the new dispensation. One such associate was the Reverend Rufus Sylvester Pope, who succeeded Spear at the Barnstable, Massachusetts, Universalist Society and remained pastor there for many years. Pope became a firm spiritualist after visiting mediums while on vacation in Moravia, New York, in the summer of 1874. During several séances on succeeding nights, he and his wife saw the materialized forms of their two sons and his mother. Pope told spiritualist and journalist Epes Sargent,

> I saw them face to face as distinctly as I see you now. They were visible to all the spectators. There could be no delusion. It was a reality. My mother, who came first, proclaimed to the company my name (till then unknown to all); and my son Milton said, "Preach this truth when you go home"—thus revealing my profession. My mother had on her head a cap on luminous whiteness. *Solid light* will best express its appearance.

Although these luminous conjurings convinced Pope, the emphasis in spiritualism on *full-form materialization,* as it was called (which increased after the Civil War)—in which spirits walked out from dark "séance cabinets" among the members of a credulous audience—signaled a decline of sorts in the fortunes of spiritualism. With this sort of performance, spiritualism became more of a magic show than a philosophy aimed at the progressive elevation of the human race.

Coming Events Cast Their Shadows Before

IN DECEMBER 1858, RUSSELL AMBLER spoke to a large crowd at Dodworth's Hall in New York City, where he was the lecturer and medium in residence. He closed his speech with a paean to the eternality of spiritualism:

> Spiritualism—we cannot make or unmake it; and it grows, independent of human effort; and, like the morning light which waits not for the sleeper, it comes—and no detection of personal fraud—no recantation can stop its onward course. It is not a plan of human invention—it has the Divine impetus—and under its glad light we may go with joy to worship in that land where morn knows no sunset, and day no night.

Nevertheless, in January 1862, Sylvanus Cobb's *The Christian Freeman* ran a notice that the Universalists had again extended the hand of fellowship to Ambler (meaning that he had abandoned spiritualism). In a later issue, Ambler explained that he now regarded the spiritualism he had earlier thought was a blessing as "a gigantic evil." He wrote,

> This discovery came to me not suddenly, but slowly and by degrees, one evidence after another presenting itself in the cases of different individuals, until at last I was led, by which I had observed in others, to look down into the well of my own experience; and if I found there the stars which heaven always sets on the darkened mirrors of earth, they were dim and troubled images, obscured by the perverting effects of abnormal conditions.

Now, Ambler was willing to say that spiritualism was "a sore on the body of humanity." Its tendency, he wrote, was "to destroy every sentiment of worship, to crush out all reverence for the sacred things of the past, to lay the axe at the root of all Christian institutions, to break down the barriers of moral restraint, to substitute ungoverned license for liberty, and to let in upon the world a flood of fanatical vagaries for which there is no name or limit."

Spiritualists were incredulous at first but then saddened that one of their foremost proponents had fallen away. Ambler became a minister again and settled into a Universalist Society in Philadelphia, Pennsylvania. Years later, his former spiritualist colleague, Warren Chase, would write in resentment,

> R. P. Ambler tried for a time to sustain himself by lecturing; but it was too hard and the pay too meagre for one who had been a clergyman, and he slid back into his old society of Universalists, repented of his heresy, and ever since has been preaching for them, and is little known and of as little account in the great cause of reform as a farmer in the mountains of Pennsylvania.

Hearing Ambler say that spiritualism promoted infidelity and immorality must have been a bitter experience for his fellow Universalists who had found a refuge in spiritualism. This was just what the orthodox had always said about Universalism: that it promoted unbelief and, by eliminating the threat of eternal damnation, spawned immorality.

In 1867, George Quinby, editor of *The Gospel Banner*, wrote that no "talented and far-seeing Universalist clergyman" had left the Universalist denomination and become a spiritualist. James Martin Peebles responded in print, "We had supposed it generally conceded that S. B. Brittan, Adin Ballou, Wm. Fishbough, Fernald, Ingalls, Barrett and others were talented and exemplary men. Had they remained with him, working for his sect, his creed, and his church, he would have doubtless thought the same." Peebles also took issue with another part of Quinby's argument: "His reference to a stampede from the ranks of the Spiritualist lecture field toward Universalism is literally laughable. Who are they? How many? R. P. Ambler; that's *all!*"

As the number of Universalists dropped over the next few years, however, fewer felt tempted to cross over into spiritualism. Even John Spear became mindful of the mixed consequences of highly public spirit missions. In early 1869, the London Dialectical Society conducted a study of spiritualism. Its committee invited testimony from many witnesses, and Spear, then in London, offered his. He did not speak in trance but gave the committee a glimpse of his life as a medium. There had been difficulties, he said, especially with those who had come to him for counsel from the spirits. He said,

> Advice has been given. Following, in whole or in part, directions or suggestions, results have not always been as pleasant or satisfactory as they anticipated, and they have blamed me. In vain have I said to such, "I did not, as a person, give you the counsel you have followed. I did but give you what, at the time, was given me." Disappointed, they have heaped abuse on my head.

In addition, Spear said, his mission had required him to undertake actions that brought not peace but rather discord to the "individuals, families, and neighborhoods" to whom he had ministered and that because of this, he had been called "a pestilent fellow" and "a mover of sedition." Under the inspiration of the spirits, he had sometimes "severely reproved" people "for unwise or wicked conduct," and they had become his enemies.

Spear reported that the spirits had also directed him to search out certain people and select them for special missions, but this had made others complain "because they were not chosen." In all this, he said, he had no choice. He had only acted "under the direction and guidance of unseen intelligences who had associated to accomplish certain specified purposes." In some cases, he had been "compelled to differ with, and to separate from some, for whom [he] had had the highest respect and tenderly loved." About this, Spear admitted frankly, "These trials borne, mostly, in the secret chambers of my soul, have been hard to endure."

Spear wished to tell the London Dialectical Society's committee something else, however, which would help them understand why he had accepted the "missionary labors" the spirits had given him:

> I have had more joys, perhaps, than most persons. Dearly have I loved the work in which I was engaged. I have been helped to see that, beyond the clouds that were round about me, there was a living, guiding, intelligent beneficent purpose—the elevation, regeneration, and redemption of the inhabitants of this earth.

Many of the Universalist clergy who had previously been interested in spiritualism lost their enthusiasm for it and even their curiosity about it. As a result, the contentiousness that had marked the border between Universalism and spiritualism softened to some extent. By 1880, one could reverse the sequence that before had led many an individual from Universalist minister to spiritualist lecturer.

In that year, Cephas B. Lynn, of Charlestown, Massachusetts, who had been a trance lecturer and medium since childhood and an ardent supporter of Victoria Woodhull's spiritualistic free-love doctrines, enrolled in Tufts Divinity School. He graduated and became a Universalist minister. He went on to have a long career as a pastor with the Universalist Society of Provincetown, Massachusetts, and then with that of Danvers.

Lynn's enrollment at Tufts was ironic, perhaps. He had attended the 1873 convention of the radical American Association of Spiritualists as the official representative of *The Banner of Light.* While there, he argued for the establishment of an independent educational institution for spiritualists, declaring from the platform,

> Some of our Liberalist friends, with this sort of generosity in their souls, have sent their children to seminaries throughout the length and breadth of the land, and have discovered that these institutions of learning were being manipulated by Christianity to the extent that the minds of these children were dwarfed, and they came home spiritual cripples, and that is worse than walking on crutches.

This remark was followed by cheers from the crowd, as Lynn used crutches because of a permanent handicap.

Even Andrew Jackson Davis severed his ties to the spiritualist movement because of what he thought was its growing preoccupation with phenomenal manifestations and its growing lack of interest in larger philosophical and religious issues. He obtained a degree from an eclectic medical school and began earning his living as a practicing physician, as did Brittan, Peebles, Spear, and many other old-line spiritualist activists. (Even so, they never gave up their convictions about the spirits.)

Peebles regarded spiritualism as the true Universalism in its most comprehensive sense. He wrote,

> Universalism, denying total depravity, vicarious atonement, trinity, endless torments, with other ecclesiastical absurdities, and embodying the principle of the *final restoration* of all souls to holiness and happiness, is as beautiful as rational. In this sense, so far as our knowledge extends, all Spiritualists are Universalists.

He contrasted the Universalism of the time, "with its dogmatic interpretations, creedal tendencies and gowned clergy," with its earlier, iconoclastic, "plastic form." He wrote, "The sect at present is in a state of fearful unrest. Some are crying, 'Lo, here!' and others, 'Lo, there!' It has in its ranks many Spiritualists, and *knows* it."

In June 1880, perhaps still trying to pay back the Universalists for their treatment of him decades before, Peebles wrote an article called "The Decay of Universalism," in which he argued that Universalism was no longer needed because of society's widespread adoption of its central tenet. In it, he wrote, "The visible and confessed decay of this new sect known as Universalism" was that "while it pursued open warfare, it refused its original purpose, it refused the call of the spirit."

Peebles neglected to note that spiritualism, too, was in a decline. It experienced a brief revival during the 1880s, but it lacked its earlier connection to radical reform, despite its continuing link to liberal religion. Spiritualists, at the time, flush with what would turn out to be unfounded confidence in the future of spiritualism, anticipated that Universalists who were still opposing spiritualism would duly progress or fade away, making a union between Universalism and spiritualism inevitable. The spiritualist editor of *The Religio-Philosophical Journal*, John Curtis Bundy, wrote,

> As among the Unitarians who went through this crisis years ago, the hard feelings will die away, the conservatives will yield, all will agree to disagree, and the advanced views now feared will be the future Universalism. Bible infallibility and lawless miracles will drift back out of sight, natural religion will gain and the world will be better for it. Spiritualism and the new activity in psychic science will come before them ere long, as a great uplifting power and a deeper insight. May they meet it fairly and use it wisely.

The same animated opposition to spiritualism that had arisen in Universalism over the previous forty years was causing the current "crisis" to which he referred. The issues were still the nature of the Bible, of Jesus, and of the Christian tradition. But by the late 1880s, opponents of spiritualism were also able to articulate a form of progressive rationalism, in which spiritualism and mysticism had little or no place. In this later generation, the Universalist leaders who opposed spiritualism included Alonzo Ames Miner (past president of Tufts College), Alpheus Baker Hervey (president of St. Lawrence University), and John Murray Atwood (president of the Clinton Liberal Institute). Those who were publicly willing or eager to accommodate spiritualism included the Reverends Charles Fluhrer, of Grand Rapids, Michigan; Ahaz Nicholas Alcott of Elgin and Peoria, Illinois; Winfred Scott Crowe, editor of *The Universalist Record*, published in Newark, New Jersey; and Everett L. Rexford, of Boston.

Fletcher Wilson, minister of the Universalist church in Delphos, Kansas, declared himself in 1885 to have been a Universalist for twenty-five years and a spiritualist for ten. He continued trying to effect a reconciliation between Universalism and spiritualism by pointing out that Universalism, in its doctrines, was closer to spiritualism than it was to orthodox Christianity. He wrote,

> The doctrine of plenary inspiration of the Bible, the Trinity, the Fall of Man, the vicarious atonement, endless punishment, and above all, the narrow and selfish incentive to virtue which underlies the whole superstructure of the orthodox churches, viz., doing right here in order to escape an endless hell and gain heaven in the world to come; still worse, if possible, the uncertainty of rewards and punishments embraced in the doctrine that death-bed sin removes the possibility of reward for any good done, and this conflicts with Universalism.... Not only as a body, but individually, the Spiritualists are with the Universalists in rejecting all these theological absurdities, and laboring for their overthrow.

Bundy, however, went further by explaining what spiritualism had to offer institutional Universalism. Universalists, he wrote, now need "other proofs of man's immortality" besides mere faith in the authority of tradition or scripture. Humans needed practical, empirical evidence that would demonstrate the reality of human life as it exceeded the small confines of its individual existence. "We need to know the inner life and infinite relations of man, to study psychological laws and powers." Without the study of these practical subjects, "education, especially for the pulpit and the healing art, will soon be held as pitifully incomplete." This proved an astute prediction of the integration of psychology, psychotherapy, psychiatry, and counseling techniques into pastoral and medical curricula. Without the willingness to integrate the religious tradition into these disciplines, theology was a dead subject, for the scriptures could no longer be seriously regarded as having a practical application. Without the willingness to bring the study of psychology to the scriptures (and to those who studied them), "the Bible is a book of strange myth and miracle, but with this key to its interpretation, it becomes not infallible but valuable as a record of spiritual experiences which are not miraculous but natural, and like those of our own day."

Many Unitarian clergy, although shy of being known as spiritualists, readily identified themselves with the scientific study of spiritualistic and psychic phenomena. In the mid 1870s, for instance, James Henry Wiggin resigned his Unitarian pulpit when he became a close associate of Helena Blavatsky at the founding of the Theosophical Society, whose members thought the organization could study spiritualism scientifically. By the mid 1880s, the contradiction between occupying the pulpit and following the scientific study of spiritualistic phenomena was not severe. Indeed, in 1885, the founders of the American Society for Psychical Research, in Boston, included many Unitarians and a number of clergy, as well, such as Charles Carroll Everett, Samuel June Barrows, Octavius Brooks Frothingham, John Edwin Hurlbut, Franklin Johnson, Francis Greenwood Peabody, William Stephen Rainsford, Charles Van Norden, and Minot Judson Savage. In 1888, demonstrating another public link between spiritualism and Unitarianism, Henry Harrison Brown, a widely known spiritualist lecturer, received a call to the pulpit of the Unitarian church in Petersham, Massachusetts. (He eventually moved to San Francisco and became a leader of the new thought, or mind cure, movement, publishing such titles as *Dollars Want Me: the New Road to Opulence, How to Control Fate through Suggestion,* and *Self Healing through Suggestion.*)

When spiritualist and former Unitarian minister Herman Snow returned to Boston in 1886 for a visit, he found himself no longer shunned but welcomed by many of his old Unitarian colleagues. He wrote, "Their theology had become more radical and progressive, whilst their attitude toward Spiritualism had greatly improved." In some sense, at least, they now recognized a common ground between progressive, liberal Unitarianism and spiritualism. "I was allowed to introduce and defend our faith in the minister's Monday Club," wrote Snow, "where I found quite a number of partial and of full sympathizers."

Bundy believed that spiritualism had already won a place for itself within Unitarianism, although a hidden one. He wrote,

> Unitarian societies are used as convenient covers by a consider-able body of people wherein to conceal their paucity of religious belief, their agnosticism, or their Spiritualism, as the case may be.... There seems to be a chronic fear on the part of Unitarian editors and preachers that their orthodox brethren suspect them of sympathy with Spiritualists, or that if they extend professional courtesy to Spiritualists they will lose caste with their Evangelical friends.

Despite this, Bundy welcomed the hidden spiritualist presence among Unitarians. Yet he also supported an idea proposed by several Universalist ministers to establish a Church of the Spirit, which would draw its members from spiritualism, Universalism, and Unitarianism. The idea was never realized, however. Spiritualists nearly always found it difficult to agree, even among themselves, about the benefits and nature of any organization. Expecting all three groups to cohere was unrealistic, at least at that time.

In light of Peebles's criticism of Universalism's fossilization into an institution, spiritualists, ironically, were finally about to have some success in setting up an enduring organization: the National Association of Spiritualists. It gathered spiritualists into a relatively small denomination, much like any other denomination or national society, issuing charters for local branches and training, licensing, and ordaining its officers. Ironically, on the basis of Peebles's argument, the appearance of such an organization should have signaled the decline and loss of vitality of the movement from which it arose.

By the 1880s, reform advocates were often either members of mainstream liberal churches, who believed it inexpedient to link their causes to radicalism, or they were anarchists and atheists, who had no sympathy for religion of any kind, spiritualism included. By that time, much of spiritualism had devolved into stage magic or been co-opted by its later competitors, Mary Baker Eddy's Christ-

ian Science and Helena Blavatsky's Theosophical Society. Spiritualist mainstays were dismayed to see many from among their ranks
defect to what they believed were retrograde movements (because
of their authoritative priesthood of leaders and sanctioned scriptures and dogmas). Peebles, in high dudgeon, characterized the de-
fectors biblically as "dogs going back to their vomit."

Nevertheless, spiritualism had lost its ability to represent itself
as scientific. Year by year, it seemed less progressive, until it nearly
disappeared from liberal and radical circles. Spiritualism survived
in an antique form, enjoying fitful sparks of popular interest at the
turn of the twentieth century and during World War I. It also dif-
fused into a misty literary cult of inspirational and airy poetry
about angels or sublimated, one might say, in artistic movements
such as surrealism and in visionary fiction or fantasy, especially
science fiction.

In addition, spiritualism melted into psychology, which still
used techniques such as free association and dream analysis that
bore the historical imprint of the techniques of clairvoyant mesmerism and spiritualism. Yet the field of psychology also progres-
sively defined itself as an empirical science and distanced itself
from parapsychology.

Spiritualists often quoted poet Thomas Campbell's line "Coming
events cast their shadows before." In that light, the controversy
about spiritualism that took place within Universalism during the
years following Andrew Jackson Davis's publication of *The Principles of Nature* in 1847 was a rehearsal for two later controversies
within the denomination that would arise a century or more later.

The first controversy concerned Universalism's institutional
tie to a Christian foundation. The battle was fought in the denomination at large in the debate during the first decades of the twentieth century between the humanists and the theists. By the 1950s,
the debate had been decided in favor of the humanists in establishing a non- or post-Christian (or even post-theistic or secularist)
identity for the denomination.

This was the direction toward which the spiritualist movement had, by and large, pressed its Universalist adherents in pursuing both spiritualism and free thought and in challenging, through rationalist argument, the plenary authority of the Bible. Spiritualists in the late nineteenth century had not anticipated, however, that the movement away from orthodox dogmatism, which pervaded the liberal churches, would draw those churches away from spiritualism and toward philosophical materialism.

The second controversy for which the spiritualism/Universalism conflict served as a rehearsal occurred in Unitarian Universalism, the religious movement that resulted from the consolidation of the two denominations in 1961. Occurring under the influence of the values of the 1960s counterculture, it marked a reassertion of the importance of spirituality as opposed to intellectual, humanistic rationalism. The Unitarian Universalist Psi Forum, established in 1969, initially focused on psychical research but soon embraced alternative spiritual paths.

In the 1980s and 1990s, the denomination embraced new age, neopagan, and Earth-centered religious practices. These forms of spirituality assumed the primacy of direct experience over intellectual knowledge as well as a universe in which the parts are interdependent and every religious way is equally valid. And they held that the spiritual, inner life and judgment of the individual was utterly superior to external or abstract truths, which they regarded as coercive. This controversy, framed as a debate between spirituality and materialism, was settled on the spiritualist side of the issue, at least in the sense that new age spiritual practices found a home in Unitarian Universalism that they could find in no other denomination.

Some have located the background for this resurgence in mysticism in Unitarian Universalism in the legacy of transcendentalism. But doing so overestimates the Unitarian stream and underestimates the Universalist one. The far more important predecessor of the new age movement was nineteenth-century spiritualism, which began and found its fuller expression among Universalists and ex-Universalists.

When the anticipation of a new era turned into the vision of a new age, it was spiritualist medium Cora Scott Richmond who announced it in a public address in 1897:

> Have you ever seen the sun rise on the ocean? The first gray lines tremble on the horizon. Streaks of gold and crimson slowly rise. A gray cloud moves across the path and then it turns a crimson cloud, moving across the sky. On the verge of the horizon trembles the pale morning star, and then the full bright orb Phoebus, in his golden chariot, ascends, and a flood of light spreads over the Universe. Even thus will dawn the new age of humanity, and not only slavery, but fear, darkness and death will be conquered in the light of the new morning.

Richmond acquired the phrase "dawn of the new age," which she used as the title of her address, from Simon Hewitt's explanation of the illustration of angels descending on the masthead of the Boston newspaper *The New Era* back in 1854. These uses of the phrase bracketed spiritualism's vital growth in the nineteenth century. But seven decades later, many others can envision "the new age," as well.

Notes

The Reconciliation of Religion and Science

Doctor of Electropsychology

"'. . . a new era of light was soon to dawn on earth.'" p. 3: Alonzo Eliot Newton, "Dr. Dods' Experience," *The New-England Spiritualist,* March 15, 1856.

"'. . . across the room, with great force.'" p. 4: Henry Spicer, *Sights and Sounds; The Mystery of the Day: Comprising an Entire History of the American "Spirit" Manifestations* (London: T. Bosworth, 1853), pp. 39–43.

". . . And then she disappeared." p. 5: Spicer, p. 42.

"'. . . to forsake Calvinism and declare universal salvation.'" p. 5: Bernard Whitman, *A Lecture on Popular Superstitions* (Boston: Bowles & Dearborn, 1829), p. 57.

". . . the sermon affected the other ministers deeply." p. 5: Eunice Hale Cobb, *Autobiography of the First Forty-One Years of the Life of Sylvanus Cobb, D.D.; To Which Is Added a Memoir, by His Eldest Son, Sylvanus Cobb, Jr.* (Boston: Universalist Publishing House, 1867), p. 167.

"'. . . which seemed to him rational and philosophical.'" p. 6: Newton, "Dr. Dods' Experience."

". . . before returning to Maine." p. 6: George Horner Gibson, "The Unitarian-Universalist Church of Richmond," *Virginia Magazine of History and Biography,* April 1966, p. 324.

". . . the Christian Union Society, the Universalist church." p. 6: On Dods's preaching at Taunton, see his *Second Death Illustrated; A Sermon Delivered before the First Universalist Society in Taunton, Mass., on Sunday, February 12, 1832* (Taunton, MA: E. Anthony, 1832).

". . . by Universalist minister Nathaniel Gunnison." p. 6: Simeon Conant Smith, *Leaves from an Old Church Record Book* (Boston: Universalist Publishing House, 1922), pp. 12–20.

". . . who made his universal love available to all." p. 6: Outlined in John Bovee Dods, *Thirty Short Sermons on Various Important Subjects, Doctrinal and Practical* (Boston: G. Bazin, 1832).

219

". . . which he believed was the cause of mesmerism." p. 6: Robert C. Fuller, *Mesmerism and the American Cure of Souls* (Philadelphia: University of Pennsylvania Press, 1982), pp. 85–89.

"'. . . the picture that is made to appear.'" p. 7: William Fishbough, "A Question Answered," *The Univercoelum and Spiritual Philosopher,* March 24, 1849.

"'. . . had misgivings on the subject.'" p. 7: Newton, "Dr. Dods' Experience."

". . . a word he liked better, *spiritualism.*" p. 8: John Bovee Dods, *Six Lectures on the Philosophy of Mesmerism, January 23–28, 1843* (Boston: A. W. Hall, 1843), p. 7.

"'. . . and through this medium he governs the universe.'" p. 8: Dods, *Six Lectures,* p. 35.

"'. . . the all-pervading "psychological influence."'" p. 9: F. L. Burr, "The 'Double-Mind' Theory," *The Spiritual Telegraph,* June 24, 1854.

". . . who were critical of Dods's theory." p. 9: Josiah Wolcott, "Dr. Dods' Theory," *The Spiritual Telegraph,* January 19, 1856.

"'. . . of our volition, will, or even knowledge." p. 9: Sylvanus Cobb, "Spiritual Manifestations," *The Christian Freeman and Family Visiter,* October 25, 1851.

". . . to describe his technique." p. 10: Joseph Rodes Buchanan, "Electro-Biology," *Buchanan's Journal of Man,* February 1850, pp. 510–511; William Fishbough, "The New Phase of Psychology," *The Univercoelum and Spiritual Philosopher,* March 10, 1849; Sylvanus Cobb, "Spiritualism—No. 5," *The Christian Freeman and Family Visiter,* March 19, 1858; and Sylvanus Cobb, "The New Science of Electro Biology," *The Christian Freeman and Family Visiter,* February 1, 1850.

". . . over the course of six nights." p. 10: The series was printed as Dods, *Six Lectures.*

". . . formed a Psychological Society." p. 10: John Bovee Dods, *The Philosophy of Electrical Psychology; In a Course of Twelve Lectures* (New York: Fowlers and Wells, 1850), p. 14.

". . . the various techniques now in common use." p. 11: On Dods's techniques versus those of Methodist minister and mesmerist La Roy Sunderland, see William Fishbough, "A Question Answered," *The Univercoelum and Spiritual Philosopher,* March 24, 1849; and La Roy Sunderland, "Pathetism," *The Univercoelum and Spiritual Philosopher,* June 2, 1849. On Sunderland's career, see Ann Taves, *Fits, Trances & Visions: Experiencing Religion and Explaining Experience from Wesley to James* (Princeton: Princeton University Press, 1999), pp. 128–161.

". . . blown up into a deliberate slander." p. 11: John Bovee Dods, Ministers' Files, Manuscripts Division, Andover-Harvard Theological Library.

"'. . . responsible for none of its acts.'" p. 11: Asa Mayo Bradley, Reminiscence and History of Universalism on Cape Cod, Manuscripts Division, Andover-Harvard Theological Library.

"'. . . under the approbation of Universalists.'" p. 12: Thomas Whittemore, "J. B. Dods," *The Trumpet and Universalist Magazine*, May 20, 1848.

". . . lecturing, experimenting, and treating patients." p. 12: On Dods's instant healing of a paralytic, see Fishbough, "A Question Answered."

"'. . . throughout all his works.'" p. 12: Dods, *The Philosophy of Electrical Psychology*, pp. 223–224.

". . . to give a series of lectures on his ideas." p. 12: These lectures are collected as John Bovee Dods, *The Philosophy of Electro-Biology, or Electrical Psychology. In a Course of Nine Lectures, Delivered by J. B. Dods, before the United States Senate, at Washington, in 1850, with Rules for Experiment, Together with [James Stanley] Grimes's Philosophy of Credencive Induction, and Cures Performed by the Editor,* comp. and ed. G. W. Stone (London: H. Balliere, 1852).

"'. . . to his brethren of the human race.'" p. 13: Newton, "Dr. Dods' Experience."

"'No telling tales out of school.'" p. 14: Samuel Byron Brittan, "Dr. Dods and Spiritualism," *The Spiritual Telegraph*, January 20, 1855.

". . . in the objective reality of the spirits." p. 14: Alonzo Eliot Newton, "Dr. Dods a Spiritualist," *The New-England Spiritualist*, January 5, 1857.

"'. . . and come out a full-fledged spiritualist.'" p. 14: "The Literature of Spiritualism," *New Englander and Yale Review*, August 1, 1858, pp. 666–691.

"'. . . from other persons to put me in it.'" p. 15: John Bovee Dods, "Letter from Dr. Dods," *The Spiritual Telegraph*, October 27, 1855.

"'. . . under *spirit-direction* and by *spirit-skill*.'" p. 15: Samuel Byron Brittan, "Healing the Sick at Provincetown," *The Spiritual Age*, July 4, 1857.

". . . from 1843 to 1844, recorded similar observations." p. 16: Phineas Parkhurst Quimby, Papers: Lucius Burkmar's Journal, January 4, 1844, Manuscript Division, Library of Congress.

". . . inspiring in her idea of mental cures." p. 16: The extent of this indebtedness is indicated in William Gill's 1887 article "My Experience in the Eddy Camp of Christian Scientists," *The Religio-Philosophical Journal*, April 2, 1887; and the unsigned article "The Origin of Christian Science," *The New York Times*, July 10, 1904.

". . . debated against spiritualists on the subject." p. 16: For example, James Stanley Grimes, *Great Discussion of Modern Spiritualism, between Prof. J. Stanley Grimes and Leo Miller, Esq.* (Boston: Berry, Colby & Company, 1860).

"... a prediction that clearly never panned out." p. 16: Thomas Whittemore, "Dr. J. B. Dods," *The Trumpet and Universalist Magazine,* November 5, 1853; and Sylvanus Cobb, "Dr. Dods and His Gold Discovery," *The Christian Freeman and Family Visiter,* December 9, 1853.

"Each was, therefore, 'a refuge of lies.'" p. 17: Charles Grandison Finney, "On Refuges of Lies," *The Oberlin Evangelist,* September 29, 1858.

"'O death, where is thy sting, etc.'" p. 18: George de Benneville, *A True and Remarkable Account of the Life and Trance of Doctor George de Benneville* (Philadelphia: Thomas T. Stiles, 1804). For general background on de Benneville, see David A. Johnson, "George de Benneville and the Radical Reformation," *The Journal of the Unitarian Universalist Historical Society* 8 (1969–1970): 29–32.

"... transmuted itself into living matter." p. 18: J. B. Gough, "The Fulfillment of the Stahlian Revolution," *Osiris* 4 (1988): 15–33; and Jacob Woodrow Savacool, "Illness and Therapy in Two Eighteenth-Century Physician Texts," *Caduceus* 13, no. 1 (Spring 1997): 51–66.

"... for transmuting base elements into gold." p. 18: Barbara M. Schindler, trans., *Life and Conduct of the Late Brother Ezechiel Sangmeister; Translated from the German, Leben und Wandel* (Ephrata, PA: Historical Society of the Cocalico Valley, 1986), part 4, pp. 60–62, 86; and Everett Gordon Alderfer, *The Ephrata Commune: An Early American Counterculture* (Pittsburgh: University of Pittsburgh Press, 1985), pp. 148, 150.

"... the *state of primitive innocence.*" p. 19: Julius Friedrich Sachse, *The German Sectarians of Pennsylvania; A Critical and Legendary History of the Ephrata Cloister and the Dunkers* (Philadelphia: Author, 1898), pp. 354–364.

"'... interprets and dignifies every circumstance.'" p. 19: Ralph Waldo Emerson, "Swedenborg; or, The Mystic," in *Representative Men: Seven Lectures* (Boston: Phillips, Sampson and Company, 1850), pp. 122–123.

The Seer of Poughkeepsie

"... that Paul was such a villain." p. 20: Gibson Smith, *The Gospel of Jesus: Compiled by His Disciple Matthew, from His Own Memoranda, and Those of Peter, Luke, Mark, and John; and Lastly Revised by Peter. Also the Acts of the Eleven Disciples; the Last Epistle of Peter to the Chapelites; the Acts of Paul and the Jewish Sanhedrin; and the Contents of the History of Jesus, by Peter, Translated from Parchment Manuscripts, in Latin, and Found in the Catacombs under the City of Rome* (South Shaftsbury, VT: Gibson Smith, 1858), introduction.

"'... as a brother in the Faith!'" p. 21: Andrew Jackson Davis, *The Magic Staff; An Autobiography* (Boston: Bela Marsh, 1857), pp. 199–201, 253–255; and Rodolphus Waite Joslyn and Frank W. Joslyn, *History of Kane County, Ill.* (Chicago: Pioneer

Publishing, 1908), 1: 528. Bartlett moved to Illinois, taking up the practice of homeopathic medicine, and became its most successful early advocate in the Midwest. Davis continued his friendship with him until Bartlett's death in 1880.

"'... and door, of the human temple!'" p. 22: Davis, *The Magic Staff*, pp. 216–217.

"... that Davis had given in trance." p. 22: Andrew Jackson Davis, *Lectures on Clairmativeness; or Human Magnetism*, ed. Gibson Smith (New York: Searing & Prall, 1845), Rand's letter, pp. 39–40. On Smith, see Davis, *The Magic Staff*, pp. 274–279.

"'... and obtain leisure for their perusal.'" p. 23: Bartlett's letter is in Fishbough's introduction to Andrew Jackson Davis, *The Principles of Nature, Her Divine Revelations, and a Voice to Mankind. By and through Andrew Jackson Davis, the Poughkeepsie Seer and Clairvoyant* (New York: S. S. Lyon and W. Fishbough, 1847), p. x.

"'... during his conversational intercourse with them.'" p. 23: William Fishbough, "A. J. Davis—A Correction," *The Spiritual Telegraph*, June 17, 1854.

"... and 'worship God with willing hearts, all as one.'" p. 23: Davis, *Lectures on Clairmativenss*, p. 32.

"'... he put a map upon the floor.'" p. 24: Quimby, January 17, 1844.

"'... traveled psychically to other planets.'" p. 24: "The Spiritual Convention," *The Springfield Republican*, April 7, 1852.

"... and publish them." p. 24: Davis, *The Magic Staff*, p. 279.

"'... of the august divine *worker* within.'" p. 24: Gibson Smith, *The Origin of Life: The Errors of Fashionable, Scientific Materialism, Examined and Exposed* (Ayer, MA: n.p., 1883), p. 38. He also wrote *The Gravitation of the Heavenly Bodies, and the Cause of Light* (Ayer, MA: n.p., 1884).

"... born in 1816 in Canaan, Maine." p. 25: Florence Osgood Rand, *Genealogy of the Rand Family* (New York: Republic Press, 1898), p. 193.

"... and sold their church to the Baptists." p. 25: Eli Ballou, "Removals," *The Universalist Watchman*, April 7, 1845; and H. L., "Poughkeepsie, N.Y.," *The Christian Ambassador*, March 2, 1850.

"'... purity and improvement of our race.'" p. 25: Luke Prescott Rand, *A Sketch of the History of the Davenport Boys; Their Mediumship, Journeyings, and the Manifestations and Tests Given in Their Presence by the Spirits; a Full Account of the Arrest and Trials of L. P. Rand and the Davenport Mediums, at Mexico [New York], and at Phoenix—Their Incarceration, and the Deliverance of L. P. Rand from the Prison by the Angels* (Oswego, NY: T. P. Ottaway, 1859), p. 14.

"'He has a mission for every one.'" p. 26: James Martin Peebles, *Seers of the Ages; Embracing Spiritualism, Past and Present; Doctrines Stated and Moral Tendencies Defined* (Boston: William White, 1869), pp. 226–230, citing the testimony of Universalist ministers Gideon S. Gowdy, James P. Sanford, Theophilus Fiske, and James Harvey Tuttle.

"'. . . their churches also expired.'" p. 26: Amasa Loring, *History of Piscataquis County, Maine. From Its Earliest Settlement to 1880* (Portland, ME: Hoyt, Fogg and Donham, 1880), p. 260; and Laura Doore Warren, *Records of Dover Cemeteries* (Dover, ME: Maine DAR Genealogical Records Committee Report, 1937), p. 18.

"'. . . advisable for him to cease preaching.'" p. 27: Clara Arlette Avery, *The Averell-Averill-Avery Family: A Record of the Descendents of William and Abigail Averell of Ipswitch, Mass.* (Cleveland: Evangelical Publishing House, 1914), 2: 620–621.

". . . and stayed there for almost a year." p. 27: They had begun their demonstrations in Buffalo in February 1854; see Stephen G. Albro, "Spiritualism in Buffalo," *The Spiritual Telegraph*, September 8, 1855, reprinted from *The Buffalo Republic*, August 11, 1855.

"'. . . though but one speaks.'" p. 28: Luke Prescott Rand, p. 9.

". . . Apostle Peter from King Herod's prison." p. 28: Acts 12:1–12.

A Voice to Humankind

". . . in Philadelphia by Abel Charles Thomas." p. 29: Abel Charles Thomas, *A Century of Universalism in Philadelphia and New York* (Philadelphia: Collins, 1872), p. 104.

". . . to preach to the Universalist Society there." p. 29: Fishbough's introduction to Davis, *The Principles of Nature*, p. xiii.

"'. . . forms of belief be sacrificed.'" p. 29: William Fishbough, "New Planets Discovered by Spiritual Sight!" *The Universalist Union*, November 28, 1846. Fishbough had already written a letter to *The New York Tribune*, which seems to have drawn at least Edgar Allan Poe to witness the New York City sessions.

"'. . . to coin an expression.'" p. 30: Philo Price, "The Newly Discovered Planet, and A. J. Davis," *The Universalist Union*, November 28, 1846.

". . . in Massachusetts 'of Puritan ancestry.'" p. 30: American Spiritualist Alliance, "In Memoriam; Samuel B. Brittan," *Proceedings of the American Spiritualist Alliance, January 21, 1883* (New York: Author, 1883); and Emma Hardinge Britten, *Modern American Spiritualism: A Twenty Years' Record of the Communion between Earth and the World of Spirits* (New York: Author, 1870), pp. 61–62.

"'. . . Mrs. Mettler's Cholera Elixir." p. 31: See, for example, her advertisement in *The New-England Spiritualist*, April 28, 1855.

"'. . . spirits would fill a volume.'" p. 31: Britten, *Modern American Spiritualism*, p. 104.

"'. . . who rise up and call her blessed.'" p. 31: Samuel Byron Brittan, "A Record of Modern Miracles," *The Banner of Light*, October 29, 1859.

"... and partner in her healing work." p. 31: Frances Harriet Greene [McDougall], *Biography of Mrs. Semantha Mettler, the Clairvoyant* (New York: The Harmonial Association, 1853); New England Spiritualists' Association, *Constitution and By-Laws, List of Officers, and Address to the Public, Organized at Boston, November, 1854* (Boston: Author, 1854); Emma Hardinge Britten, *Nineteenth Century Miracles; or, Spirits and Their Work in Every Country of the Earth; A Complete Historical Compendium of the Great Movement Known as "Modern Spiritualism"* (New York: William Britten, 1884), p. 425; also H. B., "Clairvoyance, Tried and Acquitted," *The Spiritual Telegraph,* October 21, 1854.

"'... a definite idea of what has passed.'" p. 32: Greene [McDougall], *Biography,* pp. 103–104.

"'... which his former life's images had left.'" p. 32: Britten, *Modern American Spiritualism,* p. 61.

"'... between poor humanity and celestial love.'" p. 32: Samuel Byron Brittan, "Advent Voices of the Great Spiritual Movement. The First Public Lecture ever given on the subject of Modern Spiritualism," *The Two Worlds,* November 18, 1887.

"'... and all things appeared to be transparent.'" p. 32: Samuel Byron Brittan, "History of Modern Spiritualism," in Israel Daniel Rupp, ed., *[The Charles Desilver Firm's] Religious Denominations in the United States, Their Past History, Present Condition, and Doctrines, Accurately Set Forth in Fifty-Three [. . .] Articles Written by Eminent Clerical and Lay Authors [. . .] Together with Complete and Well-Digested Statistics* (New York: AMS Press, 1975; repr. 1861 ed.), p. 620.

"'... and a purer and better life.'" p. 33: Brittan, "Advent Voices."

"'... freedom of thought and expression.'" p. 33: Brittan, "History of Modern Spiritualism," p. 620.

"'... old theology to powder." p. 33: Brittan, "Advent Voices."

"'... "the art of humbuggery, and *nothing else!*'" p. 34: George Washington Quinby, "Mesmerism in Difficulty," *The Universalist Watchman,* June 11, 1847, reprinted from *The Gospel Banner.*

"'... that it is not all a humbug after all.'" p. 34: Letter from Fishbough to Davis, June 28, 1847, from Andrew Jackson Davis, Papers, Letters, and Archival Material, Edgar Cayce Foundation Archives, Virginia Beach, Virginia.

"'... to that of *physical death.'*" p. 34: William Fishbough, "Introduction," in Davis, *The Principles of Nature,* p. xvii.

"'... to establish metaphysical hypotheses.'" p. 36: Davis, *The Principles of Nature,* pp. 374–375.

"'... incipient stages of civilization.'" p. 36: Davis, *The Principles of Nature,* p. 334.

"... at least for a while." p. 36: Davis, *The Magic Staff,* pp. 337–338.

"'... certain well known chemical elements.'" p. 37: William Fishbough, "To My Friends, Once for All," *The Univercoelum and Spiritual Philosopher,* December 18, 1847.

"'... and of these being improperly directed.'" p. 37: Davis, *The Principles of Nature,* pp. 337, 342, 410, 414, 427; on Jesus' life and nature, see pp. 481–483 and 501ff.

"'... with *you* and others of like faith?'" p. 37: Davis, *The Magic Staff,* p. 336; Robert W. Delp, "Andrew Jackson Davis and Spiritualism," in *Pseudo-Science and Society in Nineteenth-Century America,* ed. Arthur Wrobel (Lexington: University Press of Kentucky, 1987), pp. 100–121.

"... less than universal law and love." p. 37: William Henry Ferris, "The Theology of Modern Spiritualism. Its Infidelity," *The Ladies' Repository,* May 1856, p. 298.

"'... the stellar firmaments, known and unknown.'" p. 38: Brittan, "Advent Voices."

The Spirit of Inquiry Run Riot

"'... ever made by mortal man.'" p. 39: J. M. Spear, "Editors' Table. The Principles of Nature," *The Prisoner's Friend,* August 18, 1847, p. 131; and J. M. Spear, "Editors' Table. The Univercoelum," *The Prisoner's Friend,* November 17, 1847, p. 183.

"'... the infidelity of A. J. Davis' revelations.'" p. 39: Thomas Whittemore, "The 'Prisoner's Friend,'" *The Trumpet and Universalist Magazine,* January 22, 1848.

"'... in the bonds of one vast Brotherhood.'" p. 40: William Stevens Balch, "New Publications," *The Universalist Union,* August 14, 1847.

"'... for which he had an affection.'" p. 40: Thomas Jefferson Sawyer, "Br. S. Cobb on Davis' Revelations," *The Universalist Union,* September 11, 1847.

"'... the profession of this religion affords.'" p. 41: Quoted by Thomas Whittemore in "Br. Cobb's Mind Altered," *The Trumpet and Universalist Magazine,* January 29, 1848. For another Sawyer diatribe against Fishbough et al., see Thomas Jefferson Sawyer, "Davis' Revelations and its Patrons," *The Universalist Union,* October 30, 1847.

"'... a vast derangement of his plumage.'" p. 41: William Fishbough, "A Dream," *The Univercoelum and Spiritual Philosopher,* December 18, 1847.

"'... made to us from day to day.'" p. 42: Charles Partridge, *Spiritualism: Its Phenomena and Significance* (New York: Spiritual Telegraph, 1858), pp. 49–50.

"'... the sole cause of all that was done.'" p. 42: Thomas Jefferson Sawyer, "Opposition to the Bible," *The Trumpet and Universalist Magazine,* June 18, 1853.

"'. . . denominational polarity almost reversed.'" p. 42: Joseph Osgood Barrett, "Another Universalist Minister in Peril," *The Spiritual Republic*, January 12, 1867; and Joseph Osgood Barrett, "Denominational Grief," *The Spiritual Republic*, January 12, 1867.

"'. . . this suspense is terrible!'" p. 42: Samuel Byron Brittan, "Are We Christians?" *The Univercoelum and Spiritual Philosopher*, December 11, 1847.

"'. . . is second-handed, stereotyped forever!'" p. 43: Samuel Byron Brittan, "Rev. Thomas J. Sawyer," *The Univercoelum and Spiritual Philosopher*, December 4, 1847;

"'. . . than a stereotyped edition of the *fathers*.'" p. 43: Henry Knapp, "Progression and Universalism," *The Spiritual Telegraph*, September 23, 1854.

"'. . . will eternally continue their conquests.'" p. 43: Edwin A. Holbrook, "Breaking the Chains of Sectarism," *The Spiritual Age*, July 25, 1857.

"'. . . the other for a narrower creed'" p. 44: Harvey A. Jones, "Universalism vs. Spiritualism," *The Banner of Light*, December 29, 1866.

"'We need their labors.'" p. 44: Alonzo Eliot Newton, "The 'Gospel Banner,'" *The New-England Spiritualist*, February 9, 1856, quoting the *Banner* of December 29, 1855. A copy of Osgood's letter to the *Banner* is included in Alonzo Eliot Newton, "Another Clergyman Convinced," *The New-England Spiritualist*, January 5, 1856.

". . . in all its vast interconnectedness" p. 45: Another of their associates, Henry J. Horn, remembered later that Brittan had originally suggested *The Sun of Righteousness* as the title of the paper—"accounted for, partly from the fact that Bro. Brittan had not entirely freed himself from the sentimentalism of old theology"— but that Fishbough suggested *The Univercoelum and Spiritual Philosopher*. From Henry J. Horn, "Reminiscences of William Fishbough," *The Religio-Philosophical Journal*, July 9, 1881.

". . . could allow prediction of the future." p. 45: For William Fishbough's thinking as a Universalist, see *The Government of God: Considered with Reference to Natural laws and the Nature of Rewards and Punishments* (Taunton, MA: I. Amesbury, 1840). For his thinking at the full blossoming of his spiritualism, see *The Macrocosm and Microcosm; or, The Universe Without and the Universe Within: Being an Unfolding of the Plan of Creation and the Correspondence of Truths, both in the World of Sense and the World of Soul* (New York: Fowlers and Wells, 1852). And for his thinking on periodicity, see *The End of the Ages; with Forecasts of the Approaching Political, Social and Religious Reconstruction of America and the World* (New York: Continental Publishing Company, 1899). He spent the last years of his life speculating on the mystic form of the Great Pyramid at Giza.

". . . on science, rather than theology." p. 45: Samuel Byron Brittan, ""Is It a New Sect?" *The Univercoelum and Spiritual Philosopher,* May 20, 1848. For a recent look at *The Univercoelum* and the group that published it, see Sally Morita, "Unseen (and Unappreciated) Matters: Understanding the Reformative Nature of 19th-Century Spiritualism," *American Studies* 40, no. 3 (Fall 1999): 99–125.

"'. . . which that denomination does not recognize.'" p. 45: William Fishbough, "The Charge of Infidelity," *The Univercoelum and Spiritual Philosopher,* December 18, 1847.

"'. . . in full chase of the new topic.'" p 46: The article was ostensibly a review of the first volume of the second edition of Davis's work, *The Great Harmonia.* See "Literary Notes. The Great Harmonia," *The Universalist Quarterly and General Review,* July 1852, pp. 326–327.

"'. . . the armory engine house at Harper's Ferry.'" p. 46: *Biographies and Portraits of the Progressive Men of Iowa: Leaders in Business, Politics and the Professions, Together with an Original and Authentic History of the State, by Ex-Lieutenant-Governor B. F. Gue* (Des Moines, IA: Conaway & Shaw, 1899), p. 71.

"'. . . that is most dear and interesting to us.'" p. 47: As quoted from *The Christian Freeman* of November 5, 1847, by Joshua King Ingalls in "Stratification of Universalism," *The Univercoelum and Spiritual Philosopher,* January 1, 1848

"'. . . free thought and unrestricted inquiry.'" p. 47: Davis, *The Principles of Nature,* p. 5.

"'. . . and the same spiritual life.'" p. 48: Sylvanus Cobb, "A Word to Spiritualists," *The Christian Freeman and Family Visiter,* November 24, 1854.

"It is the ultimate religion." p. 48: Sylvanus Cobb, "Appeal to Spiritualists," *The Christian Freeman and Family Visiter,* January 13, 1854.

". . . as a vivification of their Christian lives." p. 48: Daniel Ballou, "Spiritualism," *The Christian Freeman and Family Visiter,* June 9, 1854.

"'. . . with greater fervor than ever before.'" p. 48: Sylvanus Cobb, "Br. Brown's Letter—Spiritualism," *The Christian Freeman and Family Visiter,* February 3, 1854.

"'. . . quite departed from the earthly.'" p. 49: Sylvanus Cobb, "Spiritual Manifestations—Correspondence—Exposition. No. 1," *The Christian Freeman and Family Visiter,* June 17, 1853.

"'. . . and anti-Christian school' of spiritualism." p. 49: Sylvanus Cobb, "Justice to the Departed," *The Christian Freeman and Family Visiter,* March 10, 1854.

"'. . . real communication with each other.'" p. 49: Sylvanus Cobb, *Autobiography of the First Forty-One Years of the Life of Sylvanus Cobb, D.D.; To Which Is Added a Memoir, by His Eldest Son, Sylvanus Cobb, Jr.* (Boston: Universalist Publishing House, 1867), pp. 511–512.

"'. . . but as a happy confirmation.'" p. 49: Sylvanus Cobb, "Clerical Testimony," *The New-England Spiritualist,* October 13, 1855.

". . . to begin this publication." p. 49: Luther Colby, "Special Notice," *The Banner of Light,* May 15, 1880.

". . . regarded as delusory, false spiritualism." p. 50: Sylvanus Cobb, "Spiritualism in Milford," *The Christian Freeman and Family Visiter,* February 12, 1858; "Br. Stoddard and Milford Spiritualism," *The Christian Freeman and Family Visiter,* February 12, 1858; and the series of numbered articles entitled "Spiritualism," published in *The Christian Freeman and Family Visiter,* February 26 through May 21, 1858.

". . . unwilling to part with Christianity." p. 50: James Martin Peebles, "Death of Rev. Sylvanus Cobb, D.D.," *The Banner of Light,* November 10, 1866; and Joseph Osgood Barrett, *The Spiritual Pilgrim; A Biography of James M. Peebles* (Boston: William White, 1872), p. 45.

". . . those who did not accept it." p. 51: James Martin Peebles, "Dr. E. H. Chapin at the Festival in Boston," *The Banner of Light,* July 7, 1866.

"'. . . in demonstration of the celestial powers.'" p. 51: Uriah Clark, "New York Correspondence—Great Interest in Western New York," *The New-England Spiritualist,* September 29, 1855.

"'. . . communicate with spirits in the flesh.'" p. 51: Quoted by James Martin Peebles in "Dr. Eli Ballou a Spiritualist," *The Banner of Light,* December 5, 1866, citing Ballou's *The Christian Repository.*

Why Seek Ye the Living Among the Dead?

"'. . . footing in the sectarian institution.'" p. 52: Samuel Byron Brittan, "J. K. Ingalls," *Brittan's Journal,* April 1874.

"'. . . a suspension of laws, or contrary thereto.'" p. 52: Joshua King Ingalls, "Immutability of God's Laws," *The Universalist Union,* November 21, 1846.

"'. . . of all things, material and spiritual.'" p. 53: Joshua King Ingalls, "Miracles: Are They Natural or Supernatural?" *The Universalist Union,* October 16, 1847; also Samuel Byron Brittan, "The Philosophy of Miracles," *The Univercoelum and Spiritual Philosopher,* December 11, 1847.

"'. . . other bodies susceptible to its influence.'" p. 54: Julia Schlesinger, "Mediumistic Experience," *The Carrier Dove,* February 1886, and "Biographical Sketch of Mrs. Laverna Mathews," *The Carrier Dove,* March 1886.

"'. . . come to know ourselves better.'" p. 55: Giles Badger Stebbins, "From Puritanism to Spiritualism. 1817–1884. Chapter 9," *The Religio-Philosophical Journal,* January 31, 1885.

"'... the authority of the Christian revelation.'" p. 56: Abel Charles Thomas, *A Century of Universalism in Philadelphia and New York* (Philadelphia: Collins, 1872), pp. 314–315.

"'... and resurrection of the Lord Jesus Christ.'" p. 56: Thomas Whittemore, "Boston Association. Extraordinary Session," *The Trumpet and Universalist Magazine,* January 1, 1848; and "Boston Association. Infidelity," *The Trumpet and Universalist Magazine,* January 1, 1848.

"'... the basis of the complaints alluded to.'" p. 56: Sylvanus Cobb, "Rev. Geo. Severance," *The Christian Freeman and Family Visiter,* November 11, 1853; Sylvanus Cobb, "Br. Mandell's Position, in Things Reformatory and Spiritual," *The Christian Freeman and Family Visiter,* May 20, 1853; and Joseph Baker, "Who Will Come to Glen's Falls?" *The Christian Freeman and Family Visiter,* February 15, 1850.

"'... as given in the Gospels, are divine truth.'" p. 57: Samuel Byron Brittan, "Fifth Universalist Society," *The Univercoelum and Spiritual Philosopher,* February 5, 1848; and Zephaniah Baker, "Is It a New Sect?" *The Univercoelum and Spiritual Philosopher,* May 20, 1848. On the New Jersey Universalist Association's creed, see Thomas Whittemore, "Universalists Sustain the Bible," *The Trumpet and Universalist Magazine,* August 19, 1848. On the Indiana State Universalist Convention's creed and the Ontario (New York) Universalist Association's creed, see Thomas Whittemore, "Infidel Notions Repudiated," *The Trumpet and Universalist Magazine,* July 8, 1848. On the St. Lawrence Universalist Association's decision to set aside its previously required creedal pledge, see Samuel Byron Brittan, "A Defunct Creed," *The Spiritual Telegraph,* July 28, 1855.

"'... to the above declaration and pledge.'" p. 58: Chautauque Universalist Association, Minutes and Notebook, Manuscript Division, Andover-Harvard Theological Library.

"'... champion of freedom, on several occasions.'" p. 58: William Cutler, *History of the State of Kansas, Containing a Full Account of Its Growth from an Uninhabited Territory to a Wealthy and Important State* (Chicago: A. T. Andreas, 1883), pp. 101–102.

"... when it adopted a creedal test." p. 58: Thomas Whittemore, "Decision of the Vermont Convention," *The Trumpet and Universalist Magazine,* September 23, 1848; and Sylvanus Cobb, "Withdrawal," *The Christian Freeman and Family Visiter,* September 22, 1854.

"'... against paganism or popular theology.'" p. 58: "Spiritual Convention at South Royalton, Vt.," *The Banner of Light,* September 4, 1858.

"'... else all men could hold intercourse.'" p. 59: Quoted in Peebles, *Seers of the Ages,* p. 231.

"'. . . definition of the word "sufficient.""" p. 59: Quoted in James Martin Peebles, "The Universalist Denomination," *The Banner of Light*, June 5, 1869, from Streeter's letter to *The Gospel Banner*.

". . . spiritualist lecturing, writing, and editing." p. 59: Thomas Whittemore, "Buffalo Association. Rev. L. S. Everett Withdrawn," *The Trumpet and Universalist Magazine*, August 12, 1848.

". . . and in Hartford and Middletown, Connecticut." p. 59: Elliot G. Storke, *The History of Cayuga County, New York* (Syracuse, NY: D. Mason, 1879), p. 206.

"'. . . to rear its head among us,' according to Whittemore." p. 60: Whittemore, "Universalists Sustain the Bible."

". . . in order to escape doctrinal scrutiny." p. 61: Thomas Whittemore, "New York State Convention of Universalists," *The Trumpet and Universalist Magazine*, June 17, 1848; and "St. Lawrence Association, N.Y.," *The Trumpet and Universalist Magazine*, August 5, 1848.

"'. . . and a life consistent with such profession.'" p. 61: Aaron Burt Grosh, "Creeds—Again," *The Trumpet and Universalist Magazine*, April 21, 1849; and "Establishing Tests," *The Trumpet and Universalist Magazine*, January 6, 1849.

". . . the idea of creeds for Universalism." p. 61: Samuel Byron Brittan, "The Pennsylvania Resolutions: Position of the Universalists," *The Univercoelum and Spiritual Philosopher*, September 16, 1848; and Thomas Whittemore, "Communications. To Rev. H. Bacon," *The Trumpet and Universalist Magazine*, October 3, 1852.

"'. . . proof of Christ's mission." p. 61: Thomas Jefferson Sawyer, "Opposition to the Bible," *The Trumpet and Universalist Magazine*, June 18, 1853.

". . . for maintaining people in fellowship." p. 62: On James Martin Peebles's reaction to the 1896–1897 Universalist debates about the Winchester Profession, see his "The Universalists' Creed," *The Philosophical Journal*, September 23, 1897.

"'. . . they have brought forth." p. 62: Quoted by Peebles in "The Universalist Denomination" from Balch's article in *The New Covenant*.

"'. . . and more determined to throw it off.'" p. 63: Elijah Case, "Incrustations of Universalism Broken Through," *The Banner of Light*, September 10, 1859.

"'. . . Christian—a *"Christian* Spiritualist.""" p. 63: Joseph Osgood Barrett, *The Spiritual Pilgrim; A Biography of James M. Peebles* (Boston: William White, 1872), pp. 40–41.

". . . when they became spiritualists." p. 63: "Call to Consider the Organization of Christian Spiritualism in America," *The Banner of Light*, July 15, 1876.

"'. . . on the altar of ecclesiastical inquisitions.'" p. 64: Uriah Clark, "From Our New York Correspondent," *The New-England Spiritualist*, March 29, 1856.

"... as it was in geology and biology." p. 64: Woodbury Melcher Fernald, "The Necessity for New and Higher Revelations, Inspirations, or Forms of Truth, for the Benefit of Mankind at the Present Day," *The Univercoelum and Spiritual Philosopher,* December 4, 1847.

"'... and all that sort of thing.'" p. 64: George Quinby quoted by Thomas Whittemore, "Rev. T. L. Harris," *The Trumpet and Universalist Magazine,* April 8, 1848.

"'... no self-consciousness reaching back to them.'" p. 65: Hosea Ballou II, "Condition of Men after Death," *The Universalist Quarterly and General Review,* January 1853, pp. 29–51.

"... to reflect his new interests." p. 66: Joshua King Ingalls, *Reminiscences of an Octogenarian in the Field of Industrial and Social Reform* (New York: M. L. Holbrook, 1897). See also his *Social Wealth: The Sole Factors and Exact Ratios in Its Acquirement and Apportionment* (New York: Social Science Publishing Company, 1885); and James Joseph Martin, *Men against the State; The Expositors of Individualist Anarchism in America, 1827–1908* (De Kalb, IL: Adrian Allen Associates, 1953), pp. 139–153.

"... within the society over spiritualism." p. 66: Joseph H. Goldsmith, "Personal and Local," *The Spiritual Age,* September 19, 1857; Samuel Byron Brittan, "Spiritual Meetings at Southold," *The Spiritual Telegraph,* June 16, 1855; "The Spirits Have Taken Southold," *The Spiritual Telegraph,* June 3, 1854; and Joella Vreeland, *This Is the Church: The Story of a Church, a Community, and a Denomination, First Universalist Church, Unitarian Universalist, Southold, New York* (Mattituck, NY: Amereon House, 1988), pp. 184–185.

"'... than all other causes combined.'" p. 66: David Henry Plumb, "Correspondence," *The Univercoelum and Spiritual Philosopher,* March 18, 1848; and "Letter from Br. Plumb," *The Univercoelum and Spiritual Philosopher,* June 3, 1848.

"'... an independent Christian position.'" p. 66: Samuel Byron Brittan, "D. H. Plumb," *The Univercoelum and Spiritual Philosopher,* September 2, 1848; and Thomas Whittemore, "Rev. D. H. Plumb," *The Trumpet and Universalist Magazine,* December 2, 1848.

"'... the worship of Almighty God.'" p. 67: David Henry Plumb, "Rev. D. H. Plumb," *The Trumpet and Universalist Magazine,* December 16, 1848.

The Pebble and the Angel

"'... the true spirit of religious progress.'" p. 68: Samuel Byron Brittan, "The Morning Stars," *Brittan's Journal,* January 1874.

"'... its truth and usefulness to mankind.'" p. 68: Woodbury Melcher Fernald, "A Clergyman's Opinion of Davis's Book," *The Prisoner's Friend,* September 15, 1847.

"... criticism from the Universalist press." p. 68: Thomas Whittemore, "Rev. Mr. Fernald against the Bible," *The Trumpet and Universalist Magazine,* December 16, 1848; and "Rev. W. M. Fernald's Paper," *The Trumpet and Universalist Magazine,* April 8, 1848. On a futile attempt in 1852 by Fernald to reconcile with the Universalist establishment, see Woodbury Melcher Fernald, "To the Universalist Denomination," *The Trumpet and Universalist Magazine,* August 14, 1852; and Thomas Whittemore, "Br. W. M. Fernald," *The Trumpet and Universalist Magazine,* October 23, 1852.

"'... Actuating Soul of the Universe.'" p. 68: Woodbury Melcher Fernald, "Pantheism," *The Univercoelum and Spiritual Philosopher,* January 22, 1847.

"'... no more than the pebble.'" p. 69: Woodbury Melcher Fernald, "To the Universalist Denomination."

"'... as a Christian preacher.'" p. 69: Thomas Whittemore, "Rev. Mr. Fernald against the Bible."

"'... and the caprices of a changeful Deity.'" p. 70: Joshua King Ingalls, "The Divine Gifts: Impartial and Immutable," *The Univercoelum and Spiritual Philosopher,* March 4, 1848.

"... in front of an audience." p. 70: In his preface to "Eureka," Poe wrote, "What I have proposed is true:—Therefore it cannot die.—or if by any means it be now trodden down so that it die, it will 'rise again to the Life Everlasting.' Nevertheless, it is as a poem only that I wish this work to be judged after I am dead."

"... as Swedenborg had described." p. 70: Contrast Woodbury Melcher Fernald's *Universalism against Partialism: In a Series of Lectures Delivered in Newburyport, Mass.* (Boston: Mussey, 1840) and his *Eternity of Heaven and Hell* (n.p., 1855).

"'... the handle of a beer-pump.'" p. 72: "Senatorial Spirit Rappings," *The New York Times,* April 19, 1854.

"... to the spiritualist movement was as an editor." p. 72: Among Brittan's published works are *An Illustration and Defense of Universalism as an Idea, in a Series of Philosophical and Scriptural Discourses* (Albany, NY: C. Killmer, 1847); *The Philosophy of Modern Miracles; or, The Relations of Spiritual Causes to Physical Effects; with Especial Reference to the Mysterious Developments at Bridgeport and Elsewhere, by "A Dweller in the Temple"* (New York: Stringer and Townsend, 1850); and *Man and His Relations; Illustrating the Influence of the Mind on the Body; the Relations of the Faculties to the Organs, and to the Elements, Objects and Phenomena of the External World* (New York: W. A. Townsend and Adams, 1864).

"... and one more hidebound institution." p. 73: Davis, *The Magic Staff,* pp. 483–490.

"'... of your philosophy and theology.'" p. 74: Letter of Fishbough to Davis, March 16, 1854, in Andrew Jackson Davis, Papers, Letters, and Archival Material.

Divine Respiration

"... regular contributors to *The Univercoelum and Spiritual Philosopher.*" p. 75: Baker had also published in 1842 Hosea Ballou's *The Ancient History of Universalism, from the Time of the Apostles to Its Condemnation in the Fifth General Council, A.D. 553. With an Appendix, Tracing the Doctrine down to the End of the Reformation,* 2nd ed., rev. (Providence, RI: Z. Baker, 1842.)

"... asked Harris to be their pastor." p. 75: Zephaniah Baker, "Circular of the 'Independent Christian Society,'" *The Univercoelum and Spiritual Philosopher,* September 30, 1848; and Samuel Byron Brittan, "The Free Church," *The Univercoelum and Spiritual Philosopher,* May 20, 1848.

"'... the Bible and its sacred institutions.'" p. 76: Thomas Whittemore, "Br. Z. Baker," *The Trumpet and Universalist Magazine,* February 12, 1853; and Thomas Whittemore, "Are They in Fellowship?" *The Trumpet and Universalist Magazine,* January 20, 1853.

"'... sensation that cannot be described.'" p. 76: Horn, "Reminiscences of William Fishbough."

"... to lecture on the new dispensation." p. 77: Thomas Lake Harris, "Progress in Cincinnati," *The Univercoelum and Spiritual Philosopher,* April 15, 1848.

"... next on his lecture tour." p. 77: Letter from Harris to Davis from Cincinnati, November 14, 1847, in Andrew Jackson Davis, Papers, Letters, and Archival Material.

"'You can not do a better work.'" p. 78: "Rev. T. L. Harris in Cincinnati," *The Trumpet and Universalist Magazine,* February 12, 1848.

"'... departed spirits in another world.'" p. 78: Whittemore, "Rev. T. L. Harris," *The Trumpet and Universalist Magazine,* April 8, 1848.

"'... is liable to repeat them.'" p. 78: Thomas Lake Harris, "A Few Words of Caution," *The Univercoelum and Spiritualist Philosopher,* September 30, 1848. Also, a letter from Fishbough to Davis, dated July 11, 1848 (in Andrew Jackson Davis, Papers, Letters, and Archival Material), suggests that Harris was unhappy about the Catherine De Wolf marriage. Fishbough wrote to Davis, "It is getting to be pretty generally known that you are married. I have not yet had one unpleasant remark made about it, but several quite pleasant ones. Harris is in the office & looks as black as the devil, but I don't exactly know what he is thinking about—Small potatoes!" Fishbough and his wife, Eliza, had served as the two witnesses at Davis's marriage to De Wolf before a justice of the peace near Fishbough's home in Williamsburgh, New York.

"'... of intellectual culture and wisdom.'" p. 79: "Critical Notices. Epic of the Starry Heavens. Thomas Lake Harris," *North American Review,* April 1854, pp. 545–546.

"... *Interior and Superior Care of Mortals.*" p. 79: Britten, *Modern American Spiritualism*, p. 215.

"'... through one of your members.'" p. 80: Britten, *Modern American Spiritualism*, pp. 207–217; and Eliab Wilkinson Capron, "Has T. L. Harris Reformed?" *The Religio-Philosophical Journal*, July 12, 1890.

"... from a couple of wealthy disciples." p. 81: Jack Ericson has collected much of the primary material about Harris, including material on his followers, in a microfilm edition, *Thomas Lake Harris and the Brotherhood of the New Life: Books, Pamphlets, Serials and Manuscripts* (New Jersey: Microfilming Corporation of America, 1974).

"'... is a question for the angels.'" p. 81: Arthur Conan Doyle, *The History of Spiritualism* (New York: Arno Press, 1975; repr. of 1926 ed.), 1: 121.

"... and 'claptrap' that accompanied it." p. 82: Samuel Byron Brittan, "The Time and the Demand," *Brittan's Journal*, July 1873.

"... and made no secret of it." p. 82: Ann Braude, *Radical Spirits: Spiritualism and Women's Rights in Nineteenth-Century America* (Boston: Beacon Press, 1989), p. 47.

The Conversation with Spirits of the Dead

Spiritual Automatists

"... who had recently moved to Rochester." p. 85: Emma Hardinge Britten, *Modern American Spiritualism: A Twenty Years' Record of the Communion between Earth and the World of Spirits* (New York: Author, 1870), pp. 49–51.

"... the gospel of universal salvation in 1830." p. 85: Most of the biographical information about Hammond before he became a spiritualist was given to me by Karen E. Dau, historian of the First Universalist Church of Rochester, New York, from her unpublished "Notes on Rev. Charles Hammond."

"... given by the Fox sisters in November 1850." p. 86: Printed from Brittan's notes by Emma Hardinge Britten. Samuel Byron Brittan, "Advent Voices of the Great Spiritual Movement. The First Public Lecture Ever Given on the Subject of Modern Spiritualism," *The Two Worlds*, November 18, 1887.

"... correspondent for Brittan's *The Spiritual Telegraph.*" p. 87: Britten, *Modern American Spiritualism*, pp. 109–111. See also Adelbert Cronise, "The Beginnings of Modern Spiritualism in and near Rochester," in *Rochester Historical Society, Publication Fund Series*, ed. Edward R. Foreman (Rochester, NY: Rochester Historical Society, 1926), 5: 1–22.

"... would soon desist, which they did." p. 87: Charles Hammond, *Light from the Spirit World; Comprising a Series of Articles on the Condition of Spirits, and the Development of Mind in the Rudimental and Second Spheres; Being Written Wholly by the Control of Spirits, Without Any Volition or Will by the Medium, or Any Thought or Care in Regard to the Matter Presented by His Hand* (Rochester, NY: W. Heughes, 1852), pp. ix–x.

"'... been unfortunate in that respect.'" p. 88: Hammond, *Light from the Spirit World; Comprising a Series of Articles on the Condition of Spirits,* p. xi.

"... a pilgrim's progress." p. 88: Charles Hammond, *Light from the Spirit World; the Pilgrimage of Thomas Paine, and Others, to the Seventh Circle in the Spirit World* (Rochester, NY: D. M. Dewey, 1852) and *Philosophy of the Spirit World; Communicated by Spirits, through the Mediumship of Rev. Charles Hammond* (New York: Partridge and Brittan, 1853).

"'... he is to be pitied.'" p. 88: William Henry Ferris, "A Review of Modern Spiritualism—Its Alleged Facts Considered," *The Ladies' Repository,* February 1856, p. 92.

"'... into so great a peril.'" p. 89: *The Christian Ambassador,* January 31, 1852.

"... answers from disembodied voices." p. 89: Dau, "Notes on Rev. Charles Hammond"; Charles Hammond, "Davenports in Rochester," *The Spiritual Age,* July 4, 1857. The magicians Penn and Teller do a version of this today.

"'... [ran] continually on that subject.'" p. 90: Thomas Whittemore, "Disease of Br. Hobbs," *The Trumpet and Universalist Magazine,* September 26, 1851.

"... letter of resignation, which was accepted." p. 90: Chenango Universalist Association, Record Book, Manuscripts Division, Andover-Harvard Theological Library.

"'... and going through the strangest ordeals.'" p. 90: As reprinted in Brittan's *The Spiritual Telegraph* and reproduced in Britten's *Modern American Spiritualism,* pp. 111–112.

"'"Spirits have power on the earth."'" p. 90: Benjamin Scovil Hobbs, "Mediumship, Nolens Volens," *The Spiritual Telegraph,* September 15, 1855.

"'... the occurrence of what he can not prevent.'" p. 91: Samuel Byron Brittan, "A Clerical Medium," *The Spiritual Age,* June 28, 1857. For Hobbs's reply, see "Rev. B. S. Hobbs and Spiritualism," *The Spiritual Age,* August 15, 1857.

"... outside their conscious volition." p. 91: Although spiritualists generally tried to espouse the calming and comforting effects of their beliefs, they often had to explain some fairly eccentric and even demented behavior by their colleagues. For examples of suicide and murder attributed by outsiders to the pernicious effect on the mind of Davis's *The Principles of Nature,* Brittan's *The Spiritual Telegraph,* and Harris's *The Mountain Cove Journal,* see "Singular Case of Suicide—Important

Coroner's Inquisition," *The New York Daily Times,* January 10, 1853; and Catherine DeWolfe Davis, "The Quincy Tragedy," *The Spirit Messenger,* March 22, 1851. Some physicians treated belief in spiritualism purely as a mental disorder, including William A. Hammond, who wrote *Spiritualism and Allied Causes and Conditions of Nervous Derangement* (New York: A. K. Butts, 1874). Yet other physicians became involved in the movement themselves. For example, Edward Payson Fowler was the medium for many wild séances in New York City while a medical student in the early 1850s. Eventually, he became a highly respected mainstream physician specializing in neurological disorders.

"'... march through even an open gate.'" p. 92: Benjamin Scovil Hobbs, "Note from Rev. B. S. Hobbs," *The Banner of Light,* December 8, 1866; Hobbs, "Spiritualism in the Pulpit," *The Banner of Light,* June 18, 1857; and Luther Colby, "Our Admonitions Attested," *The Banner of Light,* July 2, 1857. Orestes Brownson, who moved from the Universalist clergy in a direction opposite to that of most of the Universalists considered here, converted to Roman Catholicism. His novel, *The Spirit-Rapper,* written after his conversion, flails spiritualism not only for its destructive radicalism but also for the psychic damage he thought it caused in those who made themselves susceptible to trance.

Spirits Preach Universal Salvation

"... in different stages of development." p. 93: Eliab Wilkinson Capron, *Modern Spiritualism; Its Facts and Fanaticisms, Its Consistencies and Contradictions* (Boston: Bela Marsh, 1855), p. 113.

"... the explanation was intervening spirits." p. 93: Karen E. Dau provided me with selections from Austin's journal from the archives of the Austin-Harvard Theological Library. Austin's tests with spirits are detailed in entries dated January 7, 23, and 28; February 18 and 21; March 25, 27, and 28; April 19; and December 16. Austin wrote a skeptical letter about the rappings: "A Settler," *The New York Tribune,* March 27, 1850.

"'... must be something important in it.'" p. 93: John Mather Austin, Journal, December 16, 1850, Manuscripts Division, Andover-Harvard Theological Library. Boynton "found himself compelled, under an influence he could not resist, to write sentiments whose broad liberality he knew to be inimical to the dogmas of his own creed, and, what was to him a still more perplexing act, to sign to many of the heretical papers ... 'John Wesley' himself." Boynton was excommunicated by the Methodists; Britten, *Modern American Spiritualism,* p. 83.

"'... from the state of the answer.'" p. 94: Charles Spear, "Notes by the Way," *The Prisoner's Friend,* November 1850, p. 128.

"'... comprehended by a spirit.'" p. 94: Spear, "Notes by the Way," p. 128.

". . . spirits advocated 'the old theology.'" p. 94: Sylvanus Cobb, "The Speaking Mediums," *The Christian Freeman and Family Visiter,* July 21, 1853.

"'. . . "you see that Universalism is down."'" p. 95: Sylvanus Cobb, "Spiritual Manifestations—Correspondence—Exposition. No. 2," *The Christian Freeman and Family Visiter,* July 1, 1853; John Nichols, "Rev. J. Nichols on His Experiments," *The Christian Freeman and Family Visiter,* July 22, 1853.

"'. . . in the light as in the dark.'" p. 96: Dolphus Skinner, "Singular Revelations," *The Christian Ambassador,* March 2, 1850.

"'. . . this new and wonderful agency.'" p. 96: Dolphus Skinner, "The Spiritual Knockings," *The Christian Freeman and Family Visiter,* March 15, 1850; "Singular Revelations," *The Christian Ambassador,* March 2, 1850; and "Spiritual Knockings Again," *The Christian Ambassador,* May 25, 1850.

". . . on various Bible passages." p. 96: Eliza Ann Benedict et al., *Exposition of the Prophetic Scriptures of the New Testament, as Received Entirely from Spiritual Communications, at Auburn, Cayuga County, N.Y., by J. M. Brown, E. A. Benedict, Calista Sherman, Milo Webster, Sen., D. D. T. Benedict, C. Coventry, Samuel Brown and G. W. Hyatt* (Auburn, NY: E. H. Baxter and E. A. Benedict, 1850).

"'. . . immortality have not been changed.'" p. 96: Thomas Whittemore, "The Spirit Rappings," *The Trumpet and Universalist Magazine,* March 28, 1853.

"'. . . connection with the Universalist organization.'" p. 97: John Mather Austin, "Another Clerical Convert," *The Christian Ambassador,* January 2, 1858.

"'. . . we shall be most happily mistaken.'" p. 97: John Mather Austin, "Spiritualism in Battle Creek," *The Christian Ambassador,* December 11, 1858.

"'. . . arbitrary authorities and sectarian shackles.'" p. 97: Samuel Byron Brittan, "Editorial Correspondence," *The Spiritual Telegraph,* November 29, 1856.

The Detective of Toeology

". . . those who attended his séances." p. 98: Daniel Mason Knapen, "Spirit Rappings," *The Christian Freeman and Family Visiter,* July 11, 1851, and "The Spiritual Knockings. A Sermon, Delivered in Randolph, Mass.," *The Christian Freeman and Family Visiter,* March 21, 1851.

"'. . . devils that should be cast out.'" p. 98: Hannah Frances Morrill Brown, "Ohio Correspondence," *The Christian Freeman and Family Visiter,* January 11, 1850.

"'. . . over the corpse which he depicted.'" p. 99: Joseph Rodes Buchanan, "Scientific Exhibitions," *Buchanan's Journal of Man,* February 1850, p. 509.

". . . for publication in *The Univercoelum and Spiritual Philosopher.*" p. 99: Charles Chauncey Burr, "Song to Beauty," *The Univercoleum and Spiritual Philosopher,*

January 22, 1848, and "Vision of a Young Poet," *The Univercoleum and Spiritual Philosopher,* February 5, 1848. For background on Burr, see Capron, pp. 416–424, and Britten, *Modern American Spiritualism,* pp. 69–70.

"'. . . to excite [his] wonder and horror.'" p. 100: Letter from Burr to *The New York Tribune,* dated January 1852, reprinted in Capron, pp. 416–417. For earlier letters from Burr to *The New York Daily Tribune,* see these articles: "Burr against Spiritual Knockings," July 24, 1851, and "Mr. Burr on the Rappings Again," August 8, 1851.

". . . snapping one's toe joints." p. 100: Burr's pamphlet, now rare, was quoted at length in Methodist minister Hiram Mattison's *Spirit Rapping Unveiled! An Exposé of the Origin, History, Theology and Philosophy of Certain Alleged Communications from the Spirit World, by Means of "Spirit Rapping," "Medium Writing," "Physical Demonstrations," etc.* (New York: Mason Brothers, 1853). Burr's wife at the time of his mesmeric demonstrations, Celia, divorced him and remarried. In 1871, as Celia Burleigh, she became the first woman to be ordained a Unitarian minister.

"'. . . when Mr. Burr has detected forty-seven.'" p. 100: Hannah Frances Morrill Brown, "Ohio Correspondence," *The Christian Freeman and Family Visiter,* May 30, 1851.

". . . the Fox sisters' powers." p. 101: Burr, "Burr against Spiritual Knockings" and "Mr. Burr on the Rappings Again."

Burning in the Sunbeams

"'. . . with symbols of indescribable terror.'" p. 102: Uriah Clark, *Life-Sketches of Rev. George Henry Clark, by His Brother* (Boston: Abel Tompkins, 1852), pp. 15–16; and Richard Eddy, *Universalism in America. A History* (Boston: Universalist Publishing House, 1886), 2: 423.

". . . and in Chicopee and Lowell, Massachusetts." p. 102: "Lowell," *The Bay State Monthly,* March 1884, pp. 160–200.

"'. . . who were calling for my aid.'" p. 103: Uriah Clark, "Melange of Marvels—Healing, Telegraphing, Seeing, Psychometrizing," *The Banner of Light,* December 24, 1864.

". . . to infidelity and even immorality." p. 103: Thomas Whittemore, "Br. Cobb's Mind Altered," *The Trumpet and Universalist Magazine,* January 29, 1848.

"'. . . a more sublime, living, and spiritual faith.'" p. 103: Samuel Byron Brittan, "Another Lecturer in the Field," *The Spiritual Telegraph,* May 6 and July 22, 1854. See also Sylvanus Cobb, "Libertinism and the Marriage Question," *The Christian Freeman and Family Visiter,* December 10, 1854; and Stevens Sanborn Jones, "Look at It, and Spurn It from Your Door," *The Religio-Philosophical Journal,* September 20, 1873.

"... that had disfellowshipped him." p. 103: Uriah Clark, "Rev. Uriah Clark to the Public," *The Spiritual Telegraph,* July 22, 1854.

"'... may yet bless your mission!'" p. 104: Clark, "Melange of Marvels."

"'... and God was love, pervading all things.'" p. 104: Julia Schlesinger, "Mediumistic Experience," *The Carrier Dove,* February 1886, and "Biographical Sketch of Mrs. Laverna Mathews," *The Carrier Dove,* March 1886.

"'... a Hell for unfortunate spirits.'" p. 104: Julia Ann Norcross Crafts Smith, *The Reason Why; or, Spiritual Experiences of Mrs. Julia Crafts Smith, Physician, Assisted by Her Spirit Guides* (Boston: Author, 1881), pp. 10, 37–38.

"'... capable of doing, and vastly more too.'" p. 105: Andrew Rickel, *Methodism and Spiritualism: Their Agreements and Differences. A Letter of Review of Two Discourses on the Nature, Immortality and Destiny of the Human Soul, Delivered in Waterloo, Iowa, on the 12th of March, 1863, by J. Bowman, Minister of the M. E. Church. And Also, a Chapter on a New Order of Society, as Expressive of One Object of Spiritualism* (Waterloo, IA: n.p., 1865), pp. 5–6.

"'... to render them harmless or nugatory.'" p. 106: Ferdinand Canning Scott Schiller, "Spiritism," in *Encyclopaedia of Religion and Ethics,* ed. James Hastings (New York: Charles Scribner's Sons, 1920), 11: 805.

"'... and sounds of its inexplicable phenomena.'" p. 106: Uriah Clark, "The Millennium of Spiritualism," *The Spiritual Telegraph,* March 14, 1857, reprinted from Clark's newspaper *The Spiritual Clarion.* For a somewhat different angle, see Ralph Waldo Emerson, "Swedenborg; or, The Mystic," in *Representative Men: Seven Lectures* (Boston: Phillips, Sampson, 1850), p. 99: "This beatitude comes in terror, and with shocks to the mind of the receiver. 'It o'erinforms the tenement of clay,' and drives the man mad; or, gives a certain violent bias, which taints his judgment."

"... who published them in *The Spiritual Telegraph*." p. 106: For his description of becoming a trance lecturer, see Uriah Clark, "Rev. U. Clark's Spiritual Development," *The Spiritual Telegraph,* January 13, 1855.

"'... for spiritual pastors.'" p. 106: Uriah Clark, "Itinerant Etchings of U. Clark," *The Spiritual Telegraph,* July 7, 1855.

"... and from one Cape Cod town to the next." p. 107: Mary Fenn Love Davis, "Letter from Mrs. Davis," *The Spiritual Age,* October 10, 1857; Frances Harriet Greene [McDougall], "Letter from New-London," *The Spiritual Age,* September 18, 1857; Joseph H. Goldsmith, "Personal and Local," *The Spiritual Age,* September 19, 1857; James Martin Peebles, "Universalist Bigotry in Lansing, Michigan," *The Banner of Light,* December 5, 1866; and George Atkins, "Spiritualism on the Cape," *The*

Banner of Light, December 25, 1858. Traveling spiritualist Warren Chase noted lectures he gave in Universalist churches in Beloit, Wisconsin; Newport, Vermont; Manchester, New Hampshire; and Clyde, Ohio: *Life-Line of the Lone One; or, Autobiography of the World's Child* (Boston: William White, 1868), pp. 188, 254–256, and 268. Traveling test medium Ebenezer Wilson held a demonstration in the Universalist church in McHenry, Illinois: *The Truths of Spiritualism; Immortality Proved beyond a Doubt by Living Witnesses* (Chicago: Hazlitt & Reed, 1876), p. 270. Ella Gibson Hobart delivered a trance lecture in the Universalist church in Belfast, Maine, in 1857: see *Humanitarianism: Lecture Delivered in the Universalist Church, Belfast, Me., Wednesday Evening, May 6, 1857, through the Organism of Miss Ella Elvira Gibson* (Bangor, ME: Samuel S. Smith, 1857).

"... Sabbath meetings and classes for children." p. 107: Richard Mather Bayles, *History of Windham County, Connecticut* (New York: W. W. Preston, 1889), 1: 101.

"(The Farmington society later relented, however.)" p. 107: Gwen Foss, "Spiritualist Controversy," Personal Communication, March 20, 2001.

"'. . . the truth of this myself within a short time).'" p. 108: Nathaniel Randall, "Spiritualism Not a 'Wing' of Universalism," *The World's Paper,* November 12, 1858.

"'. . . of the share-holders and paying members.'" p. 108: Britten, *Modern American Spiritualism,* p. 204.

"'. . . refunded in case of failure.'" p. 108: Advertisement in *The Spiritual Telegraph,* June 30, 1855.

"... in the late summer of 1866." p. 109: "The First Great Spiritualist Camp Meeting, at Pierpont Grove, between Malden and Melrose, Mass., Aug. 30th and 31st, and Sept. 1st and 2nd, 1866," *The Banner of Light,* October 20 and 27, 1866.

"... and was again a preacher." p. 109: S. S. Jones, "Look at It, and Spurn It from Your Door," *The Religio-Philosophical Journal,* September 20, 1873.

"'. . . but for his own good.'" p. 110: Edward Whittier, "The Lecture of Mr. and Mrs. Uriah Clark," *The Stoneham Amateur,* June 24, 1871.

Do Planets Go Back?

"... and Jacob Henry Harter." p. 111: Peebles's early life and friendship with Harter is detailed in Joseph Osgood Barrett, *The Spiritual Pilgrim; A Biography of James M. Peebles* (Boston: William White, 1872). Jim Harter provided me with Harter's genealogical information: Jacob H. Harter, Personal Communication, August 17, 2000.

"...two years of revival preaching." p. 111: Woodward Vosburgh, ed., *Records of the Reformed Protestant Dutch Church of Herkimer, Herkimer County, N.Y.* (New York: New York Genealogical and Biographical Society, 1918), 1: 139–140. By August 1848, the Universalists were using the Dutch Reformed Church in Herkimer for their services. Harter was ordained by the Universalists in that church. See Jacob Henry Harter, "Rev. J. H. Harter, of Auburn, N.Y.," *The Religio-Philosophical Journal,* July 21, 1888.

"'...were as intolerant as the Calvinists.'" p. 112: Samuel Byron Brittan, "James M. Peebles," *Brittan's Journal,* April 1874, p. 161.

"'....but add to faith *knowledge.*'" p. 112: Barrett, *The Spiritual Pilgrim,* p. 56.

"...to him and his family." p. 113: Jacob Henry Harter, untitled notice, *The Religio-Philosophical Journal,* December 20, 1873.

"'...a fragment of humanity can be found.'" p. 113: For Peebles's letter, see James Martin Peebles, "Wails from the Universalists," *The Religio-Philosophical Journal,* February 28, 1880. For Harter's letter, see Jacob Henry Harter, "Letter," *The Banner of Light,* September 27, 1879, and Jacob Henry Harter, "Rev. J. H. Harter, of Auburn, N.Y. How He Obtained His Title, and What the Object of His Mission," *The Religio-Philosophical Journal,* July 21, 1888.

"'It is a glorious religion.'" p. 114: Emma Hardinge Britten, *Nineteenth Century Miracles; or, Spirits and Their Work in Every Country of the Earth; A Complete Historical Compendium of the Great Movement Known as "Modern Spiritualism"* (New York: William Britten, 1884), p. 547.

"...by undercutting spiritualism." p. 114: K. Paul Johnson, *The Masters Revealed: Madame Blavatsky and the Myth of the Great White Lodge* (Albany, NY: SUNY Press, 1994), pp. 75–79.

"...and find a place to address an audience." p. 114: Samuel Byron Brittan, "Spiritualism in the Life of John Murray," *The Spiritual Telegraph,* August 25, 1855.

"'...visions, dreams, prophecies, tongues, healings, &c.'" p. 115: James Martin Peebles, "Dr. Eli Ballou a Spiritualist," *The Banner of Light,* December 5, 1866.

"'...of the explorations in Babylon.'" p. 115: James Martin Peebles, "The Universalists' Creed," *The Philosophical Journal,* September 23, 1897.

"'...the arbiters of human destinies.'" p. 116: James Martin Peebles, *Seers of the Ages; Embracing Spiritualism, Past and Present; Doctrines Stated and Moral Tendencies Defined* (Boston: William White, 1869), pp. vi–vii.

"'...a Yogi, a Hierophant,' and 'a Magus.'" p. 118: Peebles traveled around the world five times, including extended trips to Egypt (where he first met Blavatsky) and to India (where he traveled with Henry Olcott). His travels and studies convinced him that India was "the birthplace of religion—the Eden—the conjugal circle of soul" and that religion had been corrupted when it traveled West. For a while, he took to calling Jesus *Christna* on the conviction that the Gospels had copied details of Krishna's story.

"'. . . and his wife a partial medium.'" p. 118: James Martin Peebles, "Western Flakes and Chippings," *The Banner of Light,* January 11, 1879.

"'. . . and hideous dogmas held by Orthodoxy.'" p. 119: James Martin Peebles, "The Decay of Universalism," *The Banner of Light,* June 19, 1880.

". . . just before his one-hundredth birthday." p. 119: A modern channeler whose spirit guide, he says, is James Peebles is described by Don and Linda Pendleton in *To Dance with Angels: An Amazing Journey to the Heart with the Phenomena Thomas Jacobson and the Great Spirit, "Dr. Peebles"* (New York: Kensington Books, 1996).

The Machinery of Spiritual Telegraphy

". . . who had become a spiritualist." p. 120: Joseph Osgood Barrett's journals, dating from 1846 to 1888, are in the archives of the State Historical Society of Wisconsin, Madison, WI.

"'. . . no language is adequate to describe.'" p. 120: Joseph Osgood Barrett, "Spiritual Experiences of J. Osgood Barrett," *The Spiritual Republic,* March 20 and April 6, 1867.

"'. . . to walk in the procession!'" p. 121: William H. Manning, "Quintessence of Bigotry," *The Banner of Progress,* October 19, 1867.

". . . to Boles's brand of Christianity." p. 122: Stevens Sanborn Jones, "Fishback and Braden Discussion," *The Religio-Philosophical Journal,* November 29, 1873. See also John Curtis Bundy, "A. J. Fishback, Love, Marriage, Divorce, Free Love," *The Religio-Philosophical Journal,* March 27, 1880; and Nathan S. Haynes, *History of the Disciples of Christ in Illinois, 1819–1914* (Cincinnati: Standard Publishing, 1915), pp. 472–473.

". . . after twelve years of ministerial work." p. 122: Joseph Osgood Barrett, "Spiritual Experiences" and "Our Excommunication from the Universalist Sect," *The Banner of Light,* June 5, 1869.

". . . and became a probate judge." p. 122: Pliny A. Durant, *Commemorative Biographical and Historical Record of Kane County, Illinois* (Chicago: Beers, Leggett, 1888), p. 508; Durant, "Passing in Review: Reminiscences of Men Who Have Lived in St. Charles," *St. Charles Chronicle,* September 25, 1903, p. 1; and Britten, *Nineteenth Century Miracles,* pp. 447–448.

"... in *The Religio-Philosophical Journal.*" p. 123: Jones was married at the time, but his wife was on an extended trip and her mental health was said to have been fragile. Juliet Severance stated from the platform, "Not only myself, but others in this house can testify that Mr. S. S. Jones, editor of the *Religio-Philosophical Journal*, does live in sexual relations, outside of legal marriage. The time is coming when these things shall be brought to light, and when individuals who denounce freedom in the social relationship, and yet are guilty of living a low sensual life, shall be comprehended": American Association of Spiritualists, *Proceedings of the Tenth Annual Convention of the American Association of Spiritualists, held at Grow's Opera Hall, Chicago, on Tuesday, Sept. 16* (Chicago: Author, 1873), pp. 95–96. For the denial, see Stevens Sanborn Jones, "The Late Free-Love Convention," *The Religio-Philosophical Journal*, October 11, 1873.

"... that she was Jones's paramour." p. 123: John Curtis Bundy, "The Assassination of Hon. S. S. Jones. Facts Developed at the Investigation by the Coroner's Jury," *The Religio-Philosophical Journal*, March 31, 1877. Thanks to Sue Jensen for copies of the reporting on the murder from *The Chicago Tribune*.

"... of the Universalists, Unitarians, and spiritualists." p. 123: Julia Schlesinger, *Workers in the Vineyard: A Review of the Progress of Spiritualism, Biographical Sketches, Lectures, Essays, and Poems* (San Francisco: Carrier Dove, 1896), p. 221.

The Annunciation of the New Age

This Earth and All Things Upon It

"'... unfolded and made of higher use.'" p. 127: New England Spiritualists' Association, *Constitution and By-Laws, List of Officers, and Address to the Public, Organized at Boston, November, 1854* (Boston: Author, 1854).

"'... can commit an infinite sin.'" p. 128: Hosea Ballou, *A Treatise on Atonement; in Which the Finite Nature of Sin Is Argued, Its Cause and Consequences as Such; the Necessity and Nature of Atonement; and Its Glorious Consequences, in the Final Reconciliation of All Men to Holiness and Happiness* (Randolph, VT: Sereno Wright, 1805), p. 64. See also Stephen A. Marini, *Radical Sects of Revolutionary New England* (Cambridge: Harvard University Press, 1982), pp. 144–148.

"'... and the society of angels!'" p. 129: James Martin Peebles, "The 'Death and Glory' System of Universalism," *The Banner of Light*, May 11, 1867. *Knowlton* presumably refers to Charles Knowlton, author of the 1833 work *Fruits of Philosophy* (published by former Universalist minister Abner Kneeland), which advocated (and vaguely described) birth control methods and thereby caused a scandal.

"'. . . of supreme felicity beyond death.'" p. 130: Woodbury Melcher Fernald, "Clairvoyant Revelations," *The Spirit Messenger,* March 15, 1851.

"'. . . of the theory of endless evil.'" p. 130: Samuel Byron Brittan, "Digest of Correspondence," *The Spiritual Telegraph,* July 3, 1854.

"'. . . subsequent state of higher development, etc.'" p. 131: Emma Hardinge Britten, *Modern American Spiritualism: A Twenty Years' Record of the Communion between Earth and the World of Spirits* (New York: Author, 1870), pp. 248, 257–261.

". . . were restorationists of a sort." p. 133: Samuel Byron Brittan, "A New Sect," *The Univercoelum and Spiritual Philosopher,* February 12, 1848.

"'. . . blessedness and peace.'" p. 133: Barnabas Hall, "Another Clergyman Convinced," *The Spiritual Telegraph,* November 8, 1856; and Culver M. Patterson, "A Clergyman's Testimony," *The Spiritual Telegraph,* August 23, 1856.

"'. . . and immaculate as its divine original.'" p. 134: Luther Colby, "Spiritualism vs. Old Theology," *The Banner of Light,* May 27, 1865.

"'. . . when he is legally discharged.'" p. 134: Sylvanus Cobb, "'Spiritualism in Milford," *The Christian Freeman and Family Visiter,* February 12, 1858.

". . . the final consummation of events." p. 135: John Stoddard, "The Human Soul. Natural and Spiritual Body." *The Trumpet and Universalist Magazine,* May 14, 1853.

"'. . . be both, a body and a spirit?'" p. 135: Compare with these words from Walt Whitman's "I Sing the Body Electric": "Was it doubted that those who corrupt their own bodies conceal themselves; / And if those who defile the living are as bad as they who defile the dead? / And if the body does not do as much as the Soul? / And if the body were not the Soul, what is the Soul?"

"'. . . and this mortal shall put on immortality.'" p. 135: Sylvanus Cobb, "Spiritualism—No. 2," *The Christian Freeman and Family Visiter,* February 26, 1858.

". . . immediately punished as a result." p. 135: William Ellery Channing, "The Evil of Sin," in *The Works of William E. Channing, D.D.* (Boston: Unitarian Association, 1886), p. 350; and Hosea Ballou, *A Treatise on Atonement,* pp. 12–60.

". . . against retribution in the afterlife." p. 136: Hosea Ballou, *A Candid Examination of Dr. Channing's Discourse on the Evil of Sin* (Boston: B. B. Mussey, 1833), pp. 4–5, and *An Examination of the Doctrine of Future Retribution; on the Principles of Morals, Analogy, and the Scriptures* (Boston: The Trumpet Office, 1834).

"'. . . a spirit world of demons and satans.'" p. 136: Sylvanus Cobb, "Br. Stoddard and Milford Spiritualism," *The Christian Freeman and Family Visiter,* February 12, 1858.

"... Davis was dictating *The Principles of Nature*." p. 136: Hosea Ballou II, "Analogy between the Present State and the Future," *The Universalist Quarterly and General Review*, April 1847, pp. 113–128.

"'... to make complaints against me.'" p. 137: Thomas W. Woodrow, "Pertinent Questions by a Universalist Minister," *The Religio-Philosophical Journal*, May 30, 1891.

"'... of his Universalist contemporaries.'" p. 137: John Curtis Bundy, "Note," *The Religio-Philosophical Journal*, June 6, 1891.

The Communion of Saints

"'... with marked displeasure.'" p. 139: Samuel Byron Brittan, "Science and Spiritualism," *The Spiritual Telegraph*, September 9, 1855.

"'... and, in regard to particulars, negative.'" p. 139: Ralph Waldo Emerson, "Swedenborg; or, The Mystic," in *Representative Men: Seven Lectures* (Boston: Phillips, Sampson, 1850), pp. 139–140.

"''... from the spirit world, began very low.''" p. 139: Alonzo Newton, "R. W. Emerson," *The Spiritual Telegraph*, August 9, 1856; Ralph Waldo Emerson, "Worship," in *The Conduct of Life* (Boston: Ticknor and Fields, 1860, rev. ed. 1876), p. 129; Emerson, *The Journals of Ralph Waldo Emerson*, ed. E. W. Emerson and W. E. Emerson Forbes (Boston: Houghton Mifflin, 1912), 8: 298–299; Samuel Byron Brittan, "R. W. Emerson and the Spiritualists," *The Spiritual Telegraph*, August 9, 1856; and John B. Wilson, "Emerson and the 'Rochester Rappings,'" *New England Quarterly* 41 (1968): 248–258.

"'... to confound the mighty?'" p. 139: Jesse Babcock Ferguson, *Spirit Communion; A Record of Communications from the Spirit-Spheres, with Incontestible Evidence of Personal Identity, Presented to the Public, with Explanatory Observations, by J. B. Ferguson* (Nashville: Union and American Steam Press, 1854), p. 7.

"'... who charged a pistareen a spasm!'" p. 140: Edwin P. Whipple, "Some Recollections of Ralph Waldo Emerson," *Harper's New Monthly Magazine* 65, no. 388 (September 1882): 582.

"'... and all the good things of the church.'" p. 140: Quoted in Uriah Clark, *A Plain Guide to Spiritualism; A Handbook for Skeptics, Inquirers, Clergymen, Believers, Lecturers*, 3rd ed. (Boston: William White, 1863), p. 30.

"'... from one of Mr. Parker's discourses.'" p. 140: "Theodore Parker Canonized," *The Washington Evening Star*, January 27, 1858.

"'... he was a believer in Spiritualism.'" p. 140: Ann Leah [Fox Fish] Underhill, *The Missing Link in Modern Spiritualism* (New York: Thomas R. Knox, 1885), p. 325.

"'. . . that remain in the world.'" p. 141: For example, Edwin Hubbell Chapin's essay on "the voices of the dead," in *The Crown of Thorns: A Token for the Sorrowing* (Boston: Abel Tomkins, 1855), pp. 223–242. Henry J. Horn stated, "The Rev. Dr. Chapin also felt more attraction in a gorgeous temple surrounded by the elite in a metropolis than to become a poorly paid advocate of an exalted philosophy": "Reminiscences of William Fishbough," *The Religio-Philosophical Journal*, July 9, 1881. Charles Partridge disputed Chapin's somewhat derogatory comments about spiritualism in "The New and the Old," *The Spiritual Telegraph*, February 9, 1856.

"'. . . with all my heart.'" p. 141: James Martin Peebles, *Seers of the Ages; Embracing Spiritualism, Past and Present; Doctrines Stated and Moral Tendencies Defined* (Boston: William White, 1869), pp. 219–220, 226.

". . . who utters the prayer." p. 141: Sumner Ellis, "Rev. John Pierpont," *Buchanan's Journal of Man*, July 1873, p. 301; Hudson Tuttle, "Biographical Sketch of John Pierpont," *The Religio-Philosophical Journal*, June 15, 1878; and Herman Snow, "A Reminiscence of Rev. John Pierpont," *The Religio-Philosophical Journal*, December 25, 1880.

". . . an ill-spent or ill-managed life." p. 142: Charles Partridge, "Spiritualism and Reform," *The Spiritual Telegraph*, March 14, 1857.

". . . waiting 'from time immemorial.'" p. 142: Underhill, *The Missing Link*, pp. 324–326.

". . . without a full hearing." p. 142: Britten, *Modern American Spiritualism*, pp. 173–185. According to Benjamin Coleman in *Spiritualism in America* (London: F. Pitman, 1861), "after the persecuting spirit" had driven Willis out of Harvard, he succumbed to a long illness and lay in bed, where he was "carefully nursed by several ladies who sympathized with him, as well as by spirits." As he lay in his third-floor bedroom, where two ladies were sitting with him, "Mr. Willis was suddenly covered with a quantity of red flowers which came through the open window, and they were gathered up by spirit hands into a bouquet, and presented to him" (p. 22).

". . . public recantation of spiritualism." p. 143: Conway, in an earlier letter to the *Manchester Guardian* (September 2, 1887), also had approved of the skeptical results published by the Seybert Commission of the University of Pennsylvania, which had studied spiritualism: John Curtis Bundy, "Conway on the 'Big Toe' Performance," *The Religio-Philosophical Journal*, November 17, 1888; and Samuel Byron Brittan, "Spiritualism. A Reply to Mr. Moncure Conway," *The Religio-Philosophical Journal*, September 17, 1887.

"'. . . admissible in Unitarian circles.'" p. 143: John Curtis Bundy, "Unitarianism. 1821–1881," *The Religio-Philosophical Journal*, June 4, 1881.

"'. . . by spiritually-minded people for eighteen centuries.'" p. 144: Clark, *A Plain Guide*, p. 29. Mayo's remarks are from his essay "Transcendentalism and Spiritualism."

"'. . . but infidels and Universalists?'" p. 145: Free Convention, *Proceedings of the Free Convention Held at Rutland, Vt., July 25th, 26th, and 27th, 1858* (Boston: J. B. Yerrinton and Son, 1858), pp. 161–162.

"'. . . from those nearest and dearest to them?'" p. 145: Free Convention, p. 102.

"'. . . spirits did communicate with mortals.'" p. 146: James Martin Peebles, "T. Starr King a Spiritualist," *The Banner of Light*, September 22, 1866.

"'. . . each atom is a thunder storm?'" p. 146: Quoted in Epes Sargent, *Planchette; or, The Despair of Science. Being a Full Account of Modern Spiritualism, Its Phenomena, and the Various Theories Regarding It. With a Survey of French Spiritism* (Boston: Roberts Brothers, 1869), pp. 215–216.

". . . based on their empirical investigations." p. 147: George Truesdell Flanders, "The Great Rationalist Craze," *The Christian Leader*, July 25, 1889, p. 2.

"'. . . claimed to be spiritual.'" p. 147: Uriah Clark, ""Universalism and Spiritualism," *The Spiritual Telegraph*, May 19, 1855.

". . . were unique and unquestionable." p. 148: For example, Samuel Byron Brittan, "Rejected Books of the New Testament," *The Spiritual Telegraph*, May 26, 1855.

"'. . . now we *know* it.'" p. 148: George Washington Gage, "Letter from Br. Gage," *The Star in the West*, September 22, 1855.

"'. . . there will be no sin.'" p. 149: Thomas Whittemore, "Immortal Mummies," *The Trumpet and Universalist Magazine*, April 23, 1853.

"'. . . the general condition of any one.'" p. 150: Samuel Byron Brittan, "History of Modern Spiritualism," in *[The Charles Desilver Firm's] Religious Denominations in the United States*, ed. Israel Daniel Rupp (New York: AMS Press, 1975; repr. 1861 ed.), pp. 632–633.

"'. . . forces and natural laws.'" p. 150: Brittan, "History of Modern Spiritualism," pp. 632–633.

Burning Out the Rubbish

". . . to carry out a revolution.)" p. 151: Timothy Messer-Kruse, *The Yankee International: Marxism and the American Reform Tradition, 1848–1876* (Chapel Hill: University of North Carolina Press, 1998), pp. 42–43.

". . . booking agent or business manager." p. 152: The following women were either mediums and influenced their fathers or husbands toward a deeper involvement with spiritualism or eager enthusiasts of their counterparts' spiritualistic endeavors: Andrew Jackson Davis's first wife, Catherine (Silona) DeWolfe Dodge, second wife, Mary Fenn Love, and third wife, Delphine (Della) Elizabeth Markham Youngs Dake; Uriah Clark's wife, Eliza; Adin Ballou's wife, Lucy Hunt, and daughter, Abigail Sayles Heywood; John Bovee Dods's daughter, Amelia Jane ("Jennie"), first wife, Mercy Ann Hodgson, and third wife, Phoebe Reybert; John Murray Spear's daughter, Sophronia Butler, and second wife, Caroline Hinckley; Sylvanus Cobb's wife, Eunice Hale; Jesse Babcock Ferguson's daughter, Virginia, and wife, Lucinda Mack; Samuel Byron Brittan's wife, Elizabeth Lyon; Joshua King Ingalls's wife, Amanda Gray; Woodbury Fernald's wife, Huldah Friend; Zephaniah Baker's wife, Frances; Thomas Lake Harris's second wife, Mary Isabella Waters, and third wife, Jane Lee Waring; Charles Hammond's wife, Sybil; Jacob Henry Harter's wife, Achsah Oatman; Simon Crosby Hewitt's wife, Delight Peck; John Allen's second wife, Ellen Lazarus; Lewis Feuilleteau Wilson Andrews's first wife, Jane, and second wife, Mary Lamar; Joseph Osgood Barrett's wife, Olive; and James Martin Peebles's wife, Mary Conkey.

". . . had possessed authority when living." p. 152: See Ann Braude, *Radical Spirits: Spiritualism and Women's Rights in Nineteenth-Century America* (Boston: Beacon Press, 1989), pp. 82–98; and Alex Owen, *The Darkened Room: Women, Power and Spiritualism in Late Nineteenth Century England* (London: Virago, 1989), pp. 4–12. On the gender issues for male spiritualists, see Bret E. Carroll, *Spiritualism in Antebellum America* (Bloomington: Indiana University Press, 1997), pp. 148–151, 168–170.

". . . for the rights of women." p. 155: Abel Charles Thomas, *Autobiography of Rev. Abel C. Thomas; Including Recollections of Persons, Incidents, and Places* (Boston: J. M. Usher, 1852), pp. 266; and Harriet Jane Hanson Robinson, *Loom and Spindle; or Life among the Early Mill Girls, with a Sketch of "The Lowell Offering" and Some of Its Contributors* (Kilaua, HI: Press Pacifica, 1976, repr. 1898 ed.), pp. 62–63.

"'. . . that impede mortals' progress to happiness.'" p. 156: H. F. M. Brown, "Ohio Correspondence," *The Christian Freeman and Family Visiter*, April 26, 1850.

"'. . . "an imposter" to the world.'" p. 156: Brown, "Ohio Correspondence," August 30, 1850.

"'. . . and from the world's people.'" p. 156: Brown, "Ohio Correspondence," April 11, 1851. See also Joel Tiffany, *Lectures on Spiritualism, Being a Series of Lectures on the Phenomena and Philosophy of Development, Individualism, Spirit, Immortality, Mesmerism, Clairvoyance, Spiritual Manifestations, Christianity, and Progress, Delivered at Prospect Street Church, in the City of Cleveland, during the Winter and Spring of 1851, by J. Tiffany* (Cleveland: Author, 1851).

"'. . . and God as a universal Father.'" p. 157: Brown, "Ohio Correspondence," July 18, 1851.

"'. . . lose a subscriber thereby.'" p. 157: Brown, "Ohio Correspondence," January 14, 1853.

"'. . . flowed from her heart and head.'" p. 157: Warren Chase, "Berlin Heights, Ohio. The Convention and the Spiritualists," *The Banner of Light,* September 10, 1859.

"'. . . decide their matters for them.'" p. 158: William Denton, "The Grand Jubilee at Ravenna, Ohio," *The Vanguard,* August 8, 1857.

". . . perceived as appropriate for children)." p. 158: H. F. M. Brown, *Sketches from Nature, for My Juvenile Friends,* 2nd ed. (Cleveland: Author, 1860), and *The Christmas Annual* (Cleveland: E. Cowles, 1860).

". . . her own marital difficulties." p. 158: H. F. M. Brown, *The False and True Marriage: The Reason and Results,* 2nd ed. (Cleveland: Viets and Savage, 1861).

". . . reporting them in *The Religio-Philosophical Journal.*" p. 159: H. F. M. Brown, "The Annual Festival of the Religio-Philosophical Society," *The Religio-Philosophical Journal,* August 26, 1865.

". . . lecturing in California, Utah, and Oregon." p. 159: H. F. M. Brown, "California—Its Ways and Workers," in *The Year-Book of Spiritualism for 1871,* ed. Hudson Tuttle and J. M. Peebles (Boston: William White, 1871), pp. 120–124.

". . . called *children's lyceums.*" p. 159: H. F. M. Brown, *Our Children* (Boston: William White, 1873), a collection of literature and poetry for children.

". . . and the demon will forsake the field." p. 160: H. F. M. Brown, "The Santa Barbara Lyceum," *The Banner of Light,* April 26, 1879.

". . . of the ultimate salvation of all." p. 160: E. "Miss Gibson, the Medium," *The Banner of Light,* December 4, 1858.

". . . with her husband and then worked independently." p. 161: Examples of Ella Gibson Hobart working for and preaching to the troops on the subject of moral purity are provided in *The Soldier's Gift: The Dangers and Temptations of Army Life* (Chicago: Tribune Press, 1863) and *Pledge and Signatures of the Temperance Army Corps* (Madison, WI: Atwood and Rublee, 1864).

". . . radical changes to society." p. 161: See "Woman's Kingdom, Foundation of a New Empire to Be Governed by Females," *The Chicago Tribune,* August 22, 1868. The most well-known spiritualist advocate of women's superiority over men was Eliza Woodson Farnham, whose extended essay on this subject was published by Andrew Jackson Davis after her death. See Eliza Farnham, *Woman and Her Era* (New York: A. J. Davis, 1864).

The Hierophant of Hopedale

"'. . . religion and reason must be married.'" p. 162: Quoted in Clark, *A Plain Guide,* p. 191.

"'. . . the study of human consciousness.'" p. 163: George Ripley, "Martineau's Rationale," from an 1836 article in *The Christian Examiner,* in *The Transcendentalists: An Anthology,* ed. Perry Miller (Cambridge, MA: Harvard University Press, 1950), p. 132.

"'. . . to establish a *new* sect.'" p. 163: Samuel Byron Brittan, "Spiritualism Not Sectarian," *The Spiritual Telegraph,* March 7, 1857.

"'. . . and with clear, wide open eyes.'" p. 164: Reprinted by Garrison in *The Liberator;* see Esther Ann Lukens, "Visit to Hopedale," *The Liberator,* August 8, 1851.

"'And his rest shall be glorious.'" p. 164: Adin Ballou, "J. M. Spear at Hopedale," *The Practical Christian,* July 17, 1852.

"'It is all of the devil!'" p. 164: Adin Ballou, *An Exposition of Views Reflecting the Principal Facts, Causes and Peculiarities Involved in Spirit Manifestations* (Boston: Bela Marsh, 1853), p. 89.

". . . to enter the ministry." p. 164: Adin Ballou, *Autobiography of Adin Ballou, 1803–1890: Containing an Elaborate Record and Narrative of His Life from Infancy to Old Age,* ed. William S. Heywood (Lowell, MA: Vox Populi, 1896), pp. 61–63.

". . . messages from the dead son." p. 165: Ballou collected and published these communications via Reed in *An Exposition of Views.*

". . . a spiritualist convention in Worcester, Massachusetts." p. 165: "Convention of Believers in Spiritual Manifestations," *The Massachusetts Spy,* October 6, 1852.

"'. . . method in their madness.'" p. 165: Henry Jarvis Raymond, "The Spiritual Convention," *The New York Times,* September 23, 1852.

". . . for a society of spiritualists in Milford." p. 165: Adin Ballou, *Autobiography,* p. 409.

No Eternity So Dark

". . . Universalist physician Benjamin Rush." p. 167: Julia Schlesinger, "Mrs. Cora L. V. Richmond," *The Carrier Dove,* August 1886.

". . . Cora L. V. Scott Hatch Daniels Tappan Richmond." p. 167: The initials *L. V.* are variously reported as standing for *Linn Victoria* or *Lodencia Veronica.*

"'. . . children away from them.'" p. 167: Cora L. V. Hatch, *A Discourse on the Immutable Decrees of God, and the Free Agency of Man, Delivered in the City Hall, Newburyport, Mass., Sunday, November 22d, 1857* (New York: B. F. Hatch, 1858), p. 23.

". . . better of the other in the exchange." p. 167: Charles Partridge, "Spirits Discussing with Learned Doctors," *The Spiritual Telegraph*, April 11, 1857.

"'. . . but with the living.'" p. 168: "Spiritualism and Theology. The Challenge to the Clergy Accepted by Two Learned Doctors," *The New-England Spiritualist*, April 25, 1857.

". . . was raised a Universalist." p. 168: William Emmette Coleman, "Grand Dual Celebration of the 32nd Anniversary of Modern Spiritualism in San Francisco, California," *The Religio-Philosophical Journal*, April 24, 1880.

". . . afterlife progress of the minister's spirit." p. 168: Mark Twain [Samuel Clemens], "Mark Twain a Committee Man," *Territorial Enterprise*, February 16, 1866. See also Benjamin Todd, "Mrs. Foye's Seances in Virginia, Nevada," *The Banner of Progress*, November 23, 1867.

"'. . . confirmation of their origin.'" p. 168: Harrison Delivan Barrett, *Life Work of Mrs. Cora L. V. Richmond* (Chicago: Hack and Anderson, 1895), pp. 39–43. Barrett was born in 1863 in Canaan, Maine. He graduated from the Meadville Theological School in 1869 but was not ordained because he had become a strong believer in spiritualism by then. He became a spiritualist lecturer and in 1893 co-founded the National Spiritualist Association, also serving as its first president. In 1897, he became editor of *The Banner of Light*.

"'. . . were divinely authoritative.'" p. 168: Adin Ballou, *Autobiography*, p. 462.

". . . range of opinion on the subject." p. 169: Samuel Byron Brittan, "Schism," *The Spiritual Telegraph*, November 29, 1856.

Laboring for the New Era

". . . John Murray's First Universalist Society." p. 170: Short accounts of John Murray Spear's life are provided by the following sources: John Murray Spear, *Messages from the Superior State; Communicated by John Murray, through John M. Spear, in the Summer of 1852; Containing Important Instructions to the Inhabitants of the Earth; Carefully Prepared for Publication, with a Sketch of the Author's Earthly Life, and a Brief Description of the Spiritual Experience of the Medium*, ed. Simon Crosby Hewitt (Boston: Bela Marsh, 1852), introduction; John Murray Spear, *The Educator; Beings Suggestions, Theoretical and Practical, Designed to Promote Man-Culture and Integral Reform, with a View to the Ultimate Establishment of a Divine Social State on Earth; Comprised in a Series of Revealments from Organized Associations in the Spirit-Life, through John Murray Spear*, ed. Alonzo Eliot Newton (Boston: Office of Practical Spiritualists, 1857), introduction, written by Hannah Frances Morrill Brown on his commission from the spirits; John Murray Spear,

Twenty Years on the Wing; A Brief Narrative of My Travels and Labors as a Mission-ary Sent Forth and Sustained by the Association of Beneficents in Spirit Land (Boston: William White, 1873); and Adin Ballou, *An Exposition of Views.* Spear's activities connected with the establishment of the Kiantone community and through the Civil War can be traced through the Sheldon Papers collected by Spear associate Thaddeus Spencer Sheldon and held by the University of Pitts-burgh. Sources for information about his prespiritualist period include the news-paper he published with his brother, Charles, *The Hangman* (later, *The Prisoner's Friend*), which includes annual reports he issued to his patrons on his solitary philanthropic activities. A preliminary effort at a biography is Neil Burkhart Lehman, "The Life of John Murray Spear: Spiritualism and Reform in Antebellum America" (Ph.D. Dissertation, Ohio State University, 1973).

"... to become a public speaker." p. 171: John Murray Spear, "Verification of a Mes-sage." *The Banner of Light,* September 4, 1880.

"... had brought her along from Virginia." p. 171: Kathryn Grover, *The Fugitive's Gibraltar: Escaping Slaves and Abolitionism in New Bedford, Massachusetts* (Amherst: University of Massachusetts Press, 2001), pp. 160–167.

"... facing the doctor." p. 172: Theodore K. Taylor, *The Pocket Physician, or Domes-tic Medical Advisor; Designed for Both Married and Single, Containing Valuable Hints upon the Preservation of Health and the Causes, Symptoms and Treatment of the Most Common and Obstinate Diseases Which Affect Humanity* (Boston: n.p., 1852), p. 103. Taylor listed Spear as a personal reference.

"... *The Spirit Messenger and Harmonial Guide.*" p. 172: Richard Eddy, *Universal-ism in America. A History* (Boston: Universalist Publishing House, 1886), 2: 454. For examples of the subjects of Russell Perkins Ambler's prespiritualist articles in the Universalist press, see the following: "Rationalism *versus* Miracles," *The Uni-versalist Quarterly and General Review* 5 (1849): 68; and "Christianity Contrasted with Other Systems," *The Universalist Quarterly and General Review* 7 (1851): 431.Works published after Ambler's turn to spiritualism include *The Spiritual Teacher; Comprising a Series of Twelve Lectures on the Nature and Development of the Spirit; Written by Spirits of the Sixth Circle* (New York: Author, 1852); *Elements of Spiritual Philosophy; Being an Exposition of Interior Principles; Written by Spirits of the Sixth Circle* (Springfield, MA: Author, 1852); and *The Birth of the Universe; Being a Philosophical Exposition of the Origin, Unfoldings and Ultimate of Creation; by and through R. P. Ambler* (New York: Harmonial Association, 1853).

"'... onward to an exalted destiny.'" p. 172: Russell Perkins Ambler, "The Mission of the Reformer," *The Spirit Messenger,* December 28, 1850.

"... peace in the next life." p. 173: John Murray Spear, ""Words of Comfort," *The Spirit Messenger*, August 16, 1851; and London Dialectical Society, *Report on Spiritualism of the Committee of the London Dialectical Society, Together with the Evidence, Oral and Written, and a Selection from the Correspondence* (London, England: J. Burns, 1873), p. 137.

"... naturalistic explanations for miracles." p. 174: John Prince, *Eight Historical and Critical Lectures on the Bible* (Boston: Abel Tompkins, 1846).

"'... is calculated to give.'" p. 174: Simon Crosby Hewitt, "Melodeon Meeting," *The New-England Spiritualist*, May 5, 1855.

"... nor were they necessarily benevolent." pp. 175–176: Many former Methodists could be found among spiritualists. Some of them had first passed through Universalism before moving on to spiritualism. A few Methodist clergy became spiritualist leaders and lecturers. The careers of several of them, including LaRoy Sunderland, are detailed in Ann Taves, *Fits, Trances & Visions: Experiencing Religion and Explaining Experience from Wesley to James* (Princeton, NJ: Princeton University Press, 1999). Taves follows an interesting thread that connects the ecstatic states of consciousness for which revivals became famous with the trance states common in spiritualism. The liberal denominations, however, were more conducive to spiritualists, partly because spiritualism was universally optimistic about the progress of individual souls after death. Spiritualists often wrote about revivals, criticizing their antirationalistic tone and their appeal to base instinct. Universalists and Unitarians criticized revivals on the same grounds. See "Methodistic Madness Contrasted with Spritualist Sanity," in Andrew Jackson Davis, *Mental Disorders; or, Diseases of the Brain and Nerves, Developing the Origin and Philosophy of Mania, Insanity, and Crime, with Full Direction for Their Treatment and Cure* (Boston: William White, 1871), pp. 209–215; and "Spiritualism at the Methodist Camp Meetings," in Aaron Stevens Hayward, *Nature's Laws in Human Life: An Exposition in Spiritualism; Embracing the Various Opinions of Extremists, Pro and Con; Together with the Author's Experience* (Boston: William White, 1872), pp. 153–157.

"... with her husband, Nathaniel." p. 176: Frances E. Hyer, "Louisiana," *The Banner of Light*, February 10, 1872.

"'... interposition of any foreign agency.'" p. 177: Sylvanus Cobb, "Spiritualism— No. 8," *The Christian Freeman and Family Visiter*, April 9, 1858. Cobb printed a couple of the "spirit of Murray" lectures under the title "The New Era; or Heaven Opened to Man" in *The Christian Freeman*, submitted by Simon Crosby Hewitt, but balked at printing them all.

"'... which you at all times need.'" p. 177: Spear, *Messages from the Superior State*, pp. 166–167.

". . . wrote a positive introduction to it." p. 178: John Murray Spear, *Twelve Discourses on Government; Purporting to Have Been Delivered in Boston, Mass., December, 1853, by Thomas Jefferson, of the Spirit World, through John M. Spear, Medium* (Hopedale, MA: Community Press, 1853). The Boston Public Library has Theodore Parker's copy of the pamphlet.

". . . 'in strophe and antistrophe':" p. 178: Frank Podmore, *Modern Spiritualism; A History and a Criticism* (London, England: Methuen, 1902), 2: 275. Spear's spirit guides delivered plans in many areas—health, education, government—but the Electricizers' plans are the ones described here.

"'. . . correspondingly with the population.'" p. 179: "True Creation," *The Boston Investigator,* August 23, 1863.

"'. . . it did not come sooner.'" p. 180: Simon Crosby Hewitt, "The New Motive Power, or Electrical Motor, Otherwise Called 'Perpetual Motion,'" *The New Era,* June 28, 1854.

"'. . . and harmonization of the world.'" p. 180: Adin Ballou, "Modern Spiritualism—Its Good and Evil," *The Spiritual Telegraph,* September 30, 1854, and December 16, 1854.

". . . in and out of people's pockets." p. 181: All these examples are taken from just one of Brittan's reports in "Wonders of Spiritualism," *The Spiritual Telegraph,* April 21, 1855.

"'. . . than he now does steam.'" p. 181: Reprinted from *The Spiritual Telegraph* in Britten, *Modern American Spiritualism,* p. 229.

". . . constructed a tiny settlement." p. 182: Oliver F. Chase, "The Kiantone Movement," in *Centennial History of Chautauqua County* (Jamestown, NY: Chautauqua History Company, 1904), 2: 827–830; Russell Duino, "Utopian Theme with Variations: John Murray Spear and His Kiantone Domain," *Pennsylvania History,* April 1962, pp. 140–150; Ernest C. Miller, "Utopian Communities in Warren County, Pennsylvania," *Western Pennsylvania Historical Magazine* 49 (October 1966): 301–317; and Lehman, pp. 206–288.

". . . receive, store, and transmit thoughts." p. 182: Spear, *The Educator,* pp. 248–249; and Samuel Byron Brittan, "The Spiritualist Convention in New York City," *The Spiritual Age,* June 13, 1857.

". . . the *soul-blending telegraph.*" p. 182: Spear, *The Educator,* pp. 328–329, 531–532; and "The Soul-Blending Telegraph," *The New York Tribune,* August 18, 1854.

"'. . . and the curtain fell.'" p. 182: Order of the Patriarchs, *Experience of Mrs. H. F. M. Brown with the Pschycosmon, Published by Request, and Read before the Patriarchal Order; to Which Is Appended Notes of Explanation, by Daniel Gano* (Cincinnati, OH, 1856, William Ashton Papers, Lilly Library, Indiana University, Bloomington, IN), pp. 3–5.

"... stateroom, engine room, and bridge." p. 183: David Densmore, *The Halo: An Autobiography of D. C. Densmore* (Boston: Voice of Angels, 1876), pp. 282–284; Spear, *The Educator*, pp. 252, 676, 679; and Brittan, "The Spiritualist Convention in New York City."

"'... from and to eternities!'" p. 184: Simon Crobsy Hewitt, "The Picture Gallery of the Universe," *The Agitator*, February 1, 1859.

"... that would enrich human life." p. 184: Amanda Theodocia Jones, *A Psychic Autobiography* (New York: Greaves Publishing, 1910), pp. 16–17, 137, 297–298, 338–341.

"'... combination of outward parts.'" p. 184: William Francis Channing, *The American Fire-Alarm Telegraph: A Lecture Delivered before the Smithsonian Institution, March, 1855* (Boston: Redding, 1855), pp. 3–4, 6.

"... the ringing of alarm bells)." p. 186: William Francis Channing, *The Municipal Electric Telegraph, Especially in Its Application to Fire Alarms* (New Haven, CT: B. L. Hamlen, 1852), pp. 4–5.

"... receiving guidance on its design." p. 186: Herman Snow [pseudonym "Ex-Clericus"], "Life with the Spirits," *The Religio-Philosophical Journal*, March 13 and April 10, 1880.

"... in 1816 in Sutton, Massachusetts." p. 186: Town marriage records, Wrentham, Massachusetts; and Virginia Hewitt Watterson, *Thomas Hewett of Hingham, Massachusetts and His Descendants* (Carlsbad, CA: Author, 1998), pp. 42, 88–89.

"... Massachusetts, Rhode Island, and Connecticut." p. 187: Simon Crosby Hewitt's journal, as he sent it in installments to *The Mechanic*, the weekly paper published by the Fall River organizers, can be found in Philip S. Foner, "Journal of an Early Labor Organizer," *Labor History* 10 (Spring 1969): 205–227.

"... free thought and philosophical materialism." p. 187: "Letter from Our New Boston Correspondent," *The Religio-Philosophical Journal*, April 3, 1875.

"... the kingdom of God on Earth." p. 187: Simon Crosby Hewitt's letters to *The Fall River Mechanic*, in which he described his goal of establishing on Earth the pattern of the kingdom of God, are described in Jama Lazerow, *Religion and the Working Class in Antebellum America* (Washington, DC: Smithsonian Institution Press, 1995), p. 142. Other Universalist ministers involved in the labor movement who turned to spiritualism included John Bovee Dods, John Allen, Joshua King Ingalls, Samuel Byron Brittan, and John Murray Spear. Mill workers who were radicalized by their labor experiences and wound up on the spiritualist platform included Hannah Frances Morrill Brown, Frances Harriet Greene McDougall, and Ella Elvira Gibson Hobart (among those considered here).

"...sometimes preaching and lecturing." p. 187: Simon Crosby Hewitt's *The King-dom of Heaven at Hand* was delivered there as a sermon: *The Kingdom of Heaven at Hand* (Hopedale, MA: Hopedale Community Press, 1850).

"'...of the kingdom of Heaven on earth.'" p. 188: Samuel Byron Brittan, "The Late Spiritual Convention," *The Spiritual Telegraph*, October 14, 1854.

"'...by the power of John M. Spear!'" p. 189: Henry Wickliffe, *Rappo-Mania Over-thrown: in Two Parts. Part First. The Christian Religion Triumphant, or, the Scrip-tures, Reason, Philosophy, Common-Sense and Religion Vindicated against the Claims of the "Spiritual" Rappers* (Boston: Fowlers & Welles, 1853), pp. 57–58, 85.

"'...highly important to mankind?'" p. 190: Alonzo Newton, untitled editorial, *The New-England Spiritualist*, May 19, 1856.

"'...John M. Spear will receive.'" p. 190: Andrew Jackson Davis, "A. J. Davis' Third Lecture at the Melodeon," *The New-England Spiritualist*, May 19, 1855.

"...a new age on Earth." p. 191: Simon Crosby Hewitt, "Architecture of the Fu-ture—Designs for Homes of Harmony, Transmitted from the Spirit World," *The Millennial Gazette*, July 1, 1856, pp. 3–12.

"...Rockport, Watertown, and Sterling, Massachusetts." p. 192: Eddy, *Universalism in America*, p. 256.

"...and for women's rights." p. 192: John Allen, *An Address, Delivered before the Washington Total Abstinence Society, of Rockport, February 22nd, 1842, by John Allen; Published by the Society* (Salem, MA: Salem Gazette, 1842).

"...when George Ripley was its president." p. 192: John Allen, "To the Friends of Social Reform," *The Liberator*, January 3, 1844.

"...edit its newspaper, *The Harbinger*." p. 193: John Allen reported his lecture tours in *The Harbinger*. See, for example, "Letter from Vermont," *The Harbinger*, March 7, 1845, describing his and John Orvis's stop at John Humphrey Noyes's community at Putney. See also "Capital, Its Rights," *The Harbinger*, July 31, 1847, and "Prospects in Western New York," *The Harbinger*, October 23, 1847.

"...through his work in Fourierism." p. 193: John Allen, "Committee of Thirteen," *The Harbinger*, August 7, 1847.

"...a few miles away on the Ohio River." p. 193: John Allen, "John Allen's Lectures in Cincinnati," *The Harbinger*, March–May 1848, and "The Seventh of April in Cincinnati: The First Festival of Association," *The Harbinger*, May 6, 1848.

"...in an 'age of discord.'" p. 194: Obituaries for John Allen appeared in *The Agita-tor* on November 1, 1858; *The Spiritual Age* on November 20, 1858; and *The New York Tribune* on October 23, 1858. For the postmortem communication from Allen, see also *The Agitator* on January 15, 1859.

Amen, Saith My Soul

". . . headed by Alexander Campbell." p. 195: Henry Leo Boles, *Biographical Sketches of Gospel Preachers, Including the Pioneer Preachers of the Restoration Movement and Many Other Preachers through Decades down to the Present Generation Who Have Passed to Their Reward* (Nashville: Gospel Advocate, 1932), pp. 186–191; Thomas Low Nichols, *Supramundane Facts in the Life of Rev. Jesse Babcock Ferguson, A.M., LL.D., Including Twenty Years' Observation of Preternatural Phenomena* (London, England: Spiritual Lyceum, 1865); and Johnny Tucker, *Like a Meteor across the Horizon: The Jesse B. Ferguson Story, by Johnny Tucker; History and True Position of the Church of Christ in Nashville, by Tolbert Fanning, et al.* (Fayetteville, TN: Tucker Publications, 1978).

". . . his wife, Lucinda, and daughter, Virginia." p. 195: Jesse Babcock Ferguson, *Divine Illumination. Discourse on the Ministry of Angels: The Idea of Endless Wrong an Abomination: Self-Knowledge the Knowledge of Spiritual Communion: Immortality Is Life in God: Melchisidek or Divinity in Man: God Will Teach His Creatures* (Nashville: J. F. Morgan, 1855), and *Spirit Communion; A Record of Communications from the Spirit-Spheres, with Incontestible Evidence of Personal Identity, Presented to the Public, with Explanatory Observations, by J. B. Ferguson* (Nashville: Union and American Steam Press, 1854).

"'. . . will be granted to all.'" p. 196: Joseph Rodes Buchanan, "Thirty-First Anniversary of the Advent of Modern Spiritualism," *The Banner of Light,* April 12, 1879.

"'. . . to the contrary notwithstanding.'" p. 196: This letter of Charles Shehane is quoted in Samuel Byron Brittan, "Rev. C. F. R. Shehane, a Spiritualist," *The Spiritual Telegraph,* June 2, 1855, from *The Universalist Herald.* Ferguson kept transcripts of these séances and reported them in a series of articles entitled "Spiritualism in Nashville, Tenn."

". . . the impending Northern aggression." p. 196: Alexander Campbell, "Elder J. B. Ferguson," *The Millennial Harbinger,* 1854, pp. 54–55; "Mr. Jesse B. Ferguson," *The Millennial Harbinger,* 1854, pp. 222–223; "Jesse B. Ferguson," *The Millennial Harbinger,* 1854, pp. 412–414; "Elder J. B. Ferguson's Relation of Pastor and People— No. 1," *The Millennial Harbinger,* 1854, pp. 563–568; and "The Fall of Mr. J. B. Ferguson," *The Millennial Harbinger,* 1856, pp. 636–640.

". . . little support for the idea." p. 197: Jesse Babcock Ferguson, *The Times! or, The Flag of Truce; Dedicated to the Cabinets at Washington and Richmond, by a White Republican* (Richmond, VA: Ritchie and Dunnavant, 1863).

". . . suffered as a result." p. 197: Jesse Babcock Ferguson's testimonial for the Davenports' integrity and honesty forms the last chapter of Thomas Low Nichols, *A Biography of the Brothers Davenport; with Some Account of the Physical and*

Psychical Phenomena Which Have Occurred in Their Presence, in America and Europe (London, England: Saunders, Otley, and Company, 1864).

"...messages from Spear's spirit guides." p. 197: Jesse Babcock Ferguson, *Nationality versus Sectionalism. An Estimate of the Political Crisis, the Policy of the President, and the Anomalous Legislation of the Thirty-Ninth Congress, with an Appeal to the People on the Duties and Dangers of the Hour* (Washington, DC: McGill and Witherow, 1866). For the connections with John Murray Spear, see the letters of Caroline Spear from England in the Sheldon Papers at the University of Pittsburgh. See also "Farewell Address and Testimonial to Dr. Ferguson," *The Spiritual Magazine,* June 1865, pp. 328–329, and "Experiences of the Rev. Dr. Ferguson," *The Spiritual Magazine,* June 1865, pp. 333–335.

"... a pilgrim into spiritualism." p. 197: Orson Squires Fowler, "Lewis F. W. Andrews, Biography and Phrenological Character," *American Phrenological Journal,* October 1858, pp. 550–557.

"... in Kentucky, Ohio, and Pennsylvania." p. 198: Correspondence between father and son: Lewis Feuilleteau Wilson Andrews, *Presbyterianism vs. Universalism, or, A Theological Correspondence between Rev. John Andrews, Presbyterian, and Dr. L. F. W. Andrews, Universalist* (Cincinnati: Williamson and Cantwell, 1879).

"... The Two Opinions, or, Salvation and Damnation." p. 198: Lewis Feuilleteau Wilson Andrews, *The Two Opinions; or, Salvation and Damnation* (Macon, GA: Author, 1837).

"... from the North to visit." p. 198: Britten, *Modern American Spiritualism,* pp. 430–434.

"... another newspaper, *The Christian Spiritualist.*" p. 198: I have been unable to locate a copy. This newspaper is to be differentiated from *The Christian Spiritualist* that was published in New York City.

"... regarded in the South as a threat." p. 198: Robert W. Delp, "The Southern Press and the Rise of American Spiritualism, 1847–1860," *Journal of American Culture* 7 (Fall 1984): 88–95.

Women's Power Over the Future of the Race

"... on Puget Sound in Washington State." p. 200: Charles Pierce LeWarne, *Utopias on Puget Sound, 1885–1915,* 2nd ed. (Seattle: University of Washington Press, 1995), pp. 183–184, 189.

"'... the bondage of church teachings.'" p. 200: An autobiographical essay by Waisbrooker can be found in Julia Schlesinger, *Workers in the Vineyard: A Review of the Progress of Spiritualism, Biographical Sketches, Lectures, Essays, and Poems* (San Francisco: Carrier Dove, 1896), pp. 115–117.

"... of the best of the race." p. 200: For the Order of the Patriarchs, see Britten, *Modern American Spiritualism*, pp. 362–364; John Shoebridge Williams, *The Patriarchal Order, or True Brotherhood; the Time, Place and Manner of Its Marvelous Commencement, Its Rapid Progress, Its Rare Beauties, and Its Exalted Usefulness. With an Account of an Abortive Attempt to Degrade and Expel the Writer, in which the Would-be Expellers Became the Expelled. Also, a Proposition to Re-establish the Order upon a Better Basis, and upon More Purely Patriarchal Principles* (Cincinnati: Longley Brothers, 1855); David Quinn ["A Citizen of Ohio"], *Interior Causes of the War; the Nation Demonised, and Its President a Spirit-Rapper* (New York: M. Doolady, 1863); and Order of the Patriarchs, *Complaint of Eliza J. Kenny against John M. Spear* (Cincinnati, August 1, 1858; broadside in Adin Ballou, Scrapbook, Boston Public Library; and in William Ashton Papers, Lilly Library, Indiana University, Bloomington, IN). For the Sacred Order of Unionists, see Britten, *Modern American Spiritualism*, pp. 234–239, and documents from 1858–1863 in John Murray Spear, Papers, in the [Thaddeus Spencer] Sheldon Papers, Darlington Memorial Library, University of Pittsburgh.

"... of failure and foolishness." p. 201: Spear, *Twenty Years on the Wing*, p. 17.

"'... the ultimate wretchedness thence inevitably resulting.'" p. 201: Adin Ballou, "Modern Spiritualism—Its Good and Evil"; also reprinted in *The New Era*, September 6, 1854.

"... from the spirit world." p. 202: The spirits dictated the procedures in a series of papers in April 1861: "Of Reconstruction," "Of the Order of an Unfolding," "Of Miniatures," "Of the Hand," "Of Sleep," "Personal Preparations for Constructive Labors," "Preliminaries," "Program of Labors at the Implementist's Shop," "Order of Procedures," "Of Repulsion," "Of Practical Steps to be Taken by the Implementist." All are collected in Spear, Papers.

"... their well-kept industrial secrets." p. 202: "Of the Russian Iron," March 21, 1863, Spear, Papers.

"... reproductive rights and alternative medicine." p. 203: See John Benedict Buescher, "More Lurid than Lucid: The Spiritualist Invention of the Word *Sexism*," *Journal of the American Academy of Religion* 7, no. 3 (September 2002): 561–592.

"'... reformers and benefactors of mankind.'" p. 205: Daniel Eddy, "The New Jersey Free Love Convention," *The Religio-Philosophical Journal*, April 10, 1875.

"'... will best express its appearance." p. 205: Epes Sargent, *The Proof Palpable of Immortality; Being an Account of the Materialization Phenomena of Modern Spiritualism. With Remarks on the Relations of the Facts to Theology, Morals, and Religion* (Boston: Colby and Rich, 1876), pp. 121–122.

Coming Events Cast Their Shadows Before

"'. . . and day no night.'" p. 207: Luther Colby, "R. P. Ambler at Dodworth's Hall, New York. Sunday Evening, December 12th," *The Banner of Light*, December 25, 1858.

"'. . . no name or limit.'" p. 208: Sylvanus Cobb, "Notice of Extending Fellowship to R. P. Ambler," *The Christian Freeman and Family Visiter*, January 24, 1862; R. P. Ambler, "Letter from R. P. Ambler," *The Christian Freeman and Family Visiter*, February 21, 1862; and James Steven Loveland, "Rev. R. P. Ambler, a Protest," *The Christian Freeman and Family Visiter*, February 7, 1862. See also Herman B. Storer, "R. P. Ambler," *The Banner of Light*, April 12, 1863.

". . . a Universalist Society in Philadelphia, Pennsylvania." p. 208: John Curtis Bundy, "Editorial Notes of Travel Continued," *The Religio-Philosophical Journal*, March 13, 1880.

"'. . . in the mountains of Pennsylvania." p. 208: Warren Chase, *Forty Years on the Spiritual Rostrum* (Boston: Colby and Rich, 1888), p. 42.

"'. . . R. P. Ambler; that's *all!*'" p. 208: James Martin Peebles, "'The Gospel Banner,' Again, and Universalism," *The Banner of Light*, January 12, 1867. But Orlando Miller, pastor of the First Universalist Society of Nashua, New Hampshire, "after having been a Medium for eleven years," wrote to *The Christian Freeman and Family Visiter* in February 1862 to declare spiritualism "a Humbug." See "A Repentant Miller," *Vanity Fair*, February 22, 1862, p. 98; and Orlando Dana Miller, *Har-Moad; or The Mountain of the Assembly; A Series of Archaeological Studies Chiefly from the Standpoint of the Cuneiform Inscriptions* (North Adams, MA: S. M. Whipple, 1892), pp. xi–xviii.

"'. . . heaped abuse on my head.'" p. 209: London Dialectical Society, p. 36.

". . . and then with that of Danvers." p. 210: Cephas B. Lynn, Ministers' Files, Manuscripts Division, Andover-Harvard Theological Library.

"'. . . than walking on crutches.'" p. 210: American Association of Spiritualists, *Proceedings of the Tenth Annual Convention of the American Association of Spiritualists, held at Grow's Opera Hall, Chicago, on Tuesday, Sept. 16* (Chicago: Author, 1873), p. 30.

"'. . . many Spiritualists, and *knows* it.'" p. 211: James Martin Peebles, "The Universalist Denomination," *The Banner of Light*, June 5, 1869.

"'. . . it refused the call of the spirit.'" p. 211: James Martin Peebles, "The Decay of Universalism," *The Banner of Light*, June 19, 1880.

"'. . . and use it wisely.'" p. 212: John Curtis Bundy, "Universalists Marching On," *The Religio-Philosophical Journal*, September 28, 1889.

"'. . . and laboring for their overthrow.'" p. 213: Fletcher Wilson, "Universalism and Spiritualism. A Communication from a Universalist Minister," *The Religio-Philosophical Journal*, September 12, 1885.

"'. . . and like those of our own day.'" p. 214: John Curtis Bundy, "Universalism—What It Has Done and Can Do," *The Religio-Philosophical Journal*, February 13, 1886.

". . . and *Self Healing through Suggestion.*)" p. 214: American Society for Psychical Research, *Proceedings of the American Society for Psychical Research* (Boston: Author, July 1885), pp. 1–4, 52–54. Minot Savage influenced many Unitarian clergy to adopt a stance of open-ended but intense curiosity about investigations of the afterlife. See, for example, Seth Curtis Beach, "A Masterly Sermon. Delivered by the Rev. Seth Curtis Beach in Bangor on Sunday. Subject, 'Life Beyond Death.' Is the Title of the Great Book Written by Dr. Minot J. Savage. Large Congregation in the United Church Listened with Great Interest to the Words of an Able Bangor Preacher," *The Bangor Daily Whig and Courier*, February 12, 1900. For an example of Henry Harrison Brown's Petersham sermons, see "Man Is Spirit!: An Anniversary Address Delivered at Springfield, Mass., March 31st," *The Religio-Philosophical Journal*, April 28, 1888.

"'. . . of partial and of full sympathizers.'" p. 214: Herman Snow, "Boston Spiritualism—The Unitarians," *The Religio-Philosophical Journal*, January 8, 1887.

"'. . . with their Evangelical friends.'" p. 215: John Curtis Bundy, "Unitarians and Spiritualists—Hon. R. A. Dague's Plea," *The Religio-Philosophical Journal*, January 11, 1890.

". . . from spiritualism, Universalism, and Unitarianism." p. 215: John Curtis Bundy, "Church of the Spirit," *The Religio-Philosophical Journal*, March 22, 1890; Bundy, "Unitarianism and Spiritualism," *The Religio-Philosophical Journal*, May 29, 1886; M. C. Seecey, "The New Universalism," *The Religio-Philosophical Journal*, March 29, 1890; and Ahaz Nicholas Alcott, "Church of the Spirit. One Great Advantage Which Spiritualists Enjoy for Organizing Such a Church," *The Religio-Philosophical Journal*, March 22, 1890.

"'. . . in the light of the new morning.'" p. 218: Cora L. V. Richmond, "The Dawn of the New Age," *The Philosophical Journal*, May 27, 1897.

"'. . . *The New Era* back in 1854." p. 218: Wickliffe, p. 14.

Acknowledgments

I WOULD LIKE TO THANK Peter Hughes of the Unitarian Universalist Historical Society. The online Dictionary of Unitarian and Universalist Biography, which he edits, originally inspired me to pull together the material for this book. He has been unfailingly interested in my research and helpful in pointing me to appropriate sources, answering questions about theological issues in nineteenth-century Universalism, and commenting on an early draft of the manuscript.

I also thank John Hurley of the Unitarian Universalist Association and others of the UU Historical Society, who made it possible for me to travel to Cambridge to give a talk and spend a few days doing research at the Andover-Harvard Theological Library. I thank them also for their hospitality, their good humor, and their kind interest in what I had found. I also thank Mary Benard, my indefatigable editor at Skinner House Books, and Susan Freese and her editorial staff at Communicáto, Ltd.

For their help with their research collections, I thank Tracy Arcaro of the Rare Book and Special Collections Division of the Library of Congress, Frances O'Donnell and Cliff Wunderlich of the Manuscripts and Archives Division of the Andover-Harvard Theological Library, Marcia Grodsky of the Darlington Library of the University of Pittsburgh, Dennis Laurie of the American Antiquarian Society, Roberta Zonghi of the Rare Books Department of the Boston Public Library, Jack Ericson of the Daniel Reed Library of the State University of New York at Fredonia, John Pollack of the Annenberg Rare Book and Manuscript Library of the University of Pennsylvania, Sue Presnell of the Lilly Library of Indiana University, Kathryn Grover of the New Bedford Historical Society, Diane Shephard of the Lynn Museum, Laurel Guadazno of the Provincetown Museum, Christopher Lindquist of the Sturgis Library in

Barnstable, Joyce LaJudice of the Lily Dale Assembly, and Jeanette Thomas of the Edgar Cayce Foundation.

Karen Dau of the First Universalist Society in Rochester, Aaron Payson of the Unitarian Universalist Church of Worcester, Scott Wells of the Universalist National Memorial Church in Washington, DC, and Gwen Foss of the Universalist Unitarian Church of Farmington, Michigan, all gave me important information that found its way into this book. Friends, acquaintances, and colleagues who gave me their help and support as I worked on this book include Sara Rath, Dora St. Martin, Dee Morris, Karl Petruso, Carl Bielefeldt, Adam Phillips, Bill Becker, Don Lopez, Judy Jeffrey-Howard, Pat Deveney, Sue Jensen, Sarah O'Dowd, Nancy Osgood, Leslie Price, Connie Lancaster, Jack Harder, and Sharon Seager. I also thank Michael Halpern and the other members of the Accotink Unitarian Universalist Church in Burke, Virginia, for the opportunity to speak to them on the subject of my research.

My family has supported me throughout my writing of this book, and for that, I thank my cousin, Cathy Buescher, my mother, Betty Buescher, and my sister, Siri Gian Khalsa. My wife, Belinda, and our children, Daniel and Virginia, cheerfully encouraged me in this project, and Belinda brought her editing skills to bear on the draft.

John B. Buescher

Index